FOLLOW THE LEADER

FOLLOW
THE
LEADER

Opinion Polls
and the
Modern Presidents

PAUL BRACE
BARBARA HINCKLEY

BasicBooks
A Division of HarperCollinsPublishers

Library of Congress Cataloging-in-Publication Data
Brace, Paul, 1954–
    Follow the leader: opinion polls and the modern presidents /
Paul Brace, Barbara Hinckley.
        p.   cm.
    Includes bibliographical references and index.
    ISBN 0–465–01334–1
        1. Presidents—United States.   2. Public opinion—United
States.   3. United States—Politics and government—1945–.   I.
Hinckley, Barbara, 1937–.   II. Title.
    JK518.B72 1992
    353.03'13—dc20   91-59021
                                                             CIP

Designed by Ellen Levine

92 93 94 95 CC/GL 9 8 7 6 5 4 3 2 1

Contents

List of Figures

List of Tables

Preface

PEOPLE worry about a public-relations presidency: a pattern of action in the White House that gives high priority to public support. Nowhere is this problem clearer than on questions of a president's approval ratings, as shown by the public-opinion polls. Presidents are constantly evaluated by these ratings and appear to take actions in terms of them. Yet, many of the strongest influences on the polls are beyond the presidents' control, and many of the choices they make the public might not approve of. We find an uneasy balance at best between being liked and being president. As the polls grow in importance, the balance becomes more precarious.

At the same time, there is a growing gap between what political scientists know about these approval ratings and what the public knows and learns from the media. Citizens see one president in office at a time, along with the particular cult wisdom that flourishes around the individual. Political scientists study recurring patterns among different presidents, compare their performances, and predict, with increasing accuracy, the actions they will take and the results that will follow. Consequently, the popular evaluate-the-presidents game, engaged in by journalists and the public, is played in a widening vacuum of knowledge. Citizens rally around the president in times of crisis, and political scientists predict when this rallying will occur and what impact it will have.

This book attempts to cross the knowledge gap with a new perspective both realistic and political. It examines the role public approval has played in the modern presidency—from Harry Truman to George Bush. It identifies the major influences on the polls that hold across administrations and derive from deeply rooted expectations about the presidency (Chapters 1 and 2). It also reveals the ways presidents appear to time their activities to help their standing in the polls, although some presidents do so more than others (Chapter 3). These actions and reactions have consequences for legislation and foreign policy (Chapters 4 and 5). Once the basic patterns are seen, the book looks more closely at the choices individual presidents make and at the high cost of popularity in the Bush administration (Chapters 6 and 7). A final chapter asks what might be done to bring the emphasis on the polls more in line with democratic objectives.

Should presidents chase the polls, following their ups and downs in what we will see are repetitive and predictable ways? Should they take actions in the White House regarding foreign policy, for example, in the effort to win public support? On the other hand, should they be held accountable for unrealistic expectations and for influences that they cannot control? Polls are important because they measure the public's opinion. Does the public approve of how the polls are used and what they are supposed to say? *Follow the Leader* invites people to make their own assessments once they can identify the influences all presidents face. More fundamentally, it invites them to take a more active role in shaping what this very important public approval means.

Several people helped along the way as the book grew from a series of studies into its present form. We would like to thank Bill Berry, Klaudia Brace, Youssef Cohen, Richard Fleisher, Gary King, Gary Mucciaroni, and Daniel Ward for helpful comments on earlier article drafts, as well as the editors and anonymous referees of the *Journal of Politics*. Their advice was always valuable if not always followed. Paul Brace thanks the Institute of Government and Public Affairs of the University of Illinois for generous support in the preparation of this book. We would especially like to thank editor Martin Kessler of Basic Books for his encouragement and expert advice. Akiko Takano and Michael Mueller, also of Basic Books, contributed greatly to the quality of the finished product and the pleasantness of the entire production process. Finally, this was truly a collaborative effort, and authorship was assigned alphabetically.

Paul Brace
Barbara Hinckley

1

Being Liked and Being President

WHEN the Gulf War was almost over, crowds stood on the White House lawn holding signs, each with the inscription, "We ♥ George—91%." The number on the signs did not mean the percentage of American soldiers who were still alive or uninjured, the extent of civilian damage in Iraq, or anything related to the war. Rather, it described the president's popularity: The percentage of the public who approved of the way he was doing his job. Even before the last bombers had returned to their bases, the media began speculating about what the end of the war would mean for the president's polls: How long would the hearts and the 90 percent figures remain?

This demonstrates the public-relations presidency that many feel has become a dominating force of politics—a presidency concerned primarily with maintaining and increasing public support. It was seen in the careful White House management of the war, in the media attention to Bush's popularity, and in the well-orchestrated retail support with its flags and yellow ribbons. At the time, one could even get a set of Desert Storm baseball cards, complete with both a Dick Cheney and a Sunset on the F-16.

There are obvious as well as hidden dangers suggested by this scene on the White House lawn. If popularity becomes the basis for White House decision making, then war and peace as well as issues and agendas in Congress will be chosen not on their merits but on their predicted poll impact. The public's name will be used in vain to support programs not necessarily in its interest, and presidential trips will be planned and policies chosen for their immediate benefits in popularity. Soon we will ask not what the president can do for the country, but what he can do for himself. If short, successful wars are the quickest way to boost a president's failing poll ratings (which they are), then Americans can expect more Gulf Wars and more Grenadas in the future. If issues that dramatize the nation's problems and divisions are the quickest way to hurt the president in the polls (which they are), then these problems will rarely be addressed in the White House. Consensual issues—the flag or the "war on drugs"—will be substituted, when issues are raised at all.

These are some of the obvious dangers, but there are hidden threats as well. Descriptions of how things are quickly become prescriptions of how things should be, especially in an office such as the presidency, where one case can become an instant precedent. Media cynicism fuels the fire. If journalists believe that the office is one of public relations merely, then their reporting can change the future by its description of the present. Stories on the White House's attention to falling ratings not only condone but also encourage this attention. Soon, presidents who do not have daily strategy meetings on their public approval will not be doing their job.

This book will show that modern presidents have made very different choices when confronted with the issue of popularity. Although a trend may be building, there is more than one precedent now available. The public—and journalists—need to know what the choices are.

Just as television's obsession with ratings often prohibits quality shows from developing an audience, so commentary on presidents' popularity foreshortens their goals and eliminates the work necessary to fulfill them. Presidents cannot afford the time to gain experience, work with Congress, check their information, and communicate with the public long enough to develop serious programs. "The clock is always ticking," advisers have said of the decline of presidential popularity during a term. Today it seems that the clock is running faster and time growing shorter. Several recent presidents were advised to let agenda items wait for their second term, when they could better "afford" a drop in popularity. If the obsession with polls is increasing, then the short-term goals must be getting shorter. Even as a war approaches its last stages, for example, the White House must work not to let the recent upsurge of popularity fall.

Even if presidents did not want to manipulate events for popularity's sake, they would still be strongly encouraged to do so by the media. By holding out, they risk invidious comparisons with their predecessors and analyses in editorials and weekly magazines of what they are doing wrong. These analyses then convince other commentators and the public that the president is not doing a good job—and the polls fall further.

The Reagan White House employed public-opinion expert Richard Wirthlin, previously a university professor who had gone into business for himself. Wirthlin was paid by the Republican National Committee, which shared his services with the White House. For an estimated $1 million per year, Wirthlin provided polls, special techniques, frequent consultations with Reagan, and almost daily consultations with Chief of Staff Donald Regan. His techniques included a "speech pulse," by which people holding special computerized dials could test-market presidential speeches. The dials not only tapped positive and negative reaction but also measured very specific things, such as responses to the speaker's credibility. They measured reactions moment by moment and word by word. The results could identify "power phrases" and "resonators," the lines and tones most effective in altering feelings. As Wirthlin pointed out, the system allowed pretesting and fine-tuning of presidential messages and "tells us what themes we can play after the speech, what phrases we can use again."[1]

This rule by resonator helped advisers select issues and themes in the second Reagan White House; it also shaped the antidrug issue Reagan used in his speeches for Republican senatorial candidates in 1986. Drugs were seen as an innocuous issue that the public could widely support. The most favorable resonator, which formed the mainstay of Reagan speeches, compared the national budget to the family budget. Working with Donald Regan, Wirthlin secured the right to veto drafts of State of the Union addresses. No taxes or abortion, he counseled, and the president should downplay Nicaragua, which Wirthlin said with some prescience in 1985, is "his worst issue." The regular—and sometimes daily—polls were more than a rhetorical aid: They provided important feedback for how the White House was handling various issues. To reassure reporters that the administration was not in trouble following the Iran-Contra revelations, Regan showed them the daily polls.[2] Political campaigns had used sophisticated techniques and direct-response polling before. Now they were in the White House.

Months before the Gulf War began, the Bush administration began to receive daily poll reports on American attitudes toward the Iraqi crisis. It was not clear if the administration hoped to use this information to reflect opinion or to coach it. People were asked if they approved of the way George Bush was handling the situation in the Persian Gulf, if they thought U.S. actions had been "too tough, not tough enough, or just about right," and whether they agreed or disagreed with the statement, "Given everything that has happened, the U.S. is justified in launching an attack against Iraq to drive them out of Kuwait." The polls, targeting groups by gender, income, race, national origin, region, and age cohort, could carefully track opinion in response to the varying announcements the White House was releasing from day to day.

These polls were conducted by the Wirthlin Group, in behalf of "Citizens for a Free Kuwait." Whoever these citizens were, they reflected a White House policy that was at the time still very controversial. When people rallied to "support the troops" months later, they would not know how much forethought and preparation had been given to their patriotic fervor.

The hidden danger is that people will come to believe in a new and powerful magic that officials have at their disposal or that presidents will think that if only they improve these already sophisticated measurement techniques, their problems will be solved. Quite the contrary, Reagan's popularity *is* comparable with that of other modern presidents. Nicaragua became a very bad resonator indeed. Bush's popularity in the Gulf War exacted high costs on his political fortunes by the end of the year. As this book will show, there are constraints facing all presidents, in their juggling of popularity with the demands of government, that might surpass even Mr. Wirthlin's expertise.

Equally as dangerous for democracy is the lack of information about what public popularity means. The standard poll question, originally posed by Gallup and subsequently picked up by other polling organizations, asks if people "approve of the job President _____ is doing as president." While other questions are asked from time to time, this particular one, raised monthly by Gallup since the Truman years, is usually taken as the standard and the best overall evaluation. The *New York Times*–CBS News and the *Washington Post*–ABC News polls typically use this question as the basis for stories on the polls.

Some people apparently answer in terms of the individual in office: They do or do not like George Bush or whomever is president at the time. Human sympathy also affects these responses. Hence, a family tragedy in the White House, a surgical operation, or an attempted assassination prompts some people to be kinder in their responses. Other people answer by attempting to evaluate the president's performance on issues important to them. However, a large number of people, evidently taking the president to symbolize the nation, evaluate his performance by how well they think the nation is doing. If the nation has economic problems, for example, then they feel that somehow the president is not doing a good job.

All these ideas are mixed in the poll results, which vary with circumstances. Since people's opinions tend to be stable, the polls also will be stable, fluctuating only with the most dramatic circumstances or with how commentators interpret the circumstances. But because many events are beyond White House control, presidents will be praised or blamed for things not of their own making. A president in office during bad economic times will have lower poll ratings than one in office during stable or prosperous times. Moreover, media commentary on how popular presidents are influences future popularity. Although Ronald

Reagan and Jimmy Carter, as we will see, had very similar poll standings through much of their first four years in office, one was said to be more popular than the other. Stories of declining popularity themselves influence that popularity.

The lack of information goes further. Stories about the polls do not separate the built-in constraints on the presidency from external and chance events. One president is said to be more or less popular than another, without carefully comparing him with other presidents or controlling for chance circumstances. Imagine what would happen if people were compared for how well they managed the resources of their households or businesses, without considering their inheritance or the good and bad fortune that came their way. Some people would seem to do a better job financially than others, simply because they had better luck. This happens, however, when reporters compare the presidents' popularity at some chance point in time or compare the first one hundred days of their terms. The result is a misleading news story that combines very different circumstances and past events.

Today, we find that presidents and their advisers have become increasingly obsessed with popularity, or are encouraged in this direction by media expectations. (Some presidents might not need much encouragement.) Precedents build for the future, and short-term goals get shorter. Government becomes a ratings race, with the loser being the public in whose name all this is carried out. Meanwhile, the polls that are elevated to this new monthly referendum give misleading information at best.

Of course, the presidency is supposed to be the nation's number-one democratic office. Presidents represent all the people; their election is the basis for whatever power they have. According to this logic, polls are simply a continuation of the electoral referendum, and all we need to do is gain a better understanding of what they mean. However, when Americans ask for leadership in the White House, they do not usually want the president merely to follow public opinion. In fact, some of our greatest presidents have been those willing to disregard the opinion of the moment to do what they thought was right. Truman, ranked highest by historians of modern presidents, had the lowest poll ratings. Paradoxically, part of Truman's stature appears to be precisely that he did not care about the polls and took every opportunity to show it.

Even those who might want more public-minded presidents than Truman find the contemporary scene disturbing. Few Americans would like to think that they are manipulated by public-relations specialists holding emergency meetings in the White House or that they are "interpreted" by the same specialists in the news media, who may or may not have correct information. Nor would they like to feel that wars, presidential speeches, and White House news stories are crafted with anything but the national interest in view. They might not even like the idea that presidents often postpone what could be urgent issues, on the promptings of poll results or the electoral calendar.

The problem of balancing independence with attention to public opinion is complicated, because popularity matters, as we will see in subsequent chapters. Facing Congress, for example, presidents can do more and can implement more of their policies when they have public support. Hence, presidents with ambitious agendas scorn polls at their peril. This point, made famous in the 1960s by political scientist Richard Neustadt in his book of advice to presidents, had been noted earlier by Woodrow Wilson, writing as a political scientist in the nineteenth century. Presidential leadership requires public support.[3] The point is not unqualified, however. There are times when presidents must choose which goals they will follow. Popularity helps ambitious legislative proposals, but the efforts to pass legislation hurt at the polls. Choosing one goal means that they cannot pursue others.

At best, there is an uneasy balance between popularity and the tasks Americans expect a president to do. Both of these contradictory things, it deserves to be reemphasized, can express public opinion. At worst, the popular basis of government has slipped somehow, and democracy has been turned on its head. Presidents govern in the name of the public, using poll reports and other devices as substitutes for more basic opinions and beliefs. To know a little more about what is going on, we can ask these questions: Is being popular the same as doing the job of president? What status should the polls have? How should the polls be interpreted in a modern democracy? What does the public need to know to make these evaluations—about what it does and does not want its presidents to do? These questions help to frame our look at the modern presidency, in its recent past and in the present.

This book looks at the place of popularity in the modern presidency, showing its constraints, ironies, and impact. In the process, it points out how individual presidents have balanced governing and gaining public support and identifies the components of this balance. It invites citizens to take back some of the responsibility of evaluation from various professionals, including the presidents, who predict the public's opinions and interpret them.

WHAT THE PUBLIC NEEDS TO KNOW ABOUT THE PRESIDENCY

A Basis for Evaluation

Evaluating presidents, one of the best-loved games of American politics, is played from the first poll of an election year to the latest word of historical revisionism. Americans assume they *should* make these judgments and that they *can* do so—that there is enough information available. This game is a celebration of democracy at work. Citizens say what they like and dislike about the candidates; argue—in taxis, bars, and introductory government courses—about a president's handling of foreign policy; and answer the national surveys on how well they think the president is doing his job. Joining in and cheering the public on are the national media. Cartoonists, editorial writers, television comedians, and talk-show guests all confidently rate the current officeholder in matters large and small, on style and substance, and on his current standing. Over time, a residue trickles down into political folklore. This president was successful in dealing with Congress, but that president was not. This president was popular, but that president was not.

These judgments assume that some standard, or *base of comparison*, exists. Evaluation requires comparison. A president cannot be judged in a vacuum, but only in relation to other presidents. Yet both popular and academic commentaries cling to the notion that presidents are somehow unique and incomparable, that there is only one president. The president is seen as "the Lonely Man in the crowded White House," as shown by the famous photograph of John F. Kennedy alone at the Oval Office window. According to the mystique of uniqueness, the president's is the loneliest, and the largest, burden in the world. The mystique, carried on by journalists focusing on the individuals in office at a particular time, is reinforced by academic writing that focuses on the personalities of presidents or the decisions they made in a particular set of circumstances. People use the singular and specific "the president," instead of referring to all presidents or any president. This device provides a human symbol for the powers of government. But, in so doing, it says in effect that there is only one President of the United States. He is literally incomparable, unique and alone.

It is easy to stay caught in this "each-president-is-unique" kind of thinking. Most writers define the modern presidency as beginning after World War II, making a total of only nine presidents who have served in the forty years from Truman to Bush, each with his own very distinct personality and circumstances. Can one compare, for example, the five Republican presidents in this period? Consider Eisenhower, who presided over a time of peace and prosperity; Nixon, who was engulfed in war protests and the Watergate scandal; Ford, who faced double-digit inflation, an energy crisis, and massive Democratic majorities in Congress; and Reagan and Bush, who governed without some of these same fortunes and misfortunes. Although there are ways around these analytical difficulties, we can see why some writers find it easier to assume that each president is unique. Joining with the popular mystique and the journalist convention, they look at the office one president at a time.

Think of the kind of characterizations now current in political folklore: Eisenhower was loved as a kind of grandfatherly figure; everyone liked Ike; Nixon had deep psychological problems that allowed Watergate to happen; Johnson had psychological problems on which we can blame the war in Vietnam; Carter was unpopular and unsuccessful in Congress and did not have whatever it takes to be president; Reagan was the "Great Communicator," popular with the media and the public, although severely hampered by a short attention span. Whatever we may think of those particular individuals does not really matter now because a new president is in office. To play the presidential-rating game well as American citizens, we need better characterizations than these.

The Logic of Multiple Influences

Like card players, presidents are dealt very different hands. To evaluate their skill and success, we need to ask how well they play within the common constraints (the rules of the game), controlling for the luck of the deal. We must first separate out influences common to all administrations. For example, all presidents face a decline of support, in both the first and the second term, that continues from the first year well into the third. This decay curve can be explained by dynamics built into the modern presidency—it is something all presidents must deal with. For another example, there are built-in limits to how much leadership in legislative policy presidents can deploy. After a point, they can choose additional activity in pursuit of their policies or additional success, but they cannot have both.

We also need to see how these basic influences vary from one administration to another. Some presidents are clearly dealt stronger hands than others. Poor economic conditions, for example, hurt all presidents' popularity, but some presidents face poorer economic conditions than others. The dramatic events of a term, only some of which a president can control, also will affect the polls. Then, too, legislative activity and success are shaped by how many partisans are elected to Congress. So when a news story makes comparisons about different presidents' first few months in office, it is combining all these influences—mixing Carter, who took office in bad economic times; with Nixon, who inherited Vietnam War protests; with Reagan, who survived an assassination attempt; with Kennedy, who faced an international crisis and did not survive an assassination. The story cannot separate how the presidents did or are doing from all these other influences.

It is only when we separate out, or control for, these multiple influences that we can begin to see how each president worked within the uneasy balance of the office. Modern presidents have made different choices, some more and some less supportive of their popularity. The public needs to see these differences in order to evaluate presidential performance. Personality, style, charisma, and all the other individual traits that are described so frequently also can be seen more clearly when these other effects are known.

This book will show that these evaluation techniques are available to modern social science and that the results hold information important to the presidents themselves and to all citizens. Since presidents work within a complex political environment that they cannot entirely control, the challenge for us is to identify the various influences on a particular president and then look more closely at the individual performance.

The logic of separating out many influences is the kind of thinking we do all the time when separating performance from circumstance and sheer luck. Although statistical results are reported for those who are interested, others can freely ignore them. They should not ignore, however, the fairly clear pictures that emerge and should come to recognize the chief influences all presidents face, using these to interpret the past and to understand the future.

For example, imagine someone writing a news story about how a president was doing in terms of popularity six months into his term. (We will count Truman and Johnson from the time of their first election and use the standard Gallup poll question.) Three of the modern presidents appear to be doing well if they were the subject of the story: Kennedy, with 74 percent of the public approving of his job after six months; Eisenhower, with a 73 percent approval rating; and Johnson, with a 69 percent rating. At the other extreme, two presidents would appear not to be doing well—Truman and Reagan with only 57 percent and 58 percent, respectively, approving of their job. (This was even after Reagan inherited some support in the polls as sympathy after the assassination attempt.) In the middle are Nixon and Carter, each with 63 percent approval ratings.

Why are some presidents doing better than others? Perhaps it has to do with style or first appearances. Maybe Nixon was wrong to introduce each of his cabinet members on national television; cabinet members are not necessarily an inspiring lot. While the speculative interpretations are endless, the answers are simpler. Three of these presidents benefited from good economic conditions. Johnson and Eisenhower had record lows in unemployment and little inflation. Even though Kennedy inherited higher unemployment than Eisenhower, it remained relatively low and stable throughout his term. The other four presidents inherited economic problems varying from moderate to severe. At the same time, three of the presidents faced an international event, which, no matter what, rallies patriotism and support. These are the three presidents—Kennedy, Eisenhower, and Johnson— who were found to lead in the polls six months into their term. Two of the presidents faced negative events from conditions developing before they took office: Truman with a major strike and Nixon with protest rallies on the war.

Since poor economic conditions, such as a 10-point change in the "misery" index, cost about 10 percentage points in the polls and international rally points add about 4 percentage points, on the average, most of the results at the six-month mark simply reflect external fortune. They mirror the state of the nation at a particular point in time, a condition transitory and subject to circumstance. The news stories during each presidency would say different things, but the presidents would not necessarily be doing different things. One of the first significant events of these administrations would be the often-false interpretation of why the presidents are doing well or poorly.

The Shift from the Personal to the Political

Presidents bring their own backgrounds and skills and personal idiosyncrasies to an *office*—an institution already shaped by expectations from the public; from officials, including past presidents; and from the nation's basic constitutional design. These expectations shape their behavior and choices in fundamental ways. So if we ask what the stylish Kennedy, the genial general, the born-again Christian, the log-rolling Texan, and the professional actor have in common, the answer is a set of expectations that have grown over time. These expectations are political constraints.

Thus, each of our modern presidents came to an office already defined by widely held expectations. They held, many people said, the most democratic office in the world: elected by, and charged with representing, all the people of the United States. As the "voice of the people," they were expected to solve the nation's problems and propose new legislation. They were supposed to "lead" Congress, to be the chief legislator, because Congress, lacking the vigor and singularity of the executive, was presumably incapable of leading itself. Governing a nation that had experienced a depression, they were expected to be managers of the economy, guardians of the nation's prosperity, and responsible for its problems. They were global leaders, too—the "leader of the free world," actively engaged in helping other free nations and holding the line against the spread of international Communism. Each of the modern presidents held the nuclear football and was commander-in-chief during a time of Cold War.

These expectations were codified and publicized in a famous book by Clinton Rossiter, first published in 1956. Rossiter described the different "hats" the president wears, including Voice of the People, Chief Legislator, World Leader, and Manager of Prosperity.[4] Rossiter consciously painted an ideal of the office, as one of a school of writers who sought to increase the power of the presidency by ascribing more power to it. Nevertheless, Rossiter's hats became obligatory fare in American government books, part of the "textbook presidency" that Thomas Cronin has described so well.[5] Although by the late 1970s college textbooks began to take a more realistic view of the office, the texts for younger students repeated the litany of the hats through the late 1980s.[6] The presidents governing during this time, the advisers helping them, the journalists reporting on them, and the public evaluating them were all socialized into these expectations. They defined how the president was supposed to do his job.

Each of the modern presidents also followed Franklin D. Roosevelt, whose administration helped create these expectations. As a master of rhetoric, the only president elected for more than two terms, and head of state while the nation struggled through a depression and moved toward victory in a major war, Franklin Roosevelt cast a shadow that looms over the modern political age. His successors inherited the expectations, even though the high drama was over. The free world and financial institutions survived, leaving the modern presidents in the wake of these events seeming ordinary in comparison. If they were held to Roosevelt's standard, they were cast in a game that they could not win.

Finally, each of these presidents came to an office shaped by more basic expectations about the necessary limits on government from the original constitutional design. Their own public statements to the contrary, presidents are not the government, and they do not represent all the people equally well. They act with others, against others, and in the face of continuing problems. What this means concretely is that they make choices about the kinds of policies they pursue and how actively they pursue them. Inactivity is the most popular strategy at times, although it need not be the best for the nation. Foreign and domestic policy have different risks and benefits. Presidents can choose to be active in Congress or popular with the public; these two good things do not go together. In our complex political environment, presidents must sometimes make choices to achieve partial victories.

We thus evaluate our modern presidents as occupants of a political institution, distinguishing from what is common and what is chance. This book challenges the notion of the presidency as a series of personality profiles and challenges the splendid illusion that presidents can be all things to all people if only they try harder, have better advisers, or have more favorable character traits.

Indeed, this political perspective, by separating out what is common from what is a matter of individual choice, helps us understand the personalities better. A president's popularity with the public is shaped by choices as well as by good and bad fortune and common constraints. Once we control for these factors, we can see the individual impact more clearly. Reagan and Eisenhower rank as the most popular presidents as a result of this refined ranking, Reagan first and Eisenhower second. Both made choices, as we will show in Chapter 2, that helped their popularity, and both could be described as "passive-positive" personality types. The passive-positive president, according to one typology, is characterized by low self-esteem and a strong desire to be liked.[7] According to this interpretation, both presidents got the liking they were working for. At the other extreme, Truman, Johnson, and Ford rank lowest in popularity once we control for circumstances over which they had no control. But each also made several choices contributing to his low rating that shed further light on his personality. It is interesting that these are the three presidents who came to office through succession, raising the possibility that the normal selection process screens out those most willing to act independently of the public's opinion.

This comparison allows us to challenge conventional wisdom at several points and provide new support for other impressions. We can rate Carter, for example, higher than expected on several dimensions well beyond his current reputation. We can see that Reagan showed an uncanny ability to hug the presidential mean—he might be called the "no-lose" president—neither higher nor lower in rating than expected when compared to the other presidents. Yet, Reagan does rank as the most popular president, beating out Eisenhower, once we control for the circumstances of the time. Although distinctive, the Bush administration is similar to the Reagan administration in many ways, and the policy choices of the Bush administration show the uneasy balance in its clearest form.

What appears at first idiosyncratic then becomes more understandable. The second terms of Eisenhower, Nixon, and Reagan followed the influences seen in their first terms, although the second terms added additional constraints. These are not isolated historical curiosities: Johnson's decisions on Vietnam accorded with other decisions he made. The various presidential choices do make sense in terms of political background and experience, and we can begin to see what presidents can and cannot do.

At one level this is a book on the modern presidents and their choices and constraints. The constraints are the job expectations; the choices involve balancing presidential activities with the demands of being liked. More specifically, the book gives an anatomy of how the polls define the office and the officeholders: in the constraints the polls impose, the actions they elicit, and the substance and timing of different policies they influence. It underscores the worry that the polls turn democracy upside down, encouraging a set of actions taken in the name of the public that citizens would not approve. Yet this book also indicates where the worries might be overstated, because some of the actions thought to be taken for popularity's sake do not have the desired effect. There appears to be more White House effort than public impact. If journalists or presidential advisers plot a game plan for regaining public support, they may be surprised to find how little difference their various actions make.

We first identify the chief influences on the polls: how public expectations affect the presidents. These are the influences people should begin to recognize and adjust for, and it is at this point where broad changes could occur. A change in expectations changes what the polls would report. We next look at the presidents' actions: what they do and when and what difference their actions make. Presidents do appear to select activities based on poll ratings, with an eye toward public opinion, although some do so more than others. Combining these results, we can begin to see the temptations and the potential impact on policy and that positions taken on legislation have their costs. Actions in different kinds of foreign policy have different effects on the polls. Moreover, some of the acts that help poll ratings do appear timed to follow domestic political circumstances much more frequently than one would expect to happen by chance. An irony becomes apparent: Presidents are most able to propose legislation when the country needs it least, in times of international crisis, and are least able to make successful proposals in hard domestic times. This is only one of several ironies imposed by the curious new referendum: where experience counts against a president; second-term victories bring immediate losses of support; and the most critical times in the life of the nation become—from the standpoint of popularity—a president's good luck.

2

The New Referendum

"LET him once win the admiration and confidence of the country, and no other single force can withstand him, no combination of forces will easily overpower him," Woodrow Wilson wrote long before he became president. His words, now part of American political folklore, celebrate the power of the president as the voice of the people, holder of the nation's number-one democratic office. Presidents are the only ones (along with their vice presidents) elected from a national constituency. So, when proposing policies and making decisions, they can use their elections as grounds to speak for all the nation. The larger the electoral margin—the mandate—the more presidents have been able to claim they had the people behind them in whatever they sought to do.

However, with the advent of modern public-opinion polling, this democratic basis has changed. Presidents no longer govern for four years on the strength of one election; today, the electoral mandate is continually updated and reviewed by public-opinion polls. Consequently, Lyndon Johnson and Richard Nixon, reelected by landslide margins in 1964 and 1972, respectively, found their power—that is, their claim to be the voice of the people—undercut when polls showed they had lost substantial support.

George Bush, after being elected narrowly, climbed to high levels
of approval in his first years in office. The democratic claim of the
office remains, but the means of assessing it have changed: We
now have a continuing monthly referendum on the president's
public support.

The presidency has had to adjust to this new referendum.
Harry Truman, the first president for whom we have monthly
survey ratings, made no secret of his dislike: "I wonder how far
Moses would have gone if he'd taken a poll in Egypt? What
would Jesus Christ have preached if he'd taken a poll in Israel?
. . . It isn't polls or public opinion of the moment that counts. It
is right and wrong and leadership . . . that makes epochs in the
history of the world."[1] It is not surprising that Truman scored
lowest of all modern presidents in the polls.

Most of his successors have been less willing to risk ignoring
polls, which are now watched carefully by the president and
Congress, along with the press and the public, and studied assidu-
ously by political scientists. Presidents even conduct their own
polls and amass teams of public-relations experts to advise them.
George Bush's slide in the polls in the fall of 1990 became a
major news story, and his dramatic rise after the Persian Gulf War
made news again. Those closest to Bush said he was "obsessed"
with the polls.[2] As the basis for presidential power has changed,
the presidents appear to be changing too.

This new mandate, however, can be very confusing, since polls
are subject to more interpretation and spin than relatively clear-
cut election results. The graph in Figure 2.1 shows raw, una-
nalyzed public-approval ratings for Truman through Bush, such
as the newspapers report: the time series showing the percent of
the public approving of how the president is doing his job. There
are a few familiar landmarks in the figure: We can see the effects
of the Vietnam War and Watergate and note that the nation liked
Eisenhower but was less than warm about some of the most
recent presidents. For the most part, however, the underlying
patterns are lost amid all the fluctuations. Also, the Gallup organization, *Washington Post*–ABC News, and *New York Times*–CBS
News ask the same job-approval question, but newspapers report

these polls only when they fit in with major news stories. Thus, no one sees a full or consistent picture or wonders what lessons, if any, can be learned from it.

If the polls are as important as they seem to be, citizens need to be able to interpret them. Should we worry that international crises might be fabricated by a White House worried about popularity? Should we expect a normal decline during each term? How much of the influence on the polls is in the president's own hands, or how constrained is he by events beyond his control? At this point, the answers are unclear.

This chapter takes a close look at these monthly referenda by identifying the major influences on public approval, explaining these influences in terms of how Americans view the presidency, and assessing how this affects a president's claim to have the public's support. First, we will show how much of poll fluctuation can be explained by patterns common to all administrations, by circumstances that vary from one administration to another, and by individual effects. Then we concentrate on individual presidents. Some had much more favorable circumstances than others, and some made more of their opportunities than others. We then ask about the consequences for the office and the choices and constraints that all presidents face.

Public support is measured by the Gallup time series, which reports the percentage of people who approve of the way the president is doing his job. This same question is asked by the network and newspaper polls and helps make up the surface picture that the public sees. We will look at Gallup poll results from Truman through Reagan from the time of their first election. (Ford is included for his partial term from the time he succeeded to office.)[3] These results also hold true for Bush's early years, as we will show later. We begin with the first term only so we can compare all the modern presidents and identify common effects. Later in the chapter, we will expand the results to include the second terms of Eisenhower, Nixon, and Reagan. Although these second terms are exceptional points in recent American history, their results support and accentuate the patterns found in the first four years.[4]

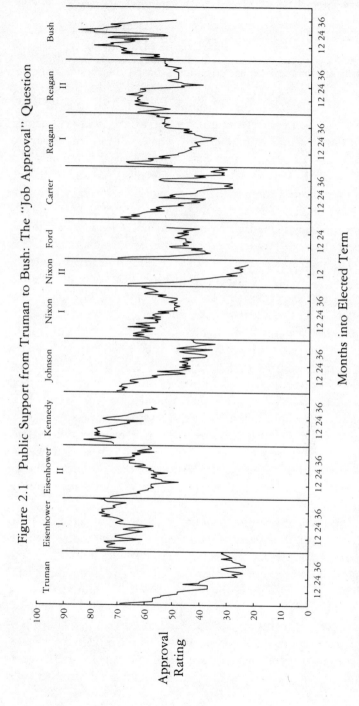

Figure 2.1   Public Support from Truman to Bush: The "Job Approval" Question

Source: Adapted from Barbara Hinckley and Sheldon Goldman, *American Politics and Government* (Glendale, Ill.: Scott, Foresman, 1990), p. 309.

INFLUENCES ON THE POLLS

People evaluate particular presidents based on general expectations of what they should do and be. Hence, the specific support—in polls, for example—should be understandable, in terms of the public's general support for the office. Political scientist Fred Greenstein has summarized "what the president means to Americans" in terms of four basic psychological functions: (1) a symbol of the nation; (2) an outlet for affect—a way of feeling good about one's country; (3) a cognitive aid, allowing an individual to symbolize the complexity of government; and (4) a means of vicarious participation through which people identify with the president and feel more a part of events occurring around them.[5]

These perceptions are found for children and adults and span many years of recent American history. The continuity should not be surprising, as textbooks teach generations of young Americans that the president is powerful and good. In a study published *after* Watergate, most persons agreed that the president "stands for our country" and that they sleep better "when a president they trust is watching over the country." The Associated Press reported the responses of a first-grade class when the teacher asked, "What should a president do for the people?" Among their replies were to help ducks; sign papers; give poor people money; tell people where to go; keep people from stealing; help a lost puppy; and help people not die. These first-graders said the same things as adults who think that presidents should "control the energy crisis" or manage the economy and "give us jobs."[6]

These public attitudes are reinforced by news coverage. Journalists equate the president with the government in their reporting of complex policy making; furthermore, they imply that presidents can solve major problems when they ask what candidates will do about inflation or the budget deficit. The attitudes also are encouraged by the presidents themselves. A study of how presidents present themselves in speeches to the nation paints a portrait that has remained consistent across the modern presidents. According to this self-portrait, presidents are symbols of the nation and moral leaders. They are one with the government and the powers of government. As unifying symbols, they abolish—that is, they do not mention—conflict within society as well as problems of past administrations. They are presidents of all the people.[7]

We thus find an idealized portrait of the office that contrasts sharply with real-world events. This contrast supplies both power and limits to individuals in office: power insofar as they inherit the unrealistic expectations, limits when these expectations cannot be fulfilled. It also shapes the kind of responses people give when asked if they think the president is doing a good job.

The Decay of Support

Within weeks of his landslide election, Lyndon Johnson explained to his White House staff why so many Great Society programs had to be broached at once: "I was just elected President by the biggest popular margin in the history of the country—16 million votes. . . . I've already lost about three of those sixteen . . . [and] I could be down to 8 million in a couple of months." A Carter adviser echoes the theme: "You know, a president starts out with a bank full of good will and slowly checks are drawn on that and it's very rare that it's replenished."[8]

Something that is patterned across time affects support for presidents, showing up in the polls, in Johnson's vote count, and in Carter's bank of goodwill. These astute political observers did not say that past approval affects the present—the polls do not stay the same, they fall over the months. Assuming a tide of decreasing influence, presidents must push out important programs as the clock starts ticking and the polls begin to fall.

Why should this be so? If unrealistic views of the office build in expectations that cannot be fulfilled, we would expect support to decline from an artificial high point as the expectations are not met.[9] According to this argument, too, presidents should rush their programs to Congress. Notice that the argument is not limited to the so-called honeymoon period, and presidents cannot expect that their votes and polls will magically return. The duration of the decline is an empirical question, as is the extent of the inflated or "soft" initial support. We thus hypothesize that time stands for something that is very real to all presidents: a cycle of deflating expectations. The cycle consists of one peak, or inflation point, and a remaining decay period. The peak occurs with the unrealistic expectations aroused from the electoral period through the inaugural celebration. The decay begins immediately after the inauguration, as presidents begin to face the realities of government, then continues until the cycle starts again. A second term will repeat the cycle and the decay. One influence, therefore, on all presidents' public approval is this decay of support over the course of the term.

Circumstances: Economic Conditions and Dramatic Events

A second kind of influence on the polls are circumstances, varying from one administration to another, that shape the public's view of the nation. Circumstances include economic conditions as well as more sharply defined events—wars, summit meetings, strikes and demonstrations, and scandals in office. The mix of circumstances is peculiar to each administration, although the effects hold for all administrations. For example, bad economic conditions hurt all presidents' ratings, although some will face worse conditions than others. Because not all these events are under a president's control, some will have much better luck than others.

The Economy.   A special kind of circumstance is posed by economic conditions. If presidents are expected to be managers of the economy, then the ups and downs in economic conditions say something about the job they are doing. Journalists ask for White House comment on the latest economic indicators; recessionary trends, inflationary spirals, and unemployment are major news. We therefore expect that the polls will respond to economic fluctuations and that presidents in office during times of prosperity will inherit more support than those facing hard economic times.

Economic conditions do appear to affect a president's support, as several studies show.[10] Changes in inflation and the growth of the gross national product (GNP) are reflected in the polls and at the ballot box.[11] People apparently do not respond to their own personal hardships or well-being but judge the national economy and the president's ability to cope with these national problems.[12] Moreover, the presidents and their advisers appear to believe that the public makes these judgments, given the amount of campaign rhetoric devoted to the subject. William Casey, manager of the 1980 Reagan-Bush campaign, summed up the theme of the campaign as "about the failure of Jimmy Carter—about the way he messed up our economy and our standing in the world." Dwight Eisenhower, not often quoted for his political observations, remarked of Nixon that "I think Dick's going to be elected President but I think he's going to be a one-term President. I think he's really going to fight inflation, and it will kill him politically."[13]

The best evidence that presidents think the economy affects their public support is the notion of a political business cycle, which some economists and political scientists have written about. In its simplest form, a political business cycle shows the behavior of the economy compared to the timing of elections. Inflation and unemployment, for example, might be at their highest early in the first term and will fall, presumably through conscious manipulation, as the election nears. Consequently, economic trends can be adjusted so that the economy will bottom out in the third year of a term so that it improves dramatically in the fourth year. We can see that such a cyclic effect does in fact occur if we look at the first-term presidencies of Truman through Reagan graphed in Figure 2.2. The graph, with the presidencies pooled together for each of the four quarters for four years, shows the "misery" index for each of the time points—that is, a combined measure of inflation and unemployment. After the first quarter, misery is highest in the first and second years and then progressively declines in the third and fourth, as the election draws closer. The same four-year cycle is shown in other studies, using a variety of economic indicators.[14]

Nevertheless, there are only so many adjustments presidents can make to steer economic conditions. With an interdependent

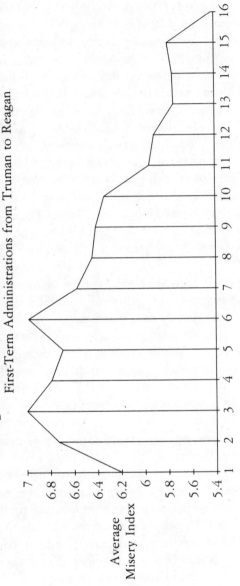

Figure 2.2 Presidential Terms and the Economic Misery Index: First-Term Administrations from Truman to Reagan

world economy and long-term trends, some of the economic conditions they are held responsible for may be beyond their control. Perceptions, however, can be shaped and adjusted. For example, in 1984 Ronald Reagan convinced people they were better off than they had been four years before, even if objective circumstances did not merit this conclusion. We suspect that the economy matters to the public's support, and presidents definitely think it matters, but we do not yet know precisely how important it is.

Dramatic Events. Very few events actually give the public evidence about how a president is doing his job. A scandal in the White House and a major diplomatic achievement are exceptions. Much more commonly, events dramatic enough to capture public attention reveal the state of the *nation:* events prompt support for the nation and its symbols, including the president, or detract from this support by emphasizing conflict and divisiveness. Since presidents serve as symbols of the nation and the government, their support will rise or fall with these events *whether or not they are themselves participants.* For instance, a president might take action to stop a racial crisis or decide to take no action: Both events dramatize conflict in the nation and can be expected to lower the president's support.

A good example of this effect occurs during international crises, when people rally around the president and the flag. The polls rise when presidents take actions that initiate rallies—Reagan's air strike on Libya or Bush's war in the Persian Gulf. However, they rise just as much when presidents take *no* action. Carter's poll ratings jumped when the hostages were first seized in the U.S. embassy in Iran and when the Soviets invaded Afghanistan. The Iranians and the Russians did the attacking, and Carter did nothing—and yet his polls jumped 20 points. Poll ratings also rise when the administration errs or is somehow responsible for a crisis. Kennedy's polls rose after the Bay of Pigs disaster, which he admitted publicly should not have occurred. Eisenhower's polls rose after a U.S. spy plane was shot down over Communist territory, causing the collapse of a planned summit meeting with the Soviet Union; unfortunately, matters were made worse when the White House first denied and then admitted that the plane was spying.

Dramatic events, then, can be predicted to have either positive or negative poll effects as they unify the nation around its symbols or dramatize its conflict and problems. An assassination attempt, the sudden use of force involving U.S. troops or personnel, and an action by a Communist nation seen as threatening U.S. interests are positive-predicted events. On the other hand, presidents have to make hard choices that provoke disagreement, or events beyond their control reveal a nation divided or a government unable to cope with its problems. Public protests and riots, economic disorders, and conflict or scandal involving government personnel are negative-predicted events. Because the president is the symbol of the government, and held responsible for it, the problems and the disunity reflect on the job he is doing.

The dramatic events in the first terms of Truman through Reagan are summarized in Appendix A. Overall, the negative-predicted events outweigh the positive, thirty-three to twenty-six. Even though all the presidents faced both kinds of events, the particular mix varied greatly. Eisenhower, Kennedy, and Johnson led in positive-predicted events. Johnson tied with Nixon for the most negative-predicted events, and Eisenhower had the fewest—only one in his first term. On balance, Kennedy, Eisenhower, and Reagan had more positive than negative events; Truman, Johnson, and Ford had more negative than positive events; and Carter had an even balance. It is also worth noting that most (twenty out of twenty-six) of the positive-predicted events consisted of international rally points, dramatic incidents which appear to be the primary means of increasing a president's support.

We should also see which of these events were under White House control. An event can be characterized as discretionary and nondiscretionary based on whether the surface impression suggests the president had some control over its timing or occurrence. Therefore, revelations about an earlier scandal are nondiscretionary because the president might have been able to avoid the scandal, but he was not able to avoid it becoming known. Also, international events that appear independent are taken at their surface value and called nondiscretionary, whether or not any behind-the-scenes manipulation might have occurred. Consequently, we assume that the shooting down of a plane is a nondiscretionary and not manipulated (discretionary) episode and that the Vietnam War protests in the Johnson years were nondiscretionary, even though, as the protesters argued, Johnson had the discretion to curtail the war and so stop the protests. Circumstances may have forced Truman to fire Douglas MacArthur, but, according to our classification, it was a discretionary act.

A president's announcing an armistice or initiating a show of force abroad is a positive discretionary event, a decision to unify the country and increase his public support. A president's announcing a controversial position or invoking the Taft-Hartley law to prevent a strike is a negative discretionary event, a decision that dramatizes conflict in the country and decreases public support. Other people take actions, too: publicizing a scandal, engaging in protests, or initiating a show of force. Large-scale events occur beyond any individual's control. Events—for example, a U.S. vessel is fired on or a sudden presidential illness strikes—that unify the country are positive nondiscretionary events predicted to increase public support. Events—for example, a strike or a war protest—that show the nation's conflicts or problems are negative nondiscretionary events predicted to decrease public support. We call these, in order, cases of *positive acts, hard choices, good luck,* and *bad luck.* People might disagree on how any one or two events are characterized, but overall they do allow a fairly straightforward coding and can be checked against the list of events in Appendix A.

Even though it seems exceedingly strange that such misfortunes as illnesses and near-assassination attempts are called positive, the term describes the impact on the polls. After Eisenhower's heart attack in October 1955, his poll ratings rose 6 percentage points. Reagan's ratings rose 7 percentage points after he was shot. That these personal misfortunes are political good fortune has been recognized by such president-watchers as David Gergen and Sam Donaldson. Gergen, speaking as a White House staffer, said that the March 1981 shooting of Reagan "gave us a second life, a second honeymoon. . . . It transformed the whole

e had new capital." Donaldson commented that one of
ns the press was so nice to Reagan in his first year was
k on his life.[15] Such are the curiosities of a president's
upport.

First-term presidents, already burdened by the fact that negative events outweigh positive ones, also confront nondiscretionary events much more frequently than discretionary ones, by a
ratio of almost two to one. In other words, presidents are more
likely to confront events predicted to affect their approval than
they are to instigate them. Nevertheless, most of the presidents
under discussion made at least one hard choice in their first
terms—that is, they announced a discretionary, negative-
predicted event: Truman fired MacArthur, Eisenhower invoked
Taft-Hartley, Johnson doubled the Vietnam draft, Nixon admitted to bombing Cambodia, and Ford pardoned Nixon. All
presidents except Ford made at least one popular choice, initiating a positive-predicted event. It can be argued that Ford did
not have very much time to arrange one. Truman, Eisenhower,
Johnson, and Carter presented peace initiatives, while Nixon
and Kennedy announced new achievements in space. All presidents except Nixon received at least one instance of good luck,
and all except Eisenhower had bad luck. Ironically, the main
"good luck" was other nations' initiating a show of force
against the United States. Bad luck included labor strife for
Truman, integration conflicts for Kennedy, war protests for
Johnson and Nixon, and economic setbacks for Carter and
Reagan. Overall, then, presidents are more constrained than
helped by events. However, some presidents are more constrained than others.

Individual Effects

Each president comes to office with a unique personality and
set of skills and occupies a unique point in history. Each differs
from the others in style and substance and perhaps in media
treatment as well. These individual characteristics also can affect
a president's popularity. Reagan was called the Great Communicator; everyone liked Ike. It is necessary to separate these effects

from the impact of circumstances. For instance, how much of Eisenhower's popularity was due to his famous smile and genial personality and how much was due to the peace and prosperity of the time? Did Carter do something wrong to cause his poll ratings to fall, or was he a victim of a failing economy and an energy crisis? Only when we separate the effects common to all administrations and the circumstances that vary among administrations can we see what the individual impact is.

We analyze presidential job approval shown in the monthly polls as a product of four components. One component is the time constraint common to all presidents, what we call the decay function or the cycle of deflating expectations. Two other components—economic conditions and dramatic events—also are common to all presidents, although the particular blend will vary with each administration. The final component is any effects that may be specific to each presidency. To perform this analysis, we pool the monthly poll ratings for the eight administrations, for all the presidents through their first terms and then for the special case of each second term. (A discussion of this technique is found in Appendix B.)

THE FIRST TERM

Each of the components shows a substantial impact on the polls, and together they account for most of the fluctuation in the ratings. High scores on the economic misery index reduce presidential approval. For each 1 percent increase in misery, the polls fall almost 1 percent. Dramatic events, positive as opposed to negative, also affect the polls, although positive events have a stronger impact than negative ones. Recall that positive-predicted events are largely international rally points. For each positive event, the polls rise over 4 percentage points. For each negative event, approval drops 2 percent beyond what one would expect from sampling error. These might seem small changes, but they add up quickly. Soon one president appears to be gaining or losing in public approval (see Appendix B).

We can also see a cycle of deflating expectations over the term, as shown dramatically in Figure 2.3. The decline becomes notice-able at the sixth month. After this initial period—presumably the "honeymoon"—presidents continue to lose support month by month, with each successive time-point producing significant effects. Approval hits its low point within the third year and begins to improve thereafter. It is important to see that this decay occurs independently of all other influences. The decay over time takes place irrespective of the economy, the president, or outside events. All presidents, it seems, must contend with this decay of support, caused by public expectations and the boundaries of a four-year term.

We can now discern the impact on the polls of individual presidencies independently of the effects of time, the economy, and dramatic events. The results indicate that significant approval variation still exists from one administration to another. This need not be due to the president's personality or skills in dealing with the public; something else—whether style, skill, or the per-ception or reports of others—affects the polls once all the other major influences are controlled. Since we have pooled all the presidents, we can also see how they compare.

The ranking of presidents in their first terms from highest to lowest approval is as follows:

1. Reagan
2. Eisenhower ⎤ tie
   Kennedy   ⎦
3. Carter
4. Nixon
5. Ford
6. Johnson
7. Truman

The ranking reveals several things of interest. There is the widespread notion that the most recent officeholders were less popular than their predecessors. People attribute this variously to a more critical stance by the media or to a new public cynicism following Watergate and Vietnam. The ranking, however, shows no chronological pattern. Truman is the lowest in approval, for

Figure 2.3   The Decay Function: The First Term

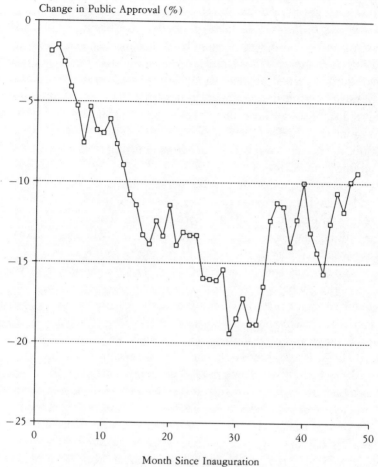

Month Since Inauguration

example, while Eisenhower is second highest; Carter ranks higher than Johnson. Perhaps the recent incumbents appear less popular because economic conditions were poor throughout their terms. Once we adjust for some of these economic effects, the chronological trend disappears. It does not appear, therefore, that any trends over time can explain these results. In other words, if the media is more critical of the most recent presidents, that treatment does not significantly impact the polls.

The ranking of Reagan is of particular interest. He leads in this modified approval rating, even surpassing the legendary Eisenhower. Eisenhower had almost no negative events in his first term, and he tied with Kennedy in positive-predicted events. Both Eisenhower and Kennedy enjoyed far better economic conditions than Reagan. Although these two presidents remain popular even in the modified ratings, they are outclassed by the gifted actor whose style and symbolism were chief features of his administration. Then, too, economic misery is an *objective* condition, the combined level of the actual consumer price index and unemployment levels. If in 1984 the Reagan White House did convince people that they were "better off financially" than they had been four years before, the *perceived* economic conditions might be far better than the objective ones. Reagan's popularity would be shaped by the perceived conditions, whereas his ranking would adjust for the more damaging objective ones.

Carter's relatively good position in the ranking also deserves attention. Richard Neustadt once observed that presidents have to guard their professional reputation, the way they are viewed by others in Washington, as well as their public reputation. Carter's position gives a clear illustration of Neustadt's advice. Observers of the Carter years tend to equate his poor relations with the press with his low public popularity.[16] This is understandable since the commentators, many professional public-relations people, see no difference between the press account and the public response. Carter was frequently *said* to be unpopular in news commentaries, but his ranking suggests that he was more popular than he was said to be. His reputation among professional president-watchers appears worse than his public reputation, suggesting that stories about killer rabbits and caricatures of Jimmy's smiling teeth meant more to the president-watchers than to the public.

Carter faced some of the worst economic conditions during his term and an even mix of negative and positive events. Once we control for these effects, we see that his public approval places him above average when compared to the other presidents. Indeed, had he confronted economic conditions like those during the Eisenhower or Kennedy years, he might have been one of our more popular presidents.

The rankings make sense when we consider the different presidential personalities: in particular, attitudes toward the public and the idea of being liked. A desire for popularity can take many different forms and fulfill various purposes; however, some people value these things more than others. Citizens might value these things differently also, some people preferring more or less public regard on the part of their presidents. In accord with these various preferences, the rankings can be read from top to bottom, from the middle, or from the bottom to the top.

The three presidents highest in the rankings do appear the most public-regarding, according to biographical and other accounts. Not only was Reagan professionally skilled at appealing to mass audiences but also his personal amiability was well known. While this amiability won liking, even from foreign heads of state, it also caused difficulties. White House advisers complained that Reagan appeared to agree with everyone, shifting his opinion according to whom he had spoken to last.

Eisenhower, too, was known as genial, with a famous grin and an ability to be liked that he used throughout his career; from the army, through all the intricacies of military politics, and into the White House. It is interesting that the other World War II generals complained of the same trait in Eisenhower that Reagan was criticized for—Ike's opinions seemed to shift depending on whom he spoke to. Each of the generals thought Eisenhower agreed with him.[17] Eisenhower certainly recognized the value of public opinion. As Fred Greenstein observes: "Eisenhower's seemingly effortless facility in winning public confidence never stopped him from also working to find additional ways to enhance support. . . . He was fully aware that his popularity was essential to his ability to exercise influence over other leaders."[18] Eisenhower commented to a friend that "One man can do a lot . . . if at that moment he happens to be ranking high in public estimation."[19] Whatever its purposes, popularity became a chief feature of the Eisenhower style.

Although Kennedy did not show the same amiability as Eisenhower or Reagan, his standing is not surprising. In the view of many observers, Kennedy tried to project a new image of personal leadership that was attractive, younger, and more vigorous than the leadership of the past. His pragmatism, too, led him to value public relations as necessary for gaining office and winning support in the White House. With Kennedy, the idea of style, skill in dealing with the press, and other public-relations efforts became more widely recognized components of the American presidency. His relative position in the ranking suggests that these efforts were in large part successful.

Ford, Johnson, and Truman are lowest in the rankings. Note that each was willing at one point in his term to take action that he knew was opposed by the public: Truman fired a popular general, Ford pardoned an unpopular president, and Johnson carried on an unpopular war. The events themselves, all negative-predicted, were supposedly controlled for; yet they signaled an attitude toward the public or the polls that might have wider impact, a kind of stubbornness in pursuing a course of action. Truman, who, as we noted earlier, had little use for polls, wrote cheerfully in his diary after he fired MacArthur: "Quite an explosion. Was expected but I had to act. Telegrams and letters of abuse by the dozens."[20] Even though Ford knew and said publicly that the American people would not stand for it, he pardoned Richard Nixon anyway, explaining that "my first consideration is to be true to my own convictions and my own conscience."[21] In the same spirit, both Truman and Ford placed among the veto leaders of the century, perhaps because they were more willing to engage in fights with Congress than to bargain and compromise. While Truman might have shown more pointedly and persistently than Ford that he did not cater to others' opinions, the two were similar in this basic approach. They did not mind conflict and did not need to be liked.

Although superficially different, Johnson fits well among the presidents who did not show a high concern about public approval. He made several major decisions to escalate the war in Vietnam as public opinion was building against the war. At the same time, he was virtually silent about his domestic program, which was sailing through the Congress, or about the favorable economic conditions of his time. Johnson achieved the lowest unemployment rate among modern presidents, but during all of 1966, he made no speeches to the public at large, except for the required State of the Union address. Advisers pleaded with him to address the "credibility gap" and speak to the public about the war, yet Johnson remained silent. "Why don't we say we achieved our objectives and go home," a senator suggested, offering a public-relations solution to the Vietnam War.[22] Johnson continued his course. While biographers have remarked that Johnson wanted to be liked, he did not act as if he did, at least as far as the public was concerned.

Johnson might have wanted to be liked, but he preferred to dominate others, according to Doris Kearns and other biographers.[23] His treatment of White House aides, his vice president, and fellow senators when he was majority leader did not suggest that he placed liking first. Yet Kearns also speaks of Johnson's conviction in pursuing any goal that he thought was right. He believed that his powers of persuasion—in Congress, for example—came from this conviction, and Kearns points out that the same belief underlaid much of his Vietnam decisions. As Kearns observes: "Failure while almost unbearable did not diminish his conviction."[24] Kearns also speaks at length of Johnson's misperception of public sentiment. As he once confided, "Deep down I knew—I simply knew—that the American people loved me. After all that I'd done for them and given to them, how could they help but love me?"[25] Accounts of Johnson's Vietnam decisions describe the same blend of conviction and misperception. As John Burke and Fred Greenstein observe: "Once Johnson had invested his ego in a policy, he could hold to it tenaciously. His convictions that he should not lose Vietnam and that he should leave as his historical legacy a massively expanded domestic welfare program are central to the politics of [the time]."[26]

To this extent, then, these three presidents drew the same line between fighting for their convictions and following a strong public opinion. Ford's "conscience," Truman's "right and wrong," and Johnson's "conviction," whether accurate or not, made them willing to make unpopular decisions.

It is interesting that the three presidents all came to office through succession; they are the accidental presidents. Perhaps this is coincidence. But it may suggest that this particular kind of stubborn conviction is not likely to withstand the obstacles of the normal election process. Nominations and elections appear to reward the more public-regarding individuals, screening out those with other key traits. Seldom do we hear election campaigns featuring the word *conviction*.

This leaves two presidents, Carter and Nixon, in the middle of the rankings. Writers have characterized each in terms of the contradictions in his approach. Nixon, the pragmatic and skilled politician, could win popularity and yet create negative impressions. Carter, caught in a conflict between principle and pragmatism, varied in how public regarding he was. Biographer Erwin Hargrove sees this conflict as central to understanding the Carter administration.[27] According to this interpretation, Carter and Nixon do not fit well in either of the other groupings, but form a separate mixed category.

Personality does appear to help explain these differences among presidents and the variation in individual impact beyond their common constraints. James David Barber, for example, presents a famous classification of presidents as either active or passive and as positive or negative in basic character traits.[28] It is interesting that two presidents Barber calls passive—Reagan and Eisenhower—lead in these approval ratings. According to the Barber scheme, these personalities are characterized by low self-esteem and concern with gaining approval. The presidents lowest in our ranking might not have shown *high* self-esteem according to many indicators of personality, but they were able to make decisions knowing that a loss of approval would follow. One does not need to follow Barber's approach, however, to see the very different styles of those high or low in the ranking.

THE SECOND TERM

While the second terms of Eisenhower, Nixon, and Reagan seem unique at first glance, they show intriguing parallels. Each of these presidents was ushered in with a large electoral victory. Eisenhower and Reagan won 58 percent and 59 percent of the popular vote, respectively, and Nixon won 61 percent. Eisenhower swept all but seven states in the electoral college, while

Nixon and Reagan swept all but one. Each administration also faced a scandal: Eisenhower had trouble when scandal engulfed his most trusted adviser, Sherman Adams; Nixon had Watergate; and Reagan had Iran-Contra.

Adams, a symbol of Yankee incorruptibility and Republican rectitude, was shown to have accepted expensive presents from a woolen manufacturer whose troubles with a federal regulatory agency led to phone calls from Adams to the agency. Eisenhower came to Adams' defense with a statement explaining that a gift is not necessarily a bribe and concluding with the famous line, "I need him." The gifts had included several thousand dollars in hotel bills, an Oriental rug, and an expensive coat woven from the wool of the exotic vicuña. Adams, who had made many enemies when guarding the door of Eisenhower's office during the first term and deciding who would get to see the president, came to be intensely criticized. Eisenhower backed down, indicating that he would not ask for Adams' resignation, but hoped he would resign. Adams did.

Biographer Peter Lyon points out that Adams' resignation left behind "a mounting swell of criticism of Eisenhower." He had appointed Adams, made him his palace guard, attempted to explain away the gifts, and then deserted him.[29] These events of the more innocent past may seem far removed from the illegalities of Watergate and Iran-Contra, yet they cast a shadow over the first half of Eisenhower's second term.

The shadow over Reagan's second term developed more gradually, undermining his administration from late 1986 until the time he left office. Reagan had argued in his 1984 campaign that he would never negotiate with terrorists. Thus, when the news broke in late 1986 of the secret arms deal with Iran, trading arms for hostages, the administration plunged into trouble. A news conference in which the president denied that he had approved the trade only made matters worse. Reagan appeared befuddled, many observers reported. Indeed, he later retracted many of his statements. The arms deal led to further disclosures about a diversion of funds to the Nicaraguan Contras and the subsequent resignations of administration officials Oliver North and John Poindexter, Reagan's national security adviser. Congress began to investigate, and the president's poll ratings plummeted. By early 1987, they had fallen 20 points from the time of the second inauguration and would remain low for the rest of Reagan's term.

Other troubles beset the Reagan White House with the indictment of former White House aide Michael Deaver for lying about his conflict of interest activities and the indictment of another former associate, Lyn Nofziger, for illegal lobbying. Edwin Meese, the attorney general and the nation's chief law enforcement officer, became the subject of investigation in the Wedtech scandal. Meese had to appoint an independent counsel to investigate himself and finally resigned in July 1988.

Nixon's troubles developed quickly when the Watergate cover-up began to unravel in early 1973. The Senate investigation began at that time, revealing that Nixon had taped his Oval Office conversations and initiating a chain of events that would culminate in his resignation in August of the following year. Nixon also faced the scandal and investigation surrounding Vice President Spiro Agnew, who finally resigned before Congress could bring charges to impeach him. Nixon's second term lasted a little more than a year and a half.

Despite all these exceptional occurrences, the influences on the polls that were seen for these presidents' first terms held equally well for the second. The decay across time, the economy, dramatic events, and individual variation continued to show substantial effects, and together they explain much of the surface fluctuation. This is a general pattern of influence, we conclude, applicable to either first or second terms and to typical as well as atypical times.

However, the second terms were different from the first in two dramatic ways. First, the ratio of negative to positive events was much larger during the second terms. Although 56 percent of the events were negative in first-term presidencies, 72 percent were negative in the second term. This is not merely a product of Watergate. All three of the second-term presidents faced more negative than positive events. Reagan did best, with thirteen negative to ten positive events. Eisenhower's good luck deserted him in his second term, with five negative to two positive events—strikes, the Sherman Adams scandal, the integration crisis at Little Rock, and the launching of the Soviet *Sputnik*. Nixon had seventeen negative events compared to one positive event, counting the separate major occurrences in the Watergate scandal. All of Nixon's negative events, except two, were Watergate-related. He also suffered the scandal surrounding Vice President Spiro Agnew and made the hard choice of announcing a price freeze to curb inflationary trends. See Appendix A for a list of events.

Nondiscretionary events also occurred more frequently in the second terms than in the first (72 percent of the events in the second terms versus 64 percent in the first). Both Reagan and Eisenhower were involved in more nondiscretionary events than discretionary ones, while Nixon's second term was dominated by events over which he had no control. Overall, the higher level of negative-predicted events, and nondiscretionary events, in the second terms suggests that second-term presidents eventually pay for things set in motion during their first terms. The illegal actions taken and approved in Watergate were *first-term* events, and discretionary ones, although they were not recognized at the time. Also, Sherman Adams had accepted his expensive presents and made his enemies in the first Eisenhower term. Although Reagan signed the secret intelligence finding to trade arms for hostages during his second term, it developed from early policy decisions. The diversion of funds to the Contras and the activities of Oliver North and CIA Director William Casey also carried over from his first term. Decisions taken in first terms came to light in the second, with significant and negative effects on the polls.

The second terms are different, too, because they show a steeper decay in public approval, what we have called the cycle of deflating expectations. The decline begins much sooner and is much steeper in the second term (see Figure 2.4). Remember that this decline is independent of the negative circumstances. It is independent of Watergate, Iran-Contra, and Eisenhower's growing troubles. Indeed, it emerges just as strongly when the Nixon years are removed. So, even though poll ratings return to a high point at the second inauguration, they begin to fall immediately, with a significant decline apparent by the third month. Substantial monthly decreases in approval continue through the middle of the third year.

The plight of second-term presidents will need to be watched in the future, when we have more than three cases to consider. These cases do show, however, how quickly landslide elections fade. Even before scandals surface, the poll ratings begin their slide. Fourteen months into Eisenhower's second term, only 50 percent of the public approved of the way he was doing his job. In Nixon's case, even before the Senate committee brought its Watergate revelations to the nation's living rooms, only 48 percent approved of how Nixon was doing his job. His ratings never were as high again.

The cases of Eisenhower, Nixon, and Reagan also bring a new meaning to the term *lame duck*. Lame-duck officeholders, known to be retiring soon, find it difficult to bargain and be persuasive because people are already thinking about their successors. Presidents already weakened in bargaining with other officials are weakened further by a withdrawal of public support. The fact that these three incumbents had scandals to contend with might be coincidence or might be a logical concomitant of the second-term plight. Perhaps potential scandals need more than one term to surface, or perhaps a more general withdrawal of support makes it easier for them to become issues. It is worth remembering that the break-in of the Democratic headquarters in the Watergate Hotel complex was known before the 1972 election and was, broadly speaking, part of reelection activity. A few journalists wanted to pursue the story, and a committee in Congress tried to start an investigation. Amid the excitement of the campaign, however, the story disappeared, and the committee could not get a majority to vote for subpoena power. The Democrat-controlled committee could not get enough support to investigate why its own headquarters was under attack by a committee to reelect the Republican president. It was only after the reelection that the Watergate story became news and Congress began thinking of an investigation.

The polls do not create lame-duck presidents, but they heighten and dramatize their debilitating effect. Having just won

Figure 2.4 The Decay Function: The Second Term

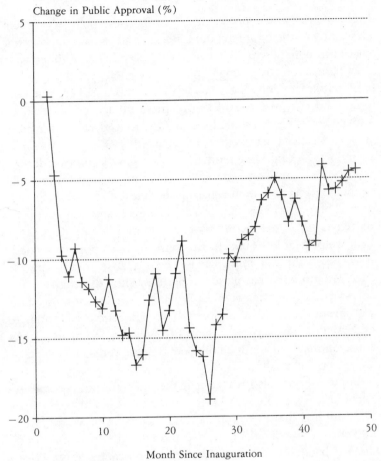

Change in Public Approval (%)

Month Since Inauguration

the highest victory American politics has to offer, second-term presidents face a withdrawal of support. If they have waited for their second term to address controversial issues or to find their place in history, they soon discover the ironies. They will find less public favor for controversial programs, and any first-term mistakes that come to light will threaten to make their place in history much less glorious.

BEHIND THE SURFACE

From the day a new president takes office, the polls begin their constantly changing referendum. Because all citizens supposedly speak through these polls, what do they need to know about what they themselves are saying?

A pattern of influences spans forty years and very different styles and circumstances. Each of these influences is linked to expectations. People should see that the polls decline over time, in what we call a decay curve, independently of anything a president does. During a first term, the polls begin a significant decline at the sixth month and continue to fall into the third year. Only as the next election approaches do the tides of approval begin to turn. The poll ratings fall quickly, however, and decrease even more sharply in the second term. So, an initially popular incumbent will appear in trouble by the third year, or a popular second-term president will immediately begin a slide. Before people speculate on what has gone wrong, they should recognize, and adjust for, this automatic effect. What was wrong, or misleading, was the inflated initial support. The time curve is central to understanding a feature of the office, which continually renews expectations that cannot be fulfilled. All presidents, quite literally, are set up for a fall.

People should also realize that the polls are not accurate reflections of the job a president is doing. A good part of the fluctuation is due to factors beyond the scope of White House influence. For example, polls rise and fall with economic conditions. Changes in economic misery significantly affect how a president is evaluated. Dramatic events that reflect the state of the nation also affect the polls, whether the president is involved in the event or not. Race riots in Chicago and a Soviet attack on a Korean plane say nothing about the job the president is doing, yet they do affect public evaluations of that job. Presidents can neither stop the decay of support over time nor reverse a bad economic report, even though they make small economic adjustments from time to time. They control only a portion of their positive and negative events. Overall, the ratio clearly favors the negative and nondiscretionary. Consequently, we note that Eisenhower and Carter were dealt two very different hands. Although the results suggest that they played those hands equally well, one president is revered for his popularity and the other is not.

Of course, presidents have some control over their popularity. They can choose some of the dramatic events that will occur in their administrations—the hard choices and the positive discretionary events. Presidents do make hard choices: fire generals, double the draft, grant unpopular pardons, and institute inflation controls. There is, then, an area of discretion remaining that includes the making of unpopular choices. They have an additional impact through their skills and personality or other individual talents. Anecdotal evidence indicates that Truman was not one to curry favor with the press or public, and that Reagan was both professionally and intuitively skilled at winning such favor. These impressions are borne out by individual rankings.

Nevertheless, the results of this chapter pose disturbing questions. Positive-predicted events had the strongest effect on approval, in both the first and second terms. Since these are largely international, they support the worries of some writers, such as Theodore Lowi, that international crises are almost the only things that will improve a president's poll ratings.[30] (Assassination attempts and other health threats would hardly be recommended as a way of buttressing falling support.) Presidents also are pressured to find something to rally falling support, but the options are few. Although the area of discretion allows presidents to rally public support, it can also tempt the more cynical occupants of the office, and their advisers, to emphasize short-term impacts over long-term goals.

Do all short military interventions mean that a president is doing a good job? Does the public wish to instruct the president to do more of these things in order to gain their valuable support? How can national problems be addressed, if a president is penalized for addressing them? People have raised these issues before; this chapter suggests that they are realistic cause for worry.

The polls have altered the time frame of democratic government, from quadrennial election to monthly review. The time is too short for presidents to learn from experience, letting programs ripen or broader judgments dictate the choice and timing of events. The time frame is not only limited but also biased, sloping downward with an inexorable decline of support. Confronting this time frame, first-term incumbents may be tempted to postpone issues until they win reelection, and those who win another term may find that their problems have only begun. Of course, it would be nice to think that presidents should be high-minded enough to discount these short-term incentives by tackling the hard problems and resisting the temptation of invading nearby small Latin American nations. Carter was perhaps the best example of a president who tried this high-minded course—and was widely *criticized* for doing exactly this. Many White House advisers felt Carter's forthrightness about the problems confronting the country was a "serious public relations liability," according to scholar Mark Rozell. Another White House staffer added that he could not remember a single program or policy that was popular and helped Carter politically. A common assessment, Rozell points out, was that "Carter insisted on pushing 'second-term issues'—ones a president emphasizes only after he does not have to worry about the electoral consequences of unpopular choices."[31] It is unlikely for Carter to be a model on how to break the pressure of the public-opinion polls.

Much of the polls' inaccuracy, as we have seen, comes from the gap between the real political world and unrealistic expectations: Presidents must bring us together, give us jobs, and solve key national problems. These expectations doom the polls to fall once the real work of government begins, discourage attention to domestic problems, and reward even the bungling of international events. They shape the influences that have been identified in this chapter: the effects of time, the economy, and dramatic national events. Consequently, if we are going to watch the polls, we also have to watch the expectations. People might argue that idealistic views of the presidency provide necessary support for incumbents. Saying that presidents have power gives them more power; reducing expectations takes something important away. Nevertheless, this chapter has indicated that the expectations are primarily constraining, or limiting, in their impact. They reduce support over time, withdraw it further in the second term, and exact penalties for a range of circumstances beyond control.

Paradoxically, more modest and realistic views of what presidents can do should allow them to do more.

More fundamentally, people might ask what kind of presidential support they expect. When individuals are elected president, they receive on average a little more than half of the votes of those American citizens who cast ballots. Only Johnson among the modern presidents won his first election by more than 55 percent of the popular vote.[32] Sweeps of the electoral college help us forget how narrow the margins are in many of the states. Kennedy won with about 50 percent of the vote, Nixon in 1968 with even less. New presidents must try to govern in the same context in which they were elected: in a plural society, with two competitive political parties and many conflicting interests. If they continue to receive somewhat more than 50 percent of the support of American citizens, they are doing well, carrying on their electoral mandate. If we expect them to do more, we transform them into the kind of symbolic figure—a leader of all Americans—who can exist only in times of external crisis. It is not surprising that it is in these times that the polls show their exceptional increase.

Democracies do not demand that all citizens have the same opinions. They typically ask for a majority vote. If we apply this principle to our interpretation of the polls, presidents will be able to govern with the same mandate on which they were elected. They might even be able to face controversies and to address problems while carrying this mandate forward.

3

Actions and Reactions

ONLY so many patriotic events in any one term can be used to bolster a president's falling approval. Other, more frequent activities, however, can offer a substitute, unifying the nation around its symbols of the president and the flag. These are the routine and ceremonial acts of office—speeches to the American people, trips abroad, and travel around the nation. Perhaps these, too, are positive acts designed to increase public support. They show in their own symbolic way that the president is doing a good job.

Consequently, presidents shuttle from London to Salt Lake City and back to the Rose Garden, with armies of staff workers coordinating each step along the way. Some people argue that presidents are increasingly "going public" and that these public-directed symbolic activities are replacing older styles of bargaining and compromise.[1] According to this line of reasoning, Jimmy Carter's series of town meetings, geographically distributed across the country, could be seen as having reasserted common democratic values and showed that the age of the imperial presidency was over. Richard Nixon's European tour, near the end of his beleaguered administration, could be seen as having reminded people of his statesmanship and foreign policy achievements. The Reagan years, according to this argument, brought such activities to a new height of professionalism: With "heavy political travel, numerous appearances before organized constituencies, and extensive use of television," every day in office became part of an ongoing election campaign.[2]

These observers note that public-relations presidencies have become more frequent and stronger in recent years and worry that presidents will soon not need programs at all—they will merely issue statements about broccoli and visit children in the hospital. Add on a few dramatic international rally points, and their popularity and reelection will be assured.

Of course, these activities need not be merely means to increase popularity. Presidents can engage in foreign trips to try to strengthen the nation's foreign policy, carving their own place in history as they do so. Domestic travel serves party or legislative policy goals—presidents can barnstorm the country to help their party in election years or bestow favors on individual members of Congress, favors that they hope will be repaid in votes on legislation. Major addresses, too, might be made to defend policies, even though studies show that the addresses do not actually change opinions. The public might like a president more after an address, but it has not changed its mind about the policy he is arguing for.

Presidents are expected to be world leaders who make foreign policy as they visit with dignitaries and travel abroad. They are supposed to speak for all Americans, even though they have been voted for by only a fraction of the people (a little more than 50 percent of the 51 percent who vote). Traveling the country and addressing the nation on prime-time television symbolically extend their constituency to all of the people. Listen to Gerald Ford in a speech to the nation in his first days: "I will be the President of black, brown, red and white Americans, of old and young . . . of the poor and the rich, of native sons and new refugees, of those who work at lathes or at desks or in mines or in the fields. . . ." With these expectations, it is no wonder that presidents cross the country speaking to one group after another—old and young, rich and poor, teachers, preachers, and Boy Scouts.[3] Ford, unelected as either president or vice president, might have felt a particular need to demonstrate the point, especially because of the swiftly approaching 1976 campaign.

This is an example of the energetic presidency that the American people have come to expect. Its roots go back to Alexander Hamilton, who wrote in *The Federalist Papers* of the executive's need for "vigor and energy." It was carried into the twentieth century by the actions of Franklin Roosevelt; the inaugural rhetoric of John Kennedy; and the memory of Woodrow Wilson, touring Europe to cheering crowds as he worked for the League of Nations and the Treaty of Versailles. In its newest form, this type of presidency is institutionalized in the modern election campaign, with its grueling schedule of traveling and speaking, typically lasting more than a year. If we can say nothing else about the candidates we elect president, we know they are energetic.

Is there a kind of institutionalized public-relations activity that can be engaged in primarily for popularity, whether in the polls or at the ballot box? Or are presidential activities more mixed, reflecting different personalities, motives, and choices? If these activities do appear to be calculated primarily for their public relations, the public should know this; if these activities do not, the public should know this, too, and so should the present and future officeholders. If presidents think that they should be public-relations experts primarily, they will attempt to follow the expectation, whether or that is what the public actually wants.

So, to paraphrase Howard Baker from the Senate Watergate hearings, we ask what did the presidents do and when did they do it? First, we examine whether the activities changed from one president to another or if there were trends developing across administrations. Activities can be selected for a number of reasons only peripherally related to popularity. Presidents might feel that they should do certain things because their predecessors did them. Or, they might make their selections more personally, following their own likes and dislikes and constraints. Second, we need to discover when the activities occurred, if they were randomly distributed or patterned over the course of each president's term. Presidents are electorally strategic actors, who, in order to gain their office, have learned to campaign, strategize, and allocate scarce resources effectively. It is unlikely that, once in the White House, they would suspend these strategic tendencies. Instead, given finite resources, we would expect them to allocate activities carefully, whether to achieve reelection or to pursue some other goal. The activities would be *strategic*—patterned in their occurrence. At the same time, presidents would need to watch their immediate political standings as reflected in the polls rather than the longer-term electoral prospects. If this were the case, they would allocate activities to maintain their public approval. These activities would be *reactive,* responsive to the ups and downs of the polls. In either case, the activities would be patterned in definite ways. Otherwise, if the activities were not being used for these purposes, they would occur randomly.

Third, we must ask if these activities helped a particular president's popularity and if some helped more than others. Not all ceremonial acts are successful. Nixon's travel did not stop the steady slide of his polls that led ultimately to his resignation. Carter's town meetings, having failed to stop his sliding popularity in his first year, were soon abandoned; people said that he did not seem imperial enough. Even Ronald Reagan, with all his professional advisers and personal experience and skill, found that travel could be politically costly, as the outcry over his trip to Bitburg, Germany, showed. (The cemetery there that he planned to visit, to demonstrate goodwill between Germany and the United States, contained graves of Nazi S.S. officers.) Certainly George Bush might have wished he had skipped his early 1992 trip to Japan, where his vomiting from stomach flu during a formal dinner at the Emperor's residence was witnessed by a worldwide television audience. Despite the sympathy Americans may have felt for this kind of ultimate embarrassment, it was hardly a diplomatic coup, and it did not begin Bush's reelection year auspiciously. This scene also suggested an unfortunate visual metaphor. Bush was in Japan to discuss the Japanese-American trade balance, which many Americans were exceedingly worried about. The sight of the American president collapsing into the arms of the prime minister was not a confidence-inspiring picture.

Chief among the presidential activities we will examine were major speeches to the nation, trips abroad, and domestic travel outside Washington, D.C., or the various presidential residences. The major speeches include all live addresses televised to a national audience.[4] Each of these ceremonial activities was part of the expected schedule from Truman to Bush. Each was covered extensively by the media. And each demonstrated in its own way that the president was on the job. Their occurrence across the modern presidency, as shown in Table 3.1, provides a reference point for the discussion that follows.

Overall, presidents are less active than people think. In their first terms, they spend an average of two to three days each month on domestic travel and an average of one day or less in travel abroad. The average corporate executive probably travels much more. However, it is true that, since Kennedy, presidents travel more than their predecessors, reflecting the technological improvements over time. Truman took no foreign trips in his first elected term; Eisenhower took one. Major speeches add little

Table 3.1

What Presidents Do

Average Number of Major Addresses and Days of Domestic and Foreign Travel per Month

	Major Addresses	Domestic Travel	Foreign Travel
Truman	.31	1.69	.00
Eisenhower	.39	1.42	.17
Kennedy	.38	2.44	.65
Johnson	.33	1.98	.69
Nixon	.48	2.00	1.23
Ford	.38	4.41	1.00
Carter	.34	2.66	1.13
Reagan	.46	3.04	.89
Average	.38	2.35	.70
Range	0–2	0–24	0–13

Note: Averages for travel are computed using total days in office.
Source: Compiled from data in the *Public Papers of the Presidents* (Washington, D.C.: Government Printing Office, various volumes).

to the work load because they are given only about four or five times a year.

While there is considerable stability evident over the years, there is variety, too. Major addresses to the nation show the stability most clearly. Nixon and Reagan gave the greatest number of speeches, and Truman and Johnson the least, although the differences are slight. Presidents not only make about the same number of major addresses but also make them on the same subjects, often using the same words. In addition to the inaugural address and the obligatory State of the Union addresses, the most frequent subjects of speeches are foreign policy and broad statements of economic policy, for a total of about five speeches a year. Only rarely—Carter on energy policy, Nixon on wage-price guidelines—have speeches dealt with specific domestic proposals. Anyone who follows these speeches over the years will notice the striking similarity in wording. For example, Nixon in an economic speech asked the nation to choose "the road of responsibility . . . , the road we are continuing on today," and Ford called on people to "choose instead the other road, the road that we know to be tested, the road that will work." In yet another economic speech, Reagan said that "Congress will stand at the fork of two roads. One road is all too familiar to us. . . . The other road promises to renew the American spirit."[5] What each president does becomes part of the institution, shaping the expectations of future presidents.

Institutional expectations affect activity, as the similarity among presidents shows. Technology also has its impact. Foreign and domestic travel increased in the Kennedy years, with the onset of the jet age. Truman and Eisenhower simply did not have available the technology to make quick trips around the world. There are seasonal influences as well. All activities decrease in the winter. About half of the days of foreign travel occur from May to August. Since this is a period when Congress is not in session, presidents might well have less government work to keep them at home. However, this is also the time when Americans are less attentive to national news. Just as television programming takes a hiatus in the summer, so presidents make a change from their daily routines.

These are not the only influences, however. Foreign travel, major addresses, and domestic travel are patterned in definite ways during each four-year term. The greatest number of major addresses occur in the first half of a reelection year (the twelfth and thirteenth quarters). Similarly, foreign trips increase as election nears, most of them occurring in the spring of the reelection year, while domestic trips reach their peak in the fall of the election year. Altogether, such presidential activities accelerate from the spring to the fall of each election year.

When we look more closely at the first terms of all the modern presidents, even clearer patterns emerge (see Appendix B). Thus we find that major addresses occur strategically, with greater frequency in each presidential reelection year. Because their frequency is lower in midterm election years, such speeches might be directed to specific reelections and not to elections generally. They are also reactive, more likely to occur in a month after a president's approval has fallen. The good luck that presidents inherit and the hard choices they make also appear to accompany their speeches. They speak both to capitalize on an event that will enhance their support and to explain a hard choice they have had to make. When they have bad luck, however, they remain silent. Major addresses also decline when inflation runs high, illustrating their inverse relationship to bad events. In short, speeches appear closely calculated to enhance popularity, for reelection and for maintaining approval in the polls.

Foreign trips show different patterns, although they also are timed in definite ways. Foreign travel is scheduled in a strategic manner, with the most trips taken in presidential reelection years, not during midterm election years. Foreign travel is also reactive, more likely to occur in response to a drop in a monthly poll. Good luck and bad luck reduce the likelihood of such travel: On these occasions, presidents stay home. The results stay the same whether we consider all the presidents or exclude Truman and Eisenhower, who had fewer opportunities to travel.

Domestic trips follow still another pattern. They, too, are allocated strategically but are taken more often in both presidential reelection and midterm election years. These trips appear to be allocated to elect members of the president's party at midterm. Like foreign trips, domestic travel is reduced by the occurrence of good luck; but unlike foreign travel, domestic travel is more likely to occur after good luck or after a president has made a hard choice, and it is positively related to higher inflation. Again, the results are essentially the same when Truman and Eisenhower are excluded.[6]

People have come to realize that presidents follow electoral cycles in many of their activities. They apparently choose major addresses and foreign travel to coincide with their own elections. They seem to direct domestic travel toward broader electoral goals when they travel at midterm to elect the loyal and defeat the opposition. But presidents do more than watch the next election. Major addresses and foreign and domestic travel are curiously timed to accord with month-to-month changes in approval ratings and the kind of events that affect those ratings. These are much shorter time frames, shaped by the polls, that the presidents appear to follow. In particular, scheduling follows the kind of circumstances that presidents cannot otherwise control.

WHAT DIFFERENCE DOES IT MAKE?

"Going public" is not one unified approach or strategy but includes a variety of activities pursued with different objectives in mind. Nevertheless, we do find some recurring patterns, both strategic and reactive. *If presidents know what they are doing,* then their activities should have an impact on the polls, although some acts would be more useful than others in extending their small supply of positive events.

To understand what effect these activities have on presidential approval ratings, we need to see them independently of the other influences: the economy, the decay over time, and dramatic events. For example, a president may take a trip at a particular point in time—when the economy is good or bad, when dramatic events are occurring, or when public support is at a particular point. We want to know what *additional* impact these activities have over and above the other influences. What impact, for example, does a speech have apart from the event the speech may be talking about? Apparently, quite a lot.

Activity	Change
Major address	→ Positive
Foreign travel	→ No difference
Domestic travel	→ Negative

The results (see Appendix B), showing the monthly change in the polls for each address or day of travel, are clear and striking: Each major address adds on average about 6 percentage points in the polls. This positive effect, independent of any dramatic event that may have prompted the speech, is also seen in other studies.[7] Domestic trips, by contrast, *hurt* a president's public standing, with each day of domestic travel costing him between 1 and 2 percentage points. Incidentally, the same negative effect is found for minor addresses, the speeches presidents make to special groups while on the road.[8] Foreign travel makes no overall difference.

Some people expect that each of these acts would have a positive impact on the polls. One writer cites Eisenhower's "good will" world tour in his second term as the first trip where popularity was the primary consideration. He also quotes Reagan staffers, who admitted frankly that the president's first trip to Europe had a public-relations goal: "Because the polls were showing a drop in the president's popularity—which made him vulnerable in Washington—his advisers decided that conferring on location with European heads of state would be good for his image as a leader."[9] The polls may have risen because of these two trips, due to any number of things; however, when we look at the trips apart from the other major influences, they do not show positive effects. Some kinds of "going public" help popularity, other kinds hurt it, and still other kinds make no difference overall.

Public activities, then, do not significantly alter the picture we saw previously. Presidents cannot expand their resources very much beyond the small supply of dramatic events. A large share of this activity actually makes no difference in public standing, it even hurts. Only major addresses, taken about four times a year, buttress dwindling support. Presidents appear to know this, since they do not travel when their polls are falling—they stay in Washington and give a major address or remain silent. Foreign trips, which do not affect the polls, are taken when there is no imminent threat of a decline in public standing. On these trips, presidents help to build their reputations as world leaders—and have vacations—but do not "go public" in the same way as when they give major addresses.

Domestic trips, by contrast, show a negative effect. The reason for this is not immediately apparent. Perhaps a president's travels at the midterm happen to coincide with the nadir of approval that typically occurs near a midterm election. Although we have tried to adjust for this cyclical impact, there some negative effect may remain. It is more likely that the politics surrounding such trips at the midterm hurt a president's approval. In their effort to support a congressional candidate, presidents may associate themselves with regional candidates or issues that may alienate others. For example, when Ronald Reagan stood on a platform with Jesse Helms, who was running for reelection to the Senate, the photographs of the smiling duo alienated citizens who liked the president but disliked the senator. Any association with domestic politics of this kind highlights national problems and, as in the case of more dramatic events, can be predicted to lower support.

Following this line of argument, we can appreciate the very different impact of the three activities we have been discussing. Each makes sense in terms of basic public expectations. Domestic travel decreases support; by drawing attention to domestic problems, it suggests that the president is not doing a good job. Foreign travel makes little difference. On the one hand, it does not occur at times of international crises, which rally public support; on the other hand, it attracts attention away from domestic events and their potentially depressing effect. Hence, its neutral effect becomes more understandable. Other forms of diplomatic activity, as we will see later, also make no difference in the polls. It is when presidents address the nation that the most positive impact appears. They control the content and timing of the speeches in large part, focusing attention on subjects important to them. Typically, they speak from the White House, with its historic and powerful symbolism. Here is the president in Washington along with the signs and symbols of office. It is easy to see why some people approve of the job he is doing at such a time.

Whether the White House knows that domestic trips hurt at the polls is another question. Trips do help gather regional support within the party before the off-year elections and presidential elections, as presidents touch base with the fund-raisers and party people they need. However, these trips are not scheduled only before off-year and presidential-year elections. They are taken throughout the four years and in times of rising and falling popularity. It is possible that the presidents themselves mistakenly think this travel will help their public standing. When his polls fell so drastically at the end of the third year, George Bush scheduled a series of domestic trips. These, according to press commentary, were supposed to rally support and show that Bush was concerned with the nation's problems. Bush's advisers would hardly have scheduled such trips if they thought the polls would fall further.

Since major speeches appear to be the one way of increasing support, why do presidents not make more of them? The record now stands at seven major speeches in one year, shared by Eisenhower, Nixon, and Reagan. Tradition suggests they may become too much of a good thing and should be used only sparingly. As no less a public-relations expert than Franklin Roosevelt once observed: "The public psychology [cannot] be attuned for long periods of time to the highest note on the scale. . . . People tire of seeing the same name, day after day, in the important headlines of the papers and the same voice, night after night, over the radio."[10]

Modern writers, quoting Roosevelt, offer the same advice: "Although major addresses may be the most dramatic and most effective approach for influencing public opinion, they also can be the most taxing," one analyst remarks. "If every presidential tribulation were taken to the country on prime time television, people would soon lose interest."[11] This apparently constitutes the approved wisdom on the subject of major speeches. Yet experience does not support the central logic of Roosevelt's argument: Certainly, modern readers do see the president's name daily in the headlines, and the White House Press Office makes sure that the name will appear. Almost without exception, a White House story appears on the front page of the major newspapers every day.[12] Perhaps people do tire of the name in the headlines *and* the face on television, but we have no way of knowing if they tire of one more than the other. No one has dared test the waters. In any case, presidents do not seem to be willing to challenge the Roosevelt dictum—and break the tradition of the office—by making a sharp increase in major speeches.

Also, it is not clear that presidents should keep silent during hard times. Nixon was the only one to speak to the nation in his first term consistently through a period of negative events. He faced widespread protests on the war and the bombing of Cambodia and other domestic divisions culminating in the killings at Kent State. Nixon's speeches featured Vietnam, domestic dissent, and the need for inflation controls. His polls did decline with the typical decay curve: from 60 percent on the average in the first year, to 57 percent in the second, and 50 percent in the third. The decline is shallow, however. One could argue on the circumstantial evidence that Nixon timed his speeches to minimize the negative effects of protests. Even after all the negative events, by the end of the third year, Nixon lost only 10 percentage points in the polls.

The example usually cited against president's addressing substantive problems is Jimmy Carter's three energy speeches, which he gave in his first year in office. In one, he wore a sweater to show that times were getting chillier and asked people to set their thermostats at 65 degrees. The media commentary was largely critical. Carter had been ineffectual or discouraging, according to some writers; the sweater did not inspire the proper presidential awe. Yet when we look at the month-to-month poll changes at the points when Carter gave these speeches, we find that the public did not necessarily agree with the commentators: Carter's poll ratings increased slightly, as one would expect following a presidential address. There is probably more room to experiment with addressing substantive problems in speeches than people might think.

THE SECOND TERM

Analyzing the activities of the presidents in their second terms is difficult for two reasons. First, only three presidents have been reelected to a second term since World War II. Second, due to Watergate, the Nixon administration was highly anomalous, suffering ever-declining polls and eventually resignation. Ordinarily we would expect activities in the second term to differ, with presidential election concerns no longer a motivating force. Yet, with the small number and, in one instance, atypical nature of these administrations, it is difficult to generalize about them. Nonetheless, some striking and plausible patterns suggest a significant drop in energy in second terms (see Appendix B).

In the first place, major addresses no longer show a reactivity to public approval: Presidents appear less motivated to speak during the second terms following a drop in the polls. Not surprisingly, major addresses are not timed to accord with the electoral clock since there is no reelection campaign to look forward to. In all, only inflation continues to exert a notable influence on major addresses during second terms, with presidents less likely to speak when inflation is high. But even this effect is slight. There is still some tendency for presidents to hide from the public as the economy worsens, but it is only a faint echo of the rule followed so carefully during first terms.[13]

Second-term travel schedules are different, too. Although domestic trips were previously not affected by the polls, during second terms they tend to follow changes in approval. In other words, presidents who suffer a drop in approval in their second terms are less likely to travel domestically. Second-term presidents are also significantly less likely to travel during midterm elections. With less direct stakes in these election outcomes, they stay in Washington instead of going across the country, as they did during their first terms. Second-term presidents do follow their previous habits in one way: They cut down domestic travel following occasions of good luck. Their foreign travel schedules maintain some of the first-term patterns. Poor economic conditions and bad luck continue to keep presidents home, although they do not alter their schedules following good luck. They are, however, much more likely to schedule foreign trips in the final year of their administrations. The idea that presidents might wish to establish a final diplomatic victory as their legacy is borne out by this result. In the final year of their first terms, presidents step up their travel schedules, both domestic and foreign. In the last year of their second terms, they cut back domestic travel and increase foreign trips.

The consequences of this activity differ even more markedly. Quite simply, *none* of it helps to maintain a president's falling approval. Even major addresses show negative results. Foreign trips make no difference, showing a very slight negative effect. When Nixon is excluded from our data, thus removing the severely negative context of Watergate, the results improve only slightly. Foreign trips emerge as very weakly positive influences of presidential approval. Major addresses and domestic trips continue to show negative effects, although their magnitude is diminished. With or without Nixon included, none of these effects is substantial (see Appendix B).

All of this underscores what appears to be a lessening of presidential impact during second terms. Activities are fewer, are less coherently structured, and show no positive effects on public approval. The change in the impact of speeches to the nation is particularly of interest. Perhaps there is a qualitative difference between terms in these speeches, with presidents more motivated to speak in publicly pleasing ways during their first terms than during their second. Or perhaps lame-duck presidents no longer convey the same aura or stature that evoked a positive response in the first term. On the other hand, the result may simply derive from the particular presidents who won second terms and the scandals surrounding them. Nixon spoke frequently on Watergate-related matters, while Reagan talked about the Iran-Contra affair, although he talked on other subjects, too. Given the subject matter of some of the speeches, a less-than-enthusiastic response is not surprising. In any case, the record thus far suggests further limits on second-term presidents. Faced with sharply falling popularity, they cannot rely on their speeches to the nation to revive public support.

By way of contrast, second terms point up even more sharply the patterns of the first terms, where activities appear to be calculated carefully and produce very clear effects. These, we might say, are the working rules of the public-relations presidency, the patterns all officeholders must confront. If they do not handle their first terms well, they will have no second chance.

THE INDIVIDUAL CASES

We can now see how individual presidents scheduled their various activities, how they varied one from another, and which presidents instinctively seemed to allocate their acts with the polls in mind. Each of the first-term presidents (except Ford) faced the same calendar: Four years to advance their programs, develop their own public personalities, and allocate their time and energies to prepare for reelection. Ford had to run on a much shorter schedule, with less than two and a half years to work within. As it turned out, of course, two presidents, Truman and Johnson, decided later not to run for reelection, and Kennedy was assassinated at the end of his third year. Nevertheless, it is interesting to see how the various choices were made.

Truman and Eisenhower present a sharp contrast. Truman's polls began to fall immediately after his 1949 inauguration and continued to fall by 30 points halfway through his second year. The high inflation and major strikes of the period certainly took their toll. However, note that he gave only three speeches (two of them required) in this period and engaged in little domestic travel until May 1950. Travel did not help him at the polls. After a brief rally point at the onset of the Korean War, Truman's polls continued to fall, even though he gave several speeches during this period. By the time he recalled General MacArthur in the spring of the third year, only 28 percent of the public approved of how Truman was doing his job. Curiously, more than half of Truman's domestic travel time occurred at the end of the fourth year, when he was no longer a candidate for reelection. He campaigned for twenty-four days in October 1952, although it is not clear how at that point he could help the Democrats. In any case, the Eisenhower tide was already beginning to crest.

Unlike Truman, Eisenhower spoke early and often, scheduling seven major addresses in the first eight months of his term. This impressive speaking schedule continued, with eleven speeches in his first fourteen months. During the relatively quiet time in the second half of his second year, Ike's popularity also declined, reaching a low of 57 percent before the off-year election. Although Ike did not speak, he traveled during this period, making the largest number of domestic trips at the end of the second year. While Eisenhower did not speak before or after his September 1955 heart attack, by the end of the year 75 percent of the public approved of the way he was doing his job. His fourth year showed routine travel, with the expected spurt in October before the election, and an average number of four speeches. All in all, one cannot say that the crowded speaking schedule of the first year helped, but a different strategy could hardly have done better.

Kennedy's popularity appears more closely linked to external events than to any choice of activities. His initial popularity on taking office climbed even higher after the Bay of Pigs crisis and remained above 70 percent for his first year. After an average beginning in number of speeches, he gave none between August and the end of the year. However, good economic times and a crisis in Berlin helped to keep his popularity high. Between March and August of his second year, when he gave no speeches, his polls began to fall by a total of 12 percentage points. The stock market also showed a decline in the same period. The polls fell further during the integration crisis at the University of Mississippi, although Kennedy gave a speech on that occasion. Then Kennedy's successful handling of the Cuban Missile Crisis restored his popularity at the end of his second year to 75 percent approval.

Kennedy's polls in his third year began to look more like the polls of other presidents. His support declined during the year: 10 percentage points from January to May, when he gave no speeches, and a further drop after the racial violence in Alabama and the civil rights march on Washington, led by Reverend Martin Luther King, Jr. During this time, he either gave no speeches or gave them on controversial subjects: one on civil rights, one on the economy, and three on the nuclear test ban treaty. Unlike those of some of the later presidents, Kennedy's speeches did not appear geared to helping his popularity so much as to serve programmatic goals. Eisenhower and Kennedy gave the same number of speeches (fifteen) in their first three years; although Eisenhower's appeared timed to help his popularity, Kennedy's appeared unrelated to popularity, either in timing or in subject.

Kennedy's travel also seemed unrelated to his public standing. His domestic travel, like Eisenhower's, was concentrated before the off-year election. He took two major foreign trips: one to Latin America in his first year, mainly to fulfill his campaign pledges to build better relations with that region; and one to Europe in his third year, when the trend of his popularity was falling. Overall, Kennedy was about average among the presidents in activity, but slightly lower than average in foreign travel.

Johnson exhibited a pattern of activity unique among the presidents. Johnson's initial speeches in his first year apparently did not go well—his polls actually went *down* after he faced the television cameras to speak to the nation. Even his inaugural address produced a slight drop. At this point he appeared to swear off public speaking and did not give a major address, except for two obligatory State of the Union addresses, from October of his first year to July of his third. Other negative events did not help his public standing: race violence in several cities and protests against the Vietnam War. Johnson maintained his silence until he had dropped almost 30 points from his inauguration.

Johnson's foreign and domestic travel also was below average. The first and longest foreign trip of his term—to Southeast Asia in fall 1966—was scheduled when other presidents were taking their domestic trips! Other presidents campaigned with a view to the upcoming congressional election; Johnson, on the other hand, drew attention to the increasingly unpopular Vietnam War. Like Truman's, most of Johnson's domestic travel was in his fourth year, after he had announced that he would not seek another term.

What did Johnson do if he did not speak or travel? Advisers have recounted at length in their biographies how he worked a sixteen- to eighteen-hour day, using his lunch and rubdown periods to schedule additional conversations. Also throughout these years, he signed into law one after another of his Great Society programs. These acts, however, were completed quietly: with only a photographer, a small circle of congressional friends, and Johnson to hand out the pens. In sharp contrast to the other presidents, Johnson gave no economic speeches, although he had more to gain than most from economic conditions. Inflation was low, and unemployment was at the record low for the post–World War II period. Whereas Kennedy appeared to act independently of the polls, Johnson appeared to act contrary to them.

No contrast is sharper than that between Johnson and Nixon. Nixon understood intuitively the results of this chapter. He timed his speeches evenly during his first term, through a period of negative events, allowing no more than three months to elapse between addresses. He gave more speeches than the other presidents, but fell below the average in domestic travel. He was the only one to reduce his domestic trips in the fourth year. Instead, Nixon scheduled his major foreign travel—to China, the Soviet Union, and eastern Europe—for the beginning of his fourth year. While the other presidents began their swings around the country for reelection, Nixon returned to the White House with news of détente.

Carter showed the reverse pattern. He was slightly under average in major speeches and above average in domestic trips. Of all the presidents, he did the greatest amount of foreign travel. Also, unlike Nixon, Carter allowed two long periods to go between speaking—from May to October in his first year and from March to August in his second. His polls fell about 10 percentage points in each period. It is quite possible that Carter was trying to be as much unlike Nixon as possible. As Chapter 2 showed, Carter's public support did not fall as badly as some people think, given the negative conditions of the time. And a different pattern of activity might have improved even that respectable record. If, for instance, Carter had spoken as frequently as Reagan, he would have gained about 8 percentage points in the polls during each year. Rather than averaging 48 percent approval in his second year, he could have been well above 50 percent. And rather than falling below 40 percent in his third year as the time for the election grew closer, he could have been only slightly below average for presidents at that time.

While Kennedy, one of the youngest of the presidents, showed average activity, one of the oldest, Reagan, appeared determined to break the records. Reagan was second only to Nixon in speaking and second only to Ford in his average rate of domestic trips. Like Nixon, Reagan allotted his speeches carefully throughout his term, allowing no more than four months of silence. He also scheduled a major European trip in his fourth year, at the same time he undertook a brutal domestic travel schedule, compiling sixty-three days in the fourth year, or more than the other three years combined. Reagan's popularity, as we saw in the preceding chapter, was quite similar to Carter's in many ways. We might say in hindsight that he did not need to do as much as he did; yet the timing of his activities may have helped his popularity marginally, although it hurt that of his predecessor.

We must look at Ford differently. He had the task, unlike all the others, of running on two political clocks: He not only had to establish a record in his first months in office, and face the usual decline in support, but also had to prepare for reelection. Consequently, he engaged in almost twice as much domestic travel per month as the other presidents, more than the average amount of foreign travel, and about the average amount of speaking engagements. For only two months during his time in office was he not on the road—December and January of 1974–75— although he addressed the nation twice in January. His choices, it is interesting to see, are similar to, although more extreme than, the ones Carter later followed. They may have helped Ford win the difficult 1976 Republican nomination and come in close on Election Day, but they clearly hurt him in the public-opinion polls.

The choice of public activities is a personal matter for the various presidents. No one pattern appears, nor is there any definite sign of a chronological trend. Moreover, presidential choices follow closely the divisions we saw in the previous chapter. Those presidents most concerned with their public standing tended to schedule their activities to help that standing; those who scorned the polls continued to disregard them when allocating their schedules and time. Truman, Johnson, and Ford, the least public-regarding of the presidents according to the ranking we used in Chapter 2, proved least likely to select activities that would help their public support. Carter, a little below average in the rankings, balanced his choices in a way that could have hurt marginally at the polls. Carter sought other balances, too, in his administration—with advisers and with different congressional strategies—that often hurt his reputation in Washington and with the public. Kennedy, average in the ranking, was also average in activity, although his choice of speeches suggest that he was more concerned with the programs than with any projected popularity increase. Reagan and Eisenhower, highest in the ranking, did appear to select activities that helped their polls.

Finally, we come to Richard Nixon, whose choices and poll standings do not match. When choosing activities to help him at the polls, he did everything right, even more so than Reagan and Eisenhower. He concentrated on major addresses and timed them carefully, playing down domestic travel, as if he knew instinctively their very different effects. Yet Nixon, like Kennedy, was willing to tackle controversial subjects. During a time of rising inflation, several of his speeches addressed the need for wage and price controls. Nixon, also, like Truman and Johnson, chose a controversial foreign policy that cost him support. Seen in this light, Nixon appears to be the most divided of the presidents on the matter of popularity. He worked for it, with the greatest of attention, but he also made choices that worked against it.

The most striking observation that can be made about the second-term presidents is their lower level of activity. Eisenhower, for example, had no days of domestic travel, and only eleven days altogether of foreign travel, in his first two years.

Nixon, too, traveled infrequently at the beginning of his second term, with no foreign travel and limited domestic trips in 1973. In 1974, Nixon took only two days of foreign travel and made only the one obligatory State of the Union address until April, when the House Judiciary Committee initiated its hearings on articles of impeachment. This means that for the three critical months prior to this event, Nixon was publicly silent. Perhaps Nixon's inactivity is not surprising when we recall that bad events caused him to reduce his first-term presidential activities. Still, Nixon was the one president willing to speak in his first term during negative events, if not in his second. Perhaps Nixon would have suffered less if he had acted more.

Ronald Reagan provides an interesting contrast. He ended his second term with a cheery wave on the White House lawn and an above-average approval rating. Many say that he left the presidency restored, even though he suffered a severe second-term scandal, with ten negative events relating to the Iran-Contra revelations alone. Investigations of the conduct of Attorney General Edwin Meese, Lyn Nofziger, and other associates continued in the background. One reporter counted more than one hundred administration members overall who had been accused of criminal or ethical misdeeds, suggesting a comparison with the Harding administration's Teapot Dome scandal.[14] Harding, himself not a part of the scandal, has been blamed by historians for his weakness and mismanagement, which allowed the scandal to occur. He is typically ranked among the least successful presidents, with the few other presidential "failures." Reagan, by comparison, emerged from his second term with his reputation only moderately bruised.

How did this happen? Reagan was called the "Teflon president" because he emerged unscathed from mistakes that would have stuck to other administrations and damaged them. Certainly he was helped by a Congress that was in no mood to investigate a president and that had its own internal investigations to worry about. He was also helped by journalists who, as author and journalist Mark Hertsgaard has argued, treated the Reagan administration kindly. Hertsgaard, in his careful analysis of press treatment of Iran-Contra and other negative events, quotes Benjamin

Bradlee, executive editor of the *Washington Post*, who said that in his opinion the press had been kinder to Reagan than to any other president since he had been at the *Post*.[15] Nevertheless, it is clear that Reagan's individual style and selection of activities should be considered factors in his popularity.

Reagan also enjoyed far more positive events than the other presidents: four in the same time period (the average is one, and the highest number for any other president is two). While we cannot say that these events were deliberately timed, they were fortuitous for an administration beset by scandal. For example, during the time that the scandals were surfacing, the nation launched an invasion on the island of Grenada and signed a major arms limitation treaty with the Soviet Union. Unlike Johnson, Reagan addressed the American people when these positive events occurred. Overall, Reagan's second term was high in what in a later chapter we will call the military-rhetorical style of foreign policy. These years were marked by many uses of U.S. force, with the president speaking to the nation on most of these occasions.

At a minimum, these events help distract the nation's attention from problems at home. Unfortunately for Nixon, no foreign crisis marred the nation's attention to Watergate. Even the crisis in Cyprus in the last weeks before his resignation brought little presidential response; it is likely that most Americans did not know there was a crisis in Cyprus. Reagan's activities during his difficult second term help illustrate how the timing of activities can effect public support. Without these international events, he might not have left the office so well restored.

All presidential choices need not be informed, of course. We can say that domestic travel hurts popularity and foreign travel makes no difference, but at any one point in time, faced with a medley of positive and negative happenings, it would be much harder for a president to know this. First, he might not be able to separate out the particular activity from everything else that is going on. Second, he might believe that "going public" is one thing whose forms are interchangeable. Nixon apparently thought this at some intuitive level, at least during his first term, since he did everything our analysis suggests. But Carter might have believed he was pursuing the best strategy possible to help in his public standing, and Reagan might have been advised to spend even more days traveling, in case fifteen days a month were not enough.

CONCLUSIONS

Presidents do appear to select activities in ways designed to increase their popularity. They make strategic choices, increasing their domestic travel in congressional and presidential election years and scheduling more foreign and domestic travel in reelection years. But they also make reactive choices, in response to the much shorter time frame of the public-opinion polls. They decide when to speak to or hide from the nation, and when to take a trip or cancel one. Of course, no one can say conclusively that presidential activities are taken consciously for public support. However, the general pattern indicates that it is very unlikely these activities could have occurred by chance. The same pattern will be seen later in the more serious affairs of foreign policy making.

On the other hand, we should not overstate the public-relations presidency.[16] First, the actual level of all this activity is quite low, so presidents have time left to turn to other affairs of government. Second, the activities are pursued in different ways, accommodating different presidential styles. Third, there is no evidence of any clear trend. Although the monthly frequency of some of these activities has increased since the Truman years, these were not found to be the kinds of activities that help public approval. Finally, some help, some hurt, and some make little difference. All in all, we see more effort than impact, more signs of presidents responding to the polls than of the public responding to designated White House cues.

Nixon, interviewed after George Bush's unfortunate Japanese trip, suggested that Bush should "cut back on a lot of the activity that's just for . . . public relations purposes."[17] In the face of exaggerated attention of White House advisers and journalistic commentators to these ceremonial acts, the results suggest their own corrective. If presidents act primarily to help their public support, they might better turn their energies to more substantive matters. Even though Americans do want an energetic executive, the present amalgam of public-relations activity is not the energy they like to see.

The ceremonial activities do not substantially change the picture seen in the preceding chapter. Presidents have a limited set of resources to apply throughout their terms, to balance negative events and the inevitable decay of support. To those limited resources we can now add the few addresses to the nation they make each year, but even these appear to be limited to first terms. Second-term addresses do not show positive effects. If we demand that presidents be supported by very high proportions of Americans—far beyond the number who elected them—we supply very few means by which they can achieve this ideal condition.

4

Activity, Popularity, and Success in Congress

IN the early weeks of the Bush administration, a political cartoonist showed an elegant president poised on a tennis court, racket in hand. Across the net was a heavyset, unshaven opponent, Congress, clutching a bowling ball. Things did not work out exactly as the cartoon predicted. Bush threw several bowling balls of his own, in the way of vetoes, to knock down congressional legislation. Congress, meanwhile, was often busy picking up pins or tying its shoelaces. Nevertheless, the cartoon is a useful reminder that there are two sides of the net and two ends of Pennsylvania Avenue to keep in perspective. As we look at the modern presidents' legislative achievements, we should keep this perspective in mind.

That presidents have the power to persuade Congress is a truism of American politics. Their popularity in the country and reputation in Washington bolster their congressional success. The *New York Times* remarked on this at the beginning of 1990: "In heading off what looked . . . like a sure defeat, President Bush proved today that a popular leader, if sufficiently aroused, can still change votes on Capitol Hill."[1] Indeed, so strong is this accepted wisdom that presidents are judged by their apparent, and superficial, success. Writers assume that presidents can persuade Congress and that some do so better than others. Wilson's New

Freedom, Roosevelt's New Deal, and Johnson's Great Society are the standards against which old and new presidents are judged.

Imagine that the country is locked in a terrible domestic crisis. A new president takes office, supported by a strong electoral mandate, and *on the first day on the job* sends sweeping new legislation to Congress to meet the crisis. Congress does not even stop to follow its own rules in its haste to pass the president's bill. The House does not have a copy of the bill but passes it anyway. Some would say that this is an example of presidential leadership. The president, with the nation behind him, acted decisively, and Congress agreed to the president's request. This occurred once in American history, in January 1933, when Congress passed Franklin Roosevelt's Emergency Banking Act, giving the president broad powers to fight the Depression. This case is not typical, nor does it accord with constitutional checks and balances. Yet, curiously, it has become a standard against which presidents governing in more normal times must compete.

Implicit in this notion of presidential leadership are at least three components: activity, approval, and success. In the now-mythic story of the Emergency Banking Act, FDR acted, the public supported him, and Congress gave him its automatic assent. The president used his mandate from the people to enact legislative agenda, winning the Congress to his point of view. Also implicit is the notion that the president's role is the critical one. The president acts, and Congress and the public respond. The public's approval is a resource to be manipulated, while Congress is a passive reactor primarily responsible for saying aye or nay. Nevertheless, three very different groups of people are making decisions. The public indicates its support in the polls, presidents take positions on pending legislation while Congress considers this legislation and conducts its roll-call votes. It is not automatically obvious how any of these activities affect the others.

If presidents' public standing increases their congressional success, the importance of the polls we have been tracking is clear. On this question, academic wisdom is somewhat at odds with popular wisdom. Some political scientists argue that a president's popularity has a very limited impact at most.[2] Others, echoing

Richard Neustadt, believe that it exerts a significant effect.[3] We are not arguing that it has the only impact or that it works so blatantly that we need not seek out other influences. This chapter points out that when we do identify other key influences, we can see just how important a president's popularity is.

We need to take a closer look at the various factors combined in the leadership notion. Impressions of leadership can be built from *activity,* or the ambitiousness of a legislative program, indicated by the number of positions that presidents take on legislation. Alternatively, presidents can be judged on the *success* of a program, large or small, indicated by the proportion of victories they score. The public's *approval* may give the illusion of success; yet, popular presidents might not succeed in Congress. In addition, all these components need not work together. Presidential success might rise, with increasing experience in dealing with Congress, at the same time that approval falls. Finally, we need to know how these components interact within the larger political context. Presidents may appear much more or less restrained— and much more or less successful—once we know these influences. Then, too, presidential activity and success may follow different paths over the years of a term: perhaps declining like the polls, increasing with experience and confidence in office, or following a congressional calendar and not a presidential one. A strategy that works at one time could fail at another. Congress has its own electoral calendar to keep its eye on.

We also need to know how these components are shaped by other influences. Just as polls reflect a mixture of presidential acts and good and bad fortune, relations with Congress show the same mixture. A particular president's success might derive in large part from popularity, from skill in dealing with Congress, or from good or bad luck. An obvious example is Lyndon Johnson, famous for his Great Society Program, with one new piece of legislation passed after another in his first years in office. Johnson, however, had so large a Democratic majority in Congress that he could have thrown away forty votes in the House at any one time and never missed them. Gerald Ford, however, had less than half as many fellow partisans in the House as Johnson: 144 compared to 295. Even if Ford had won every Republican vote in the House, he would still have needed to find 74 more for a bare majority. Both Johnson and Ford, who had been party leaders in Congress before entering the Oval Office, were experts at knowing the members and counting the votes. So, was one more skilled than the other, or did one have better luck in the congressional election returns? How much of what we call leadership is luck?

At issue are basic questions concerning the constraints and possibilities of presidential power. First, to what extent can presidents apply public support to help get their programs through Congress? Does popularity help legislative success? Second, how much of a president's activity and success is due to leadership rather than to congressional election results? Congressional elections are won in the states and districts, not through the help of the White House. The few presidents who have tried to influence these contests, including one no less skilled than Franklin Roosevelt, met with discouraging results. It is the congressional elections, then, that determine how many Democrats or Republicans there will be in Congress and which party has majority control of the Senate and the House. These elections can profoundly influence what presidents are able to do. Finally, what are the constraints and tradeoffs that presidents confront: What choices must they make? For example, in their efforts to influence Congress, do presidents lose more than they gain in approval, finding that the positions they take have costs in the polls? If so, we need to know how expensive those positions are.

The "no win" presidency some writers describe poses difficult choices between activity and success and a president's popularity.[4] Popularity can help the legislative agenda, but efforts to pass the agenda make presidents less popular. Writers evoking a leadership presidency, on the other hand, believe these difficulties can be overcome. The charisma and popularity of leaders can win people to their agendas; the vision that the agenda expresses can evoke popular support. At issue are the particular relationships among popularity, activity, and success.

We will look at modern presidents from Eisenhower to Reagan in this chapter, since common measures of legislative performance are available only from the Eisenhower years. At the outset, we will see how the presidents compare with one another on the surface: how they rank in activity, success, and approval (see Appendix B for these rankings). Activity, taken as the average number of positions the president announces on important roll-call votes in Congress, is a widely used standard as derived from the president's own speeches and messages.[5] This activity, or legislative position taking, varies greatly from one president to another. Johnson leads in activity, as might be expected, averaging more than 250 positions taken each year. Carter, Reagan, and Kennedy all rank above average. Eisenhower ranks lowest, with slightly less than one hundred positions. Ford and Nixon also appear below average in their level of activity. Yet, there are similarities among the presidents, too, as we will see more clearly later. Democrats in general take more positions than Republicans, averaging about 230 compared to the Republican's 140 each year.

However, taking a position does not spell success, which is taken as the annual percentage of these roll calls, supported by the president, that were passed by the House and Senate. Roll calls are primarily, although not exclusively, taken on controversial matters of legislation. In the Reagan years, for example, important roll calls to pass or defeat legislation occurred on controversial budget issues, such as cutbacks in education, increases in defense, tax reform, plant closings, environmental protection, abortion funding, the nation's policy toward apartheid, and aid to Nicaragua. Success on such roll calls is not a minor matter. Kennedy, Johnson, and Eisenhower were above average in their success rates, while Carter, Nixon, Reagan, and Ford were below average. Our two most successful presidents faced congresses controlled by their own party, and two of the least successful presidents faced congresses controlled by the opposition.[6] According to this first impression, Ford stands out as having been noticeably lower in success than the other presidents. We will see how this picture changes somewhat later on.

Approval, as we know, varies dramatically from one administration to another. Overall, Kennedy and Eisenhower enjoyed by far the highest average annual approval ratings of the first-term presidents surveyed.[7] Carter had the lowest average annual approval rating and, with Ford, Reagan, and Johnson, scored below average on approval.

Many impressions of presidential leadership, no doubt, are derived from these separate dimensions. Eisenhower, for example, is often viewed as having been a "hands off" leader, detached from the give-and-take of ordinary politics, while Nixon's inactivity is explained by noting that he did not like Congress or congressional bargaining. Alternatively, Kennedy, reminding people that he was the first president to be born in the twentieth century, campaigned to bring a new vigor and energy to Washington. Ford, the only appointed president, was often at odds with the large Democratic majority in Congress and in some press accounts came to be known as the "veto king." The various rankings show that these widely held but very basic impressions do have some validity. However, these impressions do not give the full picture.

We assume the political actors in the White House and Congress are well aware of each other's power. Members of Congress know that a president can reach the American public more often, more directly, and with more emotional impact than they can. Presidents know that congressional incumbents win reelection independent of anything they might do. Congress members willingly admit to being impressed with a popular president yet are also impressed by local constituency ties and their own institutional norms. Congress, in other words, can be expected to follow the polls—to be, on average, more timid when opposing a popular president and more courageous against an unpopular one. On the other hand, Congress is not a blank slate for presidents to write on: It has its own agendas and political strategies, showing stable voting alignments, by constituency and party, that persist over several presidents' terms. Interviews yield the same results: Influences shaping congressional decisions come predominantly from the constituency and from within the institution.[8] This picture accords with congressional election results, best viewed as the outcome of local contests where members run for, and win, reelection on their own. Presidents, then, wield their weapons of persuasion against powerful constraints in members' ties to their constituencies and the congressional institution.

We can also assume that these political actors are partisans, primarily Democrats and Republicans, whose agendas and strategies are set according to well-established party lines. In Congress, political parties have long been recognized as the chief predictors of roll-call voting. Members vote with their party to follow their own ideology, to accord with voters in predominantly Republican and Democratic districts, or to go along with an elaborate congressional leadership structure. Although presidents may swing a handful of congressional election results and work with their party leaders in Congress, party influence can best be seen as independent of the president. Rather, it is a given with which presidents must deal. This influence not only shapes the voting of individual members but also determines the chairs of all committees and subcommittees, dictates committee staff ratios, and gives some leaders more power than others. Party control of Congress, therefore, as shaped by congressional election results, poses a major constraint on a president's legislation. Recognizing this, presidents should act differently depending on whether they face congresses of the same or opposing parties. They should also appear more persuasive, despite varying popularity or leadership skills, in situations of same-party compared to opposing-party control. They may also act differently and receive differential support depending on whether they are Democrats or Republicans.

Even though presidents must work within these partisan and congressional constraints, they possess resources: their popularity; their sense of political timing over the cycles of the administration; an ability (or inability) to read Congress and know what bills it is likely to support. They know their limits, too: The poll ratings will fall throughout the term. Public approval, as we saw earlier, is affected by the passage of time. The president's party should also shape legislative agendas, with a Democratic administration promoting more ambitious legislative programs. All these things constitute the field on which the game of legislation is played.

That is why we will examine this phenomenon of leadership collectively and individually. From the collective perspective, we can gauge the importance of the playing field. For example, how much does same-party control of Congress help a president to pass his legislative program? How important are the polls? When we control for this and other handicaps, we can then evaluate the actual performance of individual presidents and compare them. How does Johnson, a seemingly active, successful president, look when we consider his good fortune of national economic prosperity and the large number of Democratic seats in Congress? How does he compare to Ford, who was much less active and successful but had the bad fortune of a recession and opposing-party control? In other words, what if the tables were turned?

THE COLLECTIVE PATTERNS

Time, the first problem confronting a president when advancing a legislative agenda, brings a decay in public approval. But independent of this effect, activity and success trace their own paths over a term, and these paths are somewhat contradictory. The time curve for activity, or position taking, is almost a perfect reverse image of the curve for approval (see Appendix B). Our first-term modern presidents started slow and increased their position taking through their second and third years, cutting back in their fourth. Their activity increased as their approval falls. Here we see the paradox that other writers have observed: As experience in office increases, opportunities for action decrease, due in part to the fall in approval.[9] A former governor, for example, needs time to learn the legislative ropes. Even presidents more experienced with Congress need time to conduct the necessary liaison work and put their own agendas in order. But just when their activity reaches its high point, their approval ebbs. As the polls edge upward again, their activity declines because of the demands of reelection. This is why Johnson demanded that *all* Great Society legislation be ready to go in the months following his landslide election. The former majority leader of the Senate was trying to beat the clock.

This is not the only challenge, however. Presidential success in Congress follows yet another course, staying almost constant through the first three years of a term but then falling off considerably in the fourth. If proposals are postponed into the fourth year to wait for the upswing of popular support, they must battle the downswing of congressional support. This, incidentally, is less a matter of Congress passing legislation the president does not want than of its postponing, thus saying no to, legislation the White House supports—at least until the election results are in. Thus, we see the fuller dimensions of the paradox facing presidents. Activity, approval, and success, each closely tied to impressions of leadership, follow distinct cycles that work, at least partly, against them.[10] We can see why each cycle exists without depending on the others. Each is shaped by the actions of different people: the president taking positions; the public giving or withholding approval; Congress saying aye or nay to a presidential request. But leadership, at least by the conventional notion that combines these three effects, is not necessarily something a president can control.

Circumstances—the economy and dramatic events—continue to have an impact (see Appendix B). Specifically, public approval declines with poor economic performance and the occurrence of bad events, and increases when good events occur. The fact that these findings accord so well with the results in Chapter 2 is striking.

Other circumstances, however, play a part in shaping activity and legislative success. Given the importance of party voting in Congress, we might expect that presidents facing same-party congresses would exhibit levels of activity and success higher than those of presidents facing opposing-party congresses. They would take more positions and have more victories on those positions. The results in Appendix B make this clear. Party control exerts a strong and significant effect on presidential success rates in Congress. Presidents confronting opposing parties in Congress are estimated to have about 13 percent fewer victories than presidents who face congresses controlled by their own parties. Consequently, if Nixon and Kennedy took positions on the same number of bills before Congress, Nixon would lose many more votes than Kennedy, independently of any effort or skill. These would be won or lost, we could say, by the congressional election results. Split-party control (one house the same party and one house opposing) costs about 9 percentage points in success when compared to same-party control. Reagan and Eisenhower would win more of the roll calls than Nixon, in their years of split-party control. Given these effects, it is not surprising that party differences between the White House and Congress also affect presidential position taking. Democratic presidents took significantly more positions than their Republican counterparts. And among the Republican presidents, those facing split-party control took more positions than those facing opposing-party congresses.[11] Their activity increased with the likelihood of its success.

The effects of the passage of time over a term also are evident in these results. With each year that goes by, we find a strong and significant effect on presidential position taking, success, and approval. This shows that important features of presidential-congressional relations are not static but change significantly over the course of an administration. The strategy used to usher in a new administration—and that presidents become known for—will not necessarily be the same as the strategy used later in their administration.

Party control and time exert substantial effects on activity and success, but time, the economy, and dramatic events influence public approval. How do all these interact? These results are shown in Appendix B.

Several conclusions are important. First, public approval clearly increases the chance of congressional success, *once the other influences are taken into account*. Presidents gain 7.5 percent in victories for every 10 percentage points more of approval they receive in the polls. Second, as far as the public is concerned, nothing succeeds like success. Success in Congress bolsters approval in the polls. Third, however, the relationship between the polls and position taking is *inverse*. The larger the legislative program is—that is, the more positions a president takes—the lower the approval ratings will be. Active presidents are not rewarded in the polls; popular presidents win more but generally ask less. This means that, contrary to some conventional ideas of presidential leadership, there are limits to how active presidents should be. By lowering public approval, presidents face a reduced chance for future success. This also means that presidents have to choose whether they wish to be active and "vigorous" or popular. Making one choice hurts the other.

It is not the expected *congressional* reaction that should lead presidents to limit their positions, because they do not need to prune programs to achieve higher congressional success. Indeed, the results suggest that under the same political conditions, a more cautious president will achieve a more cautious response. Activity and success go together. It is the *public* reaction that acts as the deterrent. Hence, approval ratings can function as both a help and a hindrance to passing a presidential program, assisting in gathering votes in Congress but limiting the positions the president can take.

One final question is of interest: What is the major source of influence, or the driving force, in this complex interaction? Some scholars of the presidency assume that activity is the driving force: Presidents initiate, and Congress and the public respond. Hence, the strongest paths of influence in the results should be from activity to success and activity to approval. Other scholars emphasize public relations, on the other hand, and would expect the strongest paths of influence to be from the poll ratings to activity and success. Public opinion would affect the president's position taking and Congress's response. A third interpretation, a kind of Washington insiders' approach, argues that the strongest influence is from success to activity and approval. Success in Congress provides the feedback that shapes presidential activity and public reputation.

We can now evaluate these different interpretations. (See Figure B.1 in Appendix B.) When examining typical changes in these effects over the course of administrations, we see that public approval drives the process, limiting the congressional strategies that presidents can pursue. High activity early in the term does not offset the reduction in success that results from the erosion of public support. Over the course of their term, the clearest way for presidents to succeed in Congress is to maintain high support.

Public mobilization is critical if presidents are to succeed, but our evidence indicates that such mobilization cannot be accomplished through presidential position taking or success in Congress. Approval, critical to influence in Congress, must be derived elsewhere, such as from speeches or dramatic international events. Hence, presidents without a substantial reserve of public support, or the opportunities to replenish it, would find themselves unable to move Congress by either position taking or a reputation for success.

These basic patterns remain unchanged when first and second terms are combined. Presidential activity and approval continue to exert strong positive influences on success in Congress, and the inverse relationship between activity and approval holds. Remember, however, that polls drop more rapidly during a second term. Consequently, there is even less of a window of opportunity in this term for presidents to complete their agendas for legislation.

THE INDIVIDUAL PRESIDENTS

Presidents can achieve legislative success either by being popular (and taking fewer positions) or by taking more positions but sacrificing approval. Although all presidents, we assume, would like to be popular, they make very different choices. "Choices" refer merely to courses of action that are pursued, whether consciously selected or not. Some presidents proceed with caution, taking relatively few positions and guarding their support in the polls; alternatively, some view their role as that of legislative leader, using the office to focus and prod Congress into action. How, indeed, does a president balance the tradeoff between activity and success?

Now that we have evened the playing field, we can compare the performances of the individual modern presidents, given the constraints they faced, in their first terms. This will provide us with a picture of the comparative strengths and weaknesses of each administration. In essence, we will evaluate the activity level and success rates of these presidents, adjusting for party and cycles within their administrations in activity and success.[12]

Three choice patterns emerge clearly from this comparison.

Some presidents focused on activity and appeared less interested in success (Johnson, Ford, and Kennedy), and others concentrated more on success but were less active (Nixon and Eisenhower). In addition, two presidents exhibited balanced choices (Carter and Reagan), remarkable for neither activity or success.

Presidents do fall into clusters in terms of the past experiences they brought to office. Johnson, a former Senate majority leader, and Ford, a former House minority leader, displayed levels of position taking that were substantially above those that would be expected, given the circumstances of the time. This accords with Johnson's expert advice, as told to his biographer: "There is but one way for a President to deal with the Congress, and that is continuously, incessantly, and without interruption." He goes on, warming to his subject: "If it's really going to work, the relationship between the President and the Congress has got to be almost incestuous. He's got to know them even better than they know themselves."[13]

Johnson's activity was not limited to position taking. He kept up his personal contacts in Congress and conducted some of his own liaison work.[14] One study reports that more than a fourth of all the domestic legislative initiatives introduced by presidents from 1953 to 1984 came from the Johnson White House.[15] Johnson presumably enjoyed all activity; it was not merely a matter of strategy. He liked to show people he could pick up a bill, glance at it, and recount what the rest of the bill would contain. The *Congressional Record,* clipped and summarized, was placed by his bed each morning at 7:15.[16]

Ford appears to have followed the Johnsonian strategy that Congress must be constantly prodded and urged forward. We again see a similarity between the two vice presidents who achieved office through succession. Just as they made other decisions that cost them in the polls, they took positions in Congress that hurt their public approval. This ultimately cost them congressional success. Ford's activity is important to understand, since on the surface it is not apparent. He put forth no large new initiatives and made no changes in direction but accelerated the pace of position taking from the Nixon years. While Ford's positions were largely directed at stopping Democratic programs, his activity stands out since he had far less favorable circumstances than Nixon.

Eisenhower and Nixon are similar, too, in success and downplaying activity. Nixon's dislike of Congress, and preference for foreign over domestic policy, is frequently cited to explain his low activity rate. He was quoted as saying that "all you need is a competent Cabinet to run the country at home. You need a President for foreign policy."[17] Yet these accounts miss Nixon's very respectable record of success in his first term. He attended to and won success on the few legislative initiatives he cared about.[18] In this he was quite similar to Eisenhower, who also restricted the size of his program, concentrating on a few issues. Certainly, the Republicans of the time might have been less interested in active legislative strategies than the Democrats. However, Nixon, having served as Eisenhower's vice president, had a successful model to follow as much as he chose. Former governors Reagan and Carter exhibited a balanced strategy, holding close to the baseline on both dimensions. It is remarkable that two such different presidents correspond so closely to average levels on both activity and success. Since these were the two most recent officeholders, it is possible that they benefited from institutional learning and judged more closely the various tradeoffs between activity, approval, and success.

The consistency found over the terms suggests that these strategies were consciously pursued. Three presidents—Johnson, Nixon, and Ford—made the same choices across their years in office. Johnson and Ford were consistently high in activity, and Nixon was high in success. One other president—Reagan—remained consistent for three years, increasing his relative activity in the fourth. This increase, in fact, was exactly what we would have suggested he do. His approval was stable, but his success in Congress was eroding. The slight increase in activity helped to stabilize that slide.

Only Carter varied his relative position dramatically from year to year—very high in activity in his first and third years, relative to the other presidents, and very low in his second and fourth. He admitted after he left the presidency that there were some things he might have done better with Congress: "It would have been advisable to have introduced our legislation in much more careful phases—not in such a rush," he reflected.[19] Carter seems to have compensated in his second year for what some called the "avalanche" of early legislation. After falling behind in his second year, he compensated in the following year. This wavering between different strategies, and sending different cues to Congress and the public in the process, accords with the kind of criticism often made of his administration. Yet, as Carter went on in his reminiscing: "We would not have accomplished any more, and perhaps less, but my relations with Congress would have been smoother and the image of undue haste and confusion could have been avoided."[20] He realizes what we are showing here: Reducing activity would not have helped success; it could even have hurt it in the short run. But it might have had a helpful influence over the long run by improving his standing in the polls.

Still, Carter's record is a good illustration of what an even playing field means. Presidential scholar Erwin Hargrove gives the following careful assessment:

Carter's somewhat clumsy style of policy leadership may have contributed to the early problems of his energy package, the failure of welfare reform and a number of other domestic policy measures. . . . But the political conditions surrounding these issues were very unfavorable and the economic policy dilemmas were downright intractable. . . . Many conditions were unfavorable to the exercise of leadership at all and, indeed, a number of events were simply bad luck for the president. . . . Most of the achievements were personal, and it is not clear that anyone else could have done as well.[21]

Carter himself felt that he had done "reasonably well" in his dealings with Congress.[22] We agree: He achieved about what could have been expected given the circumstances.

An obvious comparison is between Carter and his successor, Ronald Reagan. Both came to Washington as ex-governors, with no firsthand experience in Congress. However, while Carter built a bad first-year reputation for legislative relations, Reagan built a good one, primarily because of his initial budget victory. Carter grew stronger and Reagan weaker as their terms went on, but the first impressions stuck. To many people, not only was Reagan more successful than poor Jimmy Carter, but also a "Reagan Revolution" and a "Reagan Legacy" were underway. It did not matter that he would not match his first-year victories through the next seven years. As two policy analysts conclude: "For all [Reagan's] political popularity, he was unable to regain the legislative initiative he had in 1981. The domestic policy debate became a stalemate between a President determined to retain the victories he had achieved and a Congress determined to keep him from advancing further."[23] Once we account for the circumstances of the times, these two supposedly different administrations seem remarkably similar.

SUMMING UP

Popularity clearly matters. Within the broader set of influences, popularity helps a president's agenda in Congress. Success is shaped by a constellation of influences, including congressional party control, the cycles of administrations, the amount of activity the presidents pursue, and their approval as shown in the public-opinion polls. But when we consider these various influences, public approval does show a substantial effect on a president's ability to win in Congress. In this case the popular wisdom is close to the mark. For every gain of 10 percentage points in public approval, presidents can expect a change of about 7 percentage points in congressional success.

The various components of the leadership notion do not work together. Even controlling for these very different effects, presidential activity works against public approval. Taking positions on legislation helps presidents in the congressional roll-call votes but hurts them in the polls.

We find the complex situation to be expected when two powerful institutions share power while keeping a watch on the important public opinions. Public, president, and Congress are each in a position to limit or encourage the other, like the game in which the stone blunts the scissors that cut the paper that wraps the stone. Presidents are supposed to be strong enough, we said in the introductory chapter, to use their public standing to win congressional support. However, they must not be too strong. There are limits on how much legislative activity is deemed a good thing.

What does this say about the notion that presidents are supposed to lead Congress? The size and success of the legislative agenda are heavily shaped by factors presidents cannot control. Presidents who face same-party congresses enjoy significantly higher activity and success than presidents who face congresses with split or opposing-party control. Long-standing partisan ideologies affect support in Congress independent of the party of the president or the party in control of Congress. All presidents face further limits as they proceed through their terms. Position taking increases as success falls. Since public approval falls as a term proceeds, a further lowering of the success rate can be expected. But this is not all. Although public approval helps increase the success of a president's legislative program, position taking lowers that approval. Hence, presidents are confronted with a no-win situation—to increase congressional success, by bolstering approval, they must decrease the number of positions. As positions decrease, success rate falls, accompanied by a decline in the polls. Thus, popular presidents find a ceiling on their efforts to provide legislative leadership, while their less popular counterparts are forced to tread a very slippery slope in which attempts to make headway in Congress set them further behind in the polls.

The moral is clear: Presidents must look beyond their relations with Congress if legislative influence is their goal. We saw the limits of these activities in the preceding chapters. The polls fall with economic hard times and rise in times of international crisis. Ironically, then, presidents may be most able to provide legislative "leadership" when they least need it—during times of international crisis; they may be least able to supply this leadership when domestic hard times demand new legislative solutions.

Once we take the important differences into account, in essence leveling the playing field, we must revise some popular impressions. Johnson, famous author of the Great Society legislation, was not as successful as active; when push came to shove, he chose activity, not success. Ford, the other legislative leader, often viewed as a caretaker, did not act as a caretaker, but was a very active president when the adjustments are made for the circumstances of his administration. Perhaps the sharpest adjustment is needed in our pictures of Carter and Reagan. As the two most recent occupants of the office, they show a striking similarity in their balancing of activity, popularity, and legislative success.

At the same time, this chapter shows a range of discretion remaining for the presidents. Some presidents emphasized activity at the cost of success; some did the reverse; and some pursued a more even balance between the two. In the process, they expended their popularity in various ways, trading it in for activity (Johnson and Ford), balancing it (Carter and Reagan), or guarding it (Eisenhower and Nixon) and keeping an extra reserve. We saw earlier that presidents were willing to make hard choices—discretionary actions predicted to hurt at the polls. Now we see that some presidents sacrificed approval while pursuing aggressive policy agendas.

We do not have a government, 99 percent of the time, where executives can act as freely in domestic matters as FDR did with the Emergency Banking Act. The real government, where Congress, the president, and the public all have an impact on one another, can be seen at work in this chapter. Burdening presidents with an unrealistic model will only obscure the actions that are possible and the choices that must be made. Perhaps it is worth adding that Roosevelt had his share of defeats and was so unhappy with Congress that he sought a purge of some of its members in the 1938 elections. No major New Deal legislation passed Congress after 1938. Needless to say, the purge was not successful. Nor are there exceptional figures among the modern presidents who have somehow escaped the normal institutional constraints. Johnson became a legend as Senate majority leader for his skills and personal style. As president, however, his legislative record is best understood within the analysis of this chapter. Very high in legislative activity, he was no higher in success than we would expect him to be, given his circumstances and choices.

"Endless presidential bargaining, persuading, power-hoarding, managing, manipulation—is this executive leadership?" James MacGregor Burns once asked as he criticized Richard Neustadt's theory of "the power to dicker and transact."[24] However, Neustadt's perception and prescriptions seem close to the picture accorded here. Presidents can, as Neustadt suggested, use public support to help their success in Congress, juggling the support they need against the positions they wish to take. They cannot do much in the face of declining approval over the term or congressional elections results. Certainly, the term *leadership* does not adequately describe the complex and limited strategies that we begin to see as realistically available and that the presidents themselves appear to choose.

We can argue that public opinion makes a difference in legislative maneuvering. Different policies are advanced depending on whether Democrats or Republicans are elected in some states and districts of the nation. A president's popularity affects activity in the White House and Congress in very definite ways. Yet it is not clear that the American public would approve of its influence. The more public-regarding presidents may be tempted to limit their positions and initiatives, and all presidents might worry less about their various contests with Congress than about a negative reaction from the stands.

5

Long Views and Short Goals

Popularity and American Foreign Policy

PERHAPS the chief worry about a public-relations presidency has to do with the nation's foreign affairs. A president too concerned with public standing might make decisions for the wrong reasons, taking actions likely to win support and hiding those, beneath the claims of "national security," expected to be unpopular or, in extreme cases, unconstitutional. Consequently, in critical matters of war and peace, personal interest could conflict with the public interest, and immediate political goals with a longer view of national needs and obligations. It is all very well to ask for public involvement in these critical decisions, to hope that people will hold their elected officials accountable for the decisions they take. Such accountability requires information and some vigorous debate. It is quite another matter to turn things around so that the public's name is used, as in a president's high popularity ratings, to justify decisions that same public knows nothing about.

Part of the reason for the diversion of funds in the Iran-Contra scandal was the White House's perception that the Contra cause had not gained public support.[1] Hence, secret sources of funding were pursued until President Reagan could persuade the public and Congress for legitimate funding. It was not only the Iranian arms dealers and Israelis who were solicited but also the Saudis, the Taiwanese, and the South African government.[2] All knew that the United States was desperate for cash. Indeed, negotiations with the South African government proceeded as the issue of South African sanctions was being debated in Congress. In this case, the secrecy—taken in the name of public opinion but against a position assumed to be held by the public—profoundly affected our relations with other nations and our image in the world.

Even normal decisions, well within constitutional guidelines, raise the same question. The Camp David treaty signed between Israel and Egypt brought a major foreign policy triumph to the Carter administration, buttressing the president's failing popularity. Yet, much of the public did not know that the treaty had a price tag in the billions for the United States, an annual bill that would continue to come due.[3] Another example is the surprise attack in Grenada, which deflected attention from the Reagan administration's problems in Lebanon, as many observers have pointed out. Was Grenada a fortunate coincidence for the president's popularity or were the two issues—Lebanon and Grenada—paired in more conscious ways? Such questions increased in the Bush administration, as we will see later. Rightly or wrongly, people worry that the treaty or the secret arms deal or the use of force might have been decided less because of long-range national interest and more because of the public-opinion polls.

This chapter confirms the worry to some extent. Presidents do appear to take certain actions in foreign policy *reactively*—that is, in response to the polls and events predicted to affect the polls. There is reassuring news as well, since the actions do not help. A careful analysis of the polls, controlling for the influences we have seen in previous chapters, shows that foreign policy events have a much more circumscribed influence than some people think. If presidents can be lured into Faustian bargains to help their popularity, they may be surprised to find how little they receive in return.

A nation's foreign relations are shaped in part by events beyond its control. Yet, individual heads of state, along with their advisers and other policy makers, do have choices that can be shaped by domestic circumstances. Economic problems, political opposition, and strong pressure from a military bureaucracy can affect the postures a nation takes abroad. We assume, therefore, that a president has choices to make within the international constraints. We assume further that a fairly adequate set of these presidential choices can be isolated for study. Although presidents cannot personally oversee the various complex global problems, there are points at which they do take direct action. As commander-in-chief, they sign orders directing the use of force abroad. They sign treaties and engage in meetings with other foreign leaders. They send foreign policy messages to Congress and speak to the American people about the nation's foreign affairs. A closer look at the timing and impact of these four kinds of activity—military, diplomatic, legislative, and rhetorical—should tell us more about presidential foreign relations in the postwar years. While not exhaustive, it should capture both the similarities and the differences among the modern presidents on these important dimensions and should allow us to assess the poll impact of very different foreign policy making. Do peace and war, for example, suggest different domestic political costs or benefits? Is all force the same? Can one kind of activity be interchanged for another?

These questions are particularly important when it comes to U.S. military action. Political scientists have disagreed on how much international crises affect popularity. Some argue that they help, others that they hurt, and others that they make little difference.[4] We saw in Chapter 2 that nationally unifying dramatic events, consisting largely of rally points, do indeed contribute a positive effect. We now need to look more closely at the interplay of these rallies and the use of force. Rallies might work their magic with or without force. Force itself may have little effect or even a negative effect. Indeed, the mixture of these events, and their varying treatment from one administration to another, may explain the past contradictory results. For a nation that would not want to go to war to help a president's poll ratings, the question has obvious importance.

FOREIGN POLICY ACTIVITIES

It is striking how much of the time since World War II the United States has been involved in the use of force. Force, as monitored by Congress and reported in bulletins of the Congressional Reference Service (CRS), is defined as the use of military forces abroad "in situations of conflict or potential conflict to protect U.S. citizens or promote U.S. interests." The definition, widely considered the broadest and most up to date, thus includes political as well as direct military objectives, although it probably understates the amount of actual force employed. It excludes covert activity and what are called "routine training operations," as well as actions not directly involving U.S. personnel.[5] The invasion of the Bay of Pigs, for example, using Cuban nationals, is not included as a use of force. Even by this limited definition, the United States has been engaged in force somewhere in the world for most of the time since World War II. Only four years in the entire time period show no use of force: 1949, 1957, 1961 (with the Bay of Pigs), and 1977. By far the greatest number of separate occasions where force was used happened in the 1980s, with sixteen separate uses of force in the Reagan years.

This use of force can be distinguished from the dramatic events discussed earlier, many of which had to do with the nation's foreign affairs. Those dramatic events—or what we can call rally points—included U.S. uses of force as well as cases when no such force was used (see the positive-predicted events listed in Appendix A). About one-third of the rally points involved uses of U.S. force, usually in reaction to another event interpreted as hostility: the beginning of the Korean War, the Cuban Missile Crisis, the *Mayaguez* incident, the invasion of Grenada, and the air strike on Libya. Perhaps another third involved events that can be interpreted as hostile or at least threatening to the nation's interests or allies but are cases where no U.S. force was used: the shooting down of the Korean airliner, the erection of the Berlin Wall, the Iranian taking of U.S. hostages, and the Soviet invasion of Afghanistan. A final group involved peace making rather than hostilities: the various Korean and Vietnam peace agreements, the announcement of the end of bombing, the

Camp David accords, and the INF treaty. The remaining exceptional cases did not involve foreign policy.

Clearly these rally points are not the same as the use of force by the United States, although presidents and others might confuse the two categories. They did not all involve force, and they showed a mixture of major and minor issues. Presumably, the tragic and apparently mistaken Soviet firing on the Korean airliner did not raise the same kind of national security issues for the United States as the erecting of the Berlin Wall. At the same time, many uses of force did not become rally points. The evacuations of Vietnam and Cambodia in 1975 and the sending of troops to the Sinai and Lebanon in 1982 are cases in point. As we will see, rallies are primarily defined by how the issues are treated by the White House and subsequently in the press. It is also interesting how much the rallies place the nation in the role of victim, of being acted on by others who take the first hostile actions. How this confusion plays out in the actions of presidents will be clear as the chapter proceeds.

Closely related to the rally points are the foreign policy addresses that presidents give to the nation. Presidents gave a major televised address on most of these occasions: the first crossing of North Korean troops into South Korea, the forming of the Berlin Wall, the Cuban Missile Crisis, the sending of troops to the Dominican Republic, the *Mayaguez* incident, the invasion of Afghanistan, the Korean airliner attack, and the invasion of Grenada. On the other hand, they did not speak at the many other points when force was used. Although presidents do give other foreign policy speeches, many occur with these rally points and presumably help to create them.

Any attempt to trace the anatomy of rallies would require another entire study. For an event to be visible enough to be listed in the many chronologies, it requires substantial media coverage. However, it seems clear that the presidents help to create the rally points with their speeches, press releases, interviews, and other activities. None of the foreign policy rallies listed in Appendix A occurred without some presidential action. The Soviet attack on Afghanistan might have been a news story for a week, but it became much more because of its treatment by the

Carter administration. Even more clearly, the shooting down of
the Korean plane became a rally because the Reagan White
House made it one.

In extreme cases, White House efforts to create a proper scene
and dramatic effect can be all-absorbing. The invasion of Grenada in the Reagan years involved detailed planning on such
subjects as the arrangement of government photographs, a system to control how the news would be reported, and a major
presidential address. Americans did not see any combat footage
of the invasion since reporters were excluded. All they saw were
students getting off a plane and kissing the ground. The Persian
Gulf War in the Bush administration—perhaps the strongest rally
point in more than a quarter of a century—exceeded even these
efforts. Months before the war began, as we will see in the
following chapter, the Bush White House was at work on several
major speeches, regular news conferences by the president and
other officials, and an even more sophisticated system of press
censorship. Details went so far as to screen (and rehearse) the
military officers to see who could give the best briefings.

It will be important, therefore, to try to separate the rally
points from the nation's use of force and to separate both at least
in part from the surrounding rhetorical activity. These activities
can be contrasted with the diplomatic and legislative activity that
the presidents pursue. Diplomacy has been measured in past
studies as major treaties signed by the United States. We can add
to this measure the occasion of major summit meetings and, as
discussed previously, the days of foreign travel. Together, these
should give a fuller impression of the time presidents directly
spend on diplomatic affairs.

Legislative activity can be gleaned from the major foreign
policy messages sent to Congress, requesting legislation, as reported in the *Public Papers*. This excludes the informal letters sent
to members of Congress and the many routine reports that do
not request legislation. The legislative messages are subject to
many influences, of course, most of which stem from Congress.
Nevertheless, they do provide some indication of the particular
interests of an administration. Kennedy sent requests on a broad
variety of subjects but included two on the nuclear test ban treaty,

which he was strongly lobbying the Congress for. He also spoke to the nation on this subject. Reagan, by contrast, sent very few foreign policy messages but included several on aid to Central America. In 1986, for example, he sent only three foreign policy messages to Congress requesting legislation: Two directly solicited aid for the Nicaraguan Contras; the third included a Nicaraguan request as part of a more general message. Nicaragua, of course, also figured prominently in Reagan's speeches to the nation, as well as in many other activities that the administration was simultaneously pursuing.

We can now see how these different activities are distributed over a president's term. In particular, we ask whether these activities are random, reactive, or strategic. Following the logic given in Chapter 3, reactive events would occur much more frequently than expected by chance in company with other dramatic events, economic fluctuations, or shifts in presidential popularity. Strategic events would be patterned with the electoral cycles, presidential or congressional. If foreign policy activities were taken purely in terms of international goals and problems, we would find no relationship with such events. In that case, the president's activities would be randomly distributed. The use of force, to take one example, would not be related to changes in the economy or other domestic political events.

Some foreign policy activities are randomly distributed; others are not (see Appendix B). This fairly striking contrast can be summarized for the first terms of Truman through Reagan:

Use of force	Reactive
International rally point	Reactive
Foreign policy address	Reactive
Major diplomacy	Random
Message to Congress	Random

The use of force is not random, but reactive. It is significantly more likely to occur following negative dramatic events—scandals in the White House, strikes, and other signs of domestic disarray. It is also more likely to occur when economic conditions are worsening. A rise in the economic misery index significantly increases the likelihood of a use of force. The giving of foreign policy speeches is also reactive, following bad luck and the hard choices (the negative discretionary acts) that presidents decide to make. Speeches on foreign policy, in other words, are more likely to follow unpopular announcements in another area of policy. An increase in economic misery, on the other hand, does not affect the giving of such speeches. This difference is readily understandable when we recall the tendency for presidents to hide from the public during bad economic times. During such times, presidents might decide to use force, but they would not necessarily appear in public to give major foreign policy addresses.

Two writers, Charles Ostrom and Brian Job, have reported a similar pattern. They found that with a substantial worsening of economic conditions, the probability of a use of force increases by 20 percent.[6] These writers, by the way, looked only at major conflicts, what they called "nuclear-capable" situations. Indeed, when we focus on the most dramatic cases of a worsening economy—at high misery, so to speak—we find the same result. Under extreme economic conditions, the likelihood of force increases dramatically.[7] We cannot say, of course, that presidents deliberately use some foreign policy events to distract attention from domestic problems, but the problems and events are linked too closely to be seen as chance.

By contrast, other kinds of foreign policy activity are randomly distributed. Major diplomacy—the treaties, summit meetings, and other dramatic cases of peace making—are not patterned in relation to domestic political conditions. Neither are the foreign policy messages to Congress. These results make intuitive sense. Diplomacy takes long-range planning and the participation of other governments; legislation must accommodate the congressional calendar. These are not things that can be manipulated for short-term goals on the promptings of White House advisers. Of course, the same could be said for uses of force. It is interesting to see that the rally events having solely to do with peace making are randomly distributed. In this they appear similar to the other, less dramatic kinds of diplomacy.

It is true that one kind of diplomatic activity was previously found to be patterned both strategically and reactively: the taking of foreign trips. Foreign travel increased, we saw in Chapter 3, in presidential election years. It also tended to occur most frequently when presidents appeared safe from threats in the economy or at the polls. The trips were taken, in other words, when the presidents could most afford them. Trips—to somewhere in the world—certainly can be scheduled more easily than summit meetings or major treaty signings and are also more symbolic, less substantive, and probably less important activities. So, on balance, it seems that the major kinds of diplomatic activity do occur randomly. War making is patterned with domestic political events; peace making is not.

One puzzle remains. Presidents' foreign policy activities do not clearly follow declines in their popularity. In other words, events, such as poor economic conditions, predict better than the polls themselves when a use of force or a rally point will suddenly occur. The same curious result was also seen in the Ostrom and Job study. Indeed, those authors found that under some conditions, use of force was more likely when a president's popularity was high. One answer, admittedly speculative, is that these activities are taken *preemptively,* to forestall a drop in the polls; hence, they occur before the polls might decline but follow decisions that threaten a decline, such as economic misery. This does not require any hair-trigger reactions. Obviously, presidents will not jump up from an economic briefing and send troops somewhere in the world. It does mean, however, that there are enough tense international situations and negative domestic events within any term that can be linked in particular ways. Bad luck and economic misery do not *follow* rallies and uses of force, they precede them. The rallies and force follow the negative domestic circumstances with much more frequency than could be expected by chance.

The Second Term

The effects for the second term can be seen for Eisenhower, Nixon, and Reagan. We now find that all the foreign policy events are randomly distributed. Rallies and the use of force no longer follow negative domestic events in clearly patterned ways. This is especially striking since it was during the second term that the major administration scandals occurred, clearly the most negative of the domestic events. Nixon had Watergate, Reagan had Iran-Contra, and even Eisenhower had the problem of Sherman Adams and the vicuña coats and expensive hotel bills. Removing the very exceptional Watergate years from the analysis does not change these results.

It is possible that, once removed from reelection pressures, presidents would be less concerned with timing foreign policy acts to counter domestic circumstances. Actions in foreign policy would be taken more for other reasons—quite possibly pertaining to international conditions—and so would appear random in relation to domestic events. This argument is supported by the difference between first- and second-term results.

On the other hand, there was no evidence of any electoral timing in these presidents' first terms. Carter's denouncing of the Russian invasion of Afghanistan in January of his reelection year—which helped him in the polls—was an exception. Then, too, Nixon's situation in his second term was at least as critical as a reelection, if not more so. He was fighting a scandal that could have removed him from office. And yet we saw previously that he did not perform the kind of ceremonial acts that might have been expected to help his public standing; indeed, he took them much less frequently than in his first term. Throughout 1973, as the drumbeat of negative events increased—the Ervin Committee began its hearings, John Dean testified, John Erlichman and others were indicted, the Saturday night massacre occurred, and the vice presidential scandal broke—no dramatic foreign policy events occurred. No foreign trips were taken. Since Nixon engaged in these activities in his first term to better effect than that of many of the other presidents, we can see that he knew how to use them. The fact remains that in his second term, Nixon clearly did not follow the kind of reactive timing of events that might have distracted attention from problems at home, even at a point when he might have thought he could control them. By early summer of 1974, when the Cyprus crisis broke open and he took a major foreign trip, almost all of the negative events for President Nixon were over.

A closer look shows a key difference among the three presidents. Eisenhower, like Nixon, reduced his activities in his second term, although he had his share of negative events—the integration crisis in Little Rock, a major steel strike and labor controversy, and the Sherman Adams scandal. Whereas Nixon had no foreign policy events in 1973 to break the negative domestic spell, Eisenhower had but one. In June 1958, the Sherman Adams scandal broke, and in July, Eisenhower sent the marines to Lebanon at the request of the Lebanese government. The polls did rise after the Lebanese action by 6 percentage points, although we cannot necessarily impute a causal connection. Overall, however, there were few dramatic foreign policy actions in either Nixon's or Eisenhower's second terms to help mitigate the negative effects.

In the tense final days before the Nixon resignation, a curious event occurred. Secretary of Defense James Schlesinger apparently notified all U.S. commanders that no orders coming from the White House calling for the movement of troops or weapons should be followed without his countersignature.[8] Schlesinger, and presumably White House aide Alexander Haig, Jr., who was orchestrating the resignation, was apparently worried about reactivity of a particularly dangerous kind: the taking of action in foreign policy that might deflect attention from the domestic crisis. Psychological pressures on Nixon or other advisers at the time might have made this worry plausible. All we know is that the Nixon White House had not taken this kind of action in the preceding months.

In contrast to Eisenhower and Nixon, Reagan showed a more reactive pattern in his second term. Action in the Persian Gulf occurred within the same month as the beginning of the Iran-Contra hearings in May 1987. In June, as the hearings on the scandal continued, the reflagging of Kuwaiti tankers began. In April 1988, as the Edwin Meese scandal led to an investigation of the Justice Department, the marines entered Panama. Reagan's polls fell somewhat during this period, but they remained remarkably stable given the barrage of negative events. Even though we cannot show this conclusively in statistical terms because of the small number of cases, there do appear combinations of foreign and domestic events in Reagan's second term that supported the idea of reactivity.

A clearer picture, then, of second-term activity in foreign policy may need to wait for future presidents. The record is mixed, and the Schlesinger-Haig worries have not gone away.

THE INDIVIDUAL PRESIDENTS

We can now look more closely at how the individual presidents distributed their activities. Although the first-term presidencies were similar by and large, we find different emphases: Presidents make their own choices within the common constraints. These choices include military activity, as in engaging in major wars or in separate uses of force; rhetorical activity, as in speeches to the nation; legislative activity, as in foreign policy messages to Congress; and diplomatic activity, as in participating in summits or meetings with key European allies. A combined military-rhetorical emphasis is particularly worth watching for, since these are the activities most closely linked to domestic political events. How common is this pattern, and what alternative choices appear?

Noting the presidents who were above average in activity on each of these dimensions can show this variety most clearly.[9] This is a rough cut merely, but it does reveal several things. There are intriguing differences among the presidents, with some fairly distinct foreign policy styles. Further, these differences accord well with the variety we have seen previously. Finally, the military-rhetorical style is something of a late arrival. Of the incumbents from Truman to Reagan, it is Reagan who shows this emphasis most clearly. Bush also follows on the military-rhetorical style.

Most Active Presidents

Military:	Reagan I and II, Ford, Johnson
Rhetorical:	Nixon I, Kennedy, Reagan I and II, Carter
Legislative:	Truman, Nixon I, Eisenhower I, Kennedy
Diplomatic:	Nixon II, Johnson, Reagan II, Eisenhower II

Reagan, Ford, and Johnson rank highest on the separate use of force. Reagan led his predecessors in office in both his first and second terms. All of these uses of force are not equal, of course. Many of Ford's, for example, were taken for the purpose of evacuating U.S. civilians and others from various trouble spots in Vietnam, Cambodia, and Lebanon. Without the evacuations, listed as uses of force in the CRS report, Ford would have engaged force only twice. It should be added that Reagan's record does not include the bombing of Nicaraguan harbors. As a covert activity that the president agreed to in a secret "finding," it was not included in the CRS listing, even though it subsequently became very well known. Likewise, Kennedy's record does not include the stationing of advisers in Vietnam, which some could say greatly understated his use of force. These separate uses of force are far different than engagement in major wars, which produce a vastly greater number of American casualties. Truman, Johnson, and Nixon were the war-time presidents according to this latter measure.

The contrast in military activity between Carter and Reagan is particularly noteworthy. The Carter years were times of relative peace, even though the hostage crisis apparently drove out this impression. The Reagan years were very high in military activity, in separate uses of force. This impression is strengthened when we look at the foreign policy rally events that occurred in the various administrations. Only Kennedy and Reagan benefited from as many as one of these rally points each year. Kennedy faced two Berlin crises, the missiles in Cuba, and the Bay of Pigs. Reagan faced eight: Grenada, the Persian Gulf (three times), Libya (twice), Panama, and the Korean airliner shooting. Carter, however, faced only two over the course of his term. Both Carter and Reagan were high in the rhetorical activity expected of presidents in recent years, but Reagan was considerably higher in military activity. The differences may be small, but they have substantive importance: Reagan made an average of two uses of force in one year; Carter made an average of one use of force in two years.

The rhetorical leaders include Nixon in his first term, Kennedy, Reagan in both terms, and Carter. In part, this speaking on foreign policy reflects a broader rhetorical style: Some presidents simply like to talk more to the nation than others. Reagan and Nixon, with the highest average number of major addresses overall, also were high in foreign policy speaking. Truman and Johnson, with the fewest speeches overall, also were low in foreign policy. Johnson ranks the lowest, having given an average of one foreign policy speech every two years. Yet, because of the self-imposed limitation on speeches to the nation, presidents must decide the subjects on which to expend their valuable speaking time. They do not need to select foreign policy speeches. Carter, for example, ranks higher in foreign policy speaking than he ranks overall, while Eisenhower ranks lower. Eisenhower, the third most vocal president overall, ranks lower in foreign policy, outranking only Johnson and Ford. In any case, individual choice seems more important than the events themselves in deciding when presidents will speak. Both Johnson and Nixon spent their first terms fighting the war in Vietnam, but Johnson gave only one speech on Vietnam in those years; Nixon gave eleven. Some presidents, Eisenhower, for example, gave major addresses after returning from foreign trips. Events may have required Kennedy to speak on the Berlin Wall and Ford to speak after sending troops to rescue the crew of the *Mayaguez*, but they did not require Carter to speak on Afghanistan or Reagan to speak on the shooting of the Korean airliner. These were choices the individual presidents made.

Foreign policy messages to Congress may reflect some institutional trends at work. Truman and Nixon were the most inclined to send these messages, followed by Eisenhower in his first term and Kennedy. The most recent presidents rank lower in these requests. Foreign aid, once a major White House initiative and key part of any legislative foreign policy, was increasingly handled routinely and outside the Oval Office. Military aid was diversified or incorporated in a larger budget request. Hence, these two programs that Eisenhower, Kennedy, and Nixon worked hard for, no longer needed the same kind of attention. The Reagan White House, for example, could increase the military assistance budget by a variety of techniques without sending a direct request to Congress on the subject.[10]

Much of the choice, however, is still a matter of individual priorities. While Reagan ranks near the bottom among presidents sending messages to Congress in both his first and second terms, he did send messages requesting aid to the Contras. And, in 1983, when he sent no foreign policy messages at all, he sent a total of nine on other issues—the budget, the economy, school tuition, federalism, health-care incentives, tax reform, an amendment for prayer in schools, employment, and education. Clearly, Reagan chose what he wanted to send messages about. So did Johnson, whose average legislative record in foreign policy was far different from his domestic program. The same element of choice is apparent in the high ranking of Nixon and Eisenhower. These Republican presidents tended to be less active overall in legislation than the Democrats. It seems likely that the activity in foreign policy was a deliberate choice to balance the lower emphasis on the domestic agenda.

In diplomatic activity, all presidents seem to try for one major achievement that will be noted in the historical record. Truman negotiated the Japanese peace treaty ending World War II and Eisenhower the Korean War peace. Kennedy initiated and won the nuclear test ban treaty, made more difficult by the intense Cold War that was in effect at the time. Nixon, the one president with two widely regarded diplomatic achievements, negotiated the SALT treaty and opened new diplomatic relations with China. Carter won a Middle East peace treaty in the Camp David agreements, and Reagan signed the historic INF treaty with the Soviet Union, limiting the use of middle-range nuclear weapons. Only Ford is missing from this list of major diplomatic coups—presumably because he did not have time to achieve one. Given the similar expectations, it is not surprising that there is little variation in diplomatic activity among the presidents. Nevertheless, some do engage in more of this diplomacy than others by means of key summit meetings and other major trips. The leaders are Nixon, Reagan, and Eisenhower in their second terms and Johnson. Both Reagan and Eisenhower, it is interesting to see, were higher in this activity in their second terms.

The similarities are more obvious than the differences. All presidents are expected to pursue diplomatic achievements, to give the occasional foreign policy speech, and to send legislation to Congress. They must be vigilant and effective as commander-in-chief. Different relative emphases do appear within the general patterns. Nixon was uniquely active in his first term. He was high in both military activity, carrying on the war in Southeast Asia, and the rhetorical activity of foreign policy speeches. He was very high in legislative activity as well. Nixon's messages to Congress, it is worth pointing out, were not perfunctory. They included his detailed Vietnamization program, a major trade bill, a controversial Asia development program, along with several foreign aid requests. He was the one president who responded to Congress's pleading for reform of the foreign aid program by sending a detailed reform package to the Hill. (An ungrateful Congress did not pass the legislation.) Even in his abbreviated second term, Nixon still managed to score two very visible diplomatic achievements.

The other presidents created their own particular emphases. Truman and Johnson were similar: comparatively low in rhetoric and both engaged in war. Carter was about average on three of the dimensions, but was lower than average in the use of force. Reagan showed the military-rhetorical pattern most clearly, in both terms. Reagan ranks high in the use of force, quite high in foreign policy speeches, and quite low in legislation. The impression is strengthened when we recall that most of Reagan's legislative requests concerned aid to Central America. None of the administrations is under average on all four dimensions. Although each president pursued some kind of foreign policy, their particular activities differed.

These rankings accord with most subjective judgments that speak, for example, of Nixon's active record in foreign affairs or the shift to a stronger military posture in the Reagan years. People might disagree with any one of the placements, arguing, for example, that Kennedy should be placed higher in legislative activity because he pioneered new programs in foreign assistance, or higher in military activity because of his actions in Vietnam. Adjustments of this kind are possible, but the overall point is clear. Presidents do vary on these several dimensions as they carve out their own foreign policy styles. Further, no clear trend

is apparent. Two of the most recent presidents, Carter
gan, showed very different emphases. This is importa
office like the presidency, where trends develop quic
precedents appear instantly. George Bush, as we will see in
ter 7, not only followed his predecessor in a military-rhe
emphasis, but may have surpassed him. The CRS bulletin lists
four uses of force in Bush's first year in office.

FOREIGN AFFAIRS AND
THE POLLS

The domestic political context does affect the frequency and
timing of foreign policy. We now ask how these foreign policy
acts affect domestic politics—specifically, the president's standing in the polls.

We look for the effect on popularity of each of these foreign
policy activities, controlling for the other important influences:
the economy, negative events, and the decline over the term. We
particularly want to distinguish the various kinds of rally points
from the different uses of force to see what is and what is not
influential. Rally events are divided into three types: those involving force, those involving no force, and other types of rallies.
Nonrally events consist of major diplomacy, force without rallies,
messages to Congress, and treaty announcements. Much of the
headline news as reported from the White House is captured by
these events. The results for all presidents are shown in Figure
5.1. (The statistical results are reported in Appendix B.)

Not all foreign affairs have positive effects on a president's
public standing. Fewer still have a statistically significant impact
on the approval ratings. No automatic popularity accrues to
presidents in the conduct of foreign affairs. The use of force
during an international rally has the most positive, significant, and
sustained influence. The boost to popularity from these uses of
force ranges from over 6 percent in the first month to roughly 5
percent after four months. But before White House advisers urge
a president to send out the troops, they should compare this

Political Capital

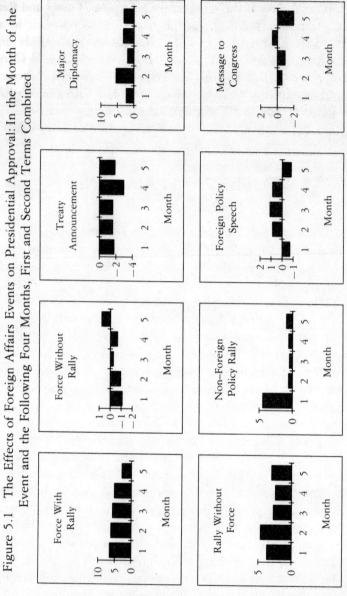

Figure 5.1 The Effects of Foreign Affairs Events on Presidential Approval: In the Month of the Event and the Following Four Months, First and Second Terms Combined

pattern with the use of force in the absence of an international rally event. Force without the dramatic attention created by a rally point is slightly negative and remains consistently so in the following months; popularity might *decline* slightly with a use of force, although not to a significant degree. Moreover, this measure of force counts all operations only once and does not include the increasing negative effects on popularity produced by the Korean and Vietnam wars. These widely understood effects have been shown in several studies.[11] Uses of force are closely tied to negative domestic conditions. Unfortunately for the presidents, these reactive uses of force show no signs of benefiting them at the polls.

Other events show some positive impact. Rally points not involving U.S. force increase presidential approval by over 4 percent in the month of the event. Presidents could announce an international crisis or that they need surgery—both statements would produce a rallying to their support, although this rallying would have nothing to do with the substance of policy. In addition, international hostilities without use of force boost presidential approval ratings by over 4 percent in the month after they occur. For example, the Russian move into Afghanistan boosted Carter's approval ratings. Lastly, acts of major diplomacy increase public support by roughly 5 percent one month after the event. Whatever criticism of a president's performance might surround these events, the summit meetings, major trips to Communist countries, and key meetings with European allies do help the approval ratings. Foreign travel, we saw earlier, generally makes no difference, although particular trips can make a difference.

Beyond these activities and events, the conduct of foreign affairs has weakly negative effects. After presidents announce treaties or send foreign policy messages to Congress, their approval will fall slightly. These endeavors can be controversial, of course, and do not provoke the unity of a threat from abroad. Nevertheless, they do suggest that foreign affairs offer a president an unfortunate set of incentives. A hostile international situation can yield a significant and sustained boost to a president's standing with the public, while a peace treaty, an arms-limitation agreement, or a new foreign aid program can impair that standing.

We must conclude that the impact on the polls has little to do with the substance of policy and much more with how the events are presented or perceived. Uses of force per se do not help a president at the polls, even apart from the negative effects of the Vietnam and Korean wars. On the other hand, rally points, whether they announce force or a prolonged presidential hospital stay, do have a substantial impact. Since both the force and the rallies occur at times of negative domestic events, it is possible that the White House has not made this important distinction.

The duration of the effects also is important. Does an event in March continue to help a president's popularity in May or June? As Figure 5.1 shows clearly, some of the effects have a very short life, with appreciable increases in support limited to one month. A dramatic event without U.S. use of force contributes to a significant increase in approval only in the month following the event. If, for example, Carter denounced the Afghanistan invasion in early January, the event might have been expected to help him in February. By March, its impact would have largely disappeared. The non–foreign policy rallies are even briefer, virtually limited to the month in which they occur. It is the rallies in which the United States employs force that last the longest: at least four months overall. If the air strike on Libya first affected polls in April 1986, it would be expected to have an impact in April, May, June, and July. By the fifth month after a dramatic use of force, the effect will be only weakly positive and will have begun to disappear. A study by political scientist Michael MacKuen also suggests four months as the average duration of these dramatic events.[12]

Two cases from the Bush administration show these durational effects at work. Before the invasion of Panama, Bush's popularity was high: Fully 68 percent of the public approved of his performance in October 1989. His popularity reached a high point of 80 percent following the invasion and the surrender of Noriega, but four months after the surrender, it returned to 65 percent. After the Gulf War victory, 86 percent of the public told Gallup they approved of the way Bush was doing his job; four months later, 70 percent approved. Bush was still very popular in the early summer of 1991: Nevertheless, his polls had fallen 16 percentage points. The fall-off rate from the momentary ia of victory was quite similar, as Gallup's mid-month sults show:

Month of Event	Panama (January 1990) (%)	Persian Gulf (March 1991) (%)
1	80	86
2	73	77
3	74	76
4	67	71
5	65	70

For any president concerned with the polls, four months can buy time to derail press stories about the administration being in trouble or to discourage people from looking for more trouble. Even a one-month boost can change the all-important momentum, something the presidents know well from their previous campaigns. Nevertheless, it is worth stressing how short-lived the rallies are. Like Fourth of July fireworks, they make a dramatic impact and quickly fade away.

IMPLICATIONS

Foreign policy and questions of presidential popularity do appear intertwined. Uses of force by the United States and dramatic rally points follow negative domestic events much more frequently than could be expected by chance. Economic conditions, in particular, make very good predictors of when some uses of force will occur: The more negative the economic news is, the more likely there will be a use of force. It is not all foreign policy, however, but only particular kinds that show this curious connection. Although force and foreign policy speeches follow negative events, acts of diplomacy and legislation do not.

Foreign affairs do affect the polls, but their impact has little to do with the substance of policy and much more to do with how events are perceived or presented. Dramatic rally points, with or without the use of force, are strongly positive in impact. Rallies having nothing to do with foreign policy are also strongly positive. Dramatic peace-making events, on the other hand, show little effect on popularity. Other diplomacy and legislation similarly show no effect. We cannot argue, however, that there is a policy at issue here—for example, that Americans support war more than peace—since they support only wars presented in a particular way. Overall, the use of force by the United States shows very weak negative effects in the polls. This result holds independently of the strongly negative effects on popularity produced by the Vietnam and Korean wars.

It appears that the presidents themselves, and perhaps the public, have confused two kinds of events. Both acts of force and rallies occur reactively, following bad economic news and other negative events. This suggests, at least circumstantially, that presidential activities are expected to help the polls, countering the negative effects. But force without rallies does not help popularity, although the reactive allocation of these acts of force suggests that presidents *think* they can boost their public standing.

These results also help explain the contradictions about rally points seen in political science studies. Rallies by and large have been equated with international crises involving hostility on the part of at least one nation. The combination cannot distinguish between two very different effects. Thus, writers concentrating on the period from Truman to Johnson can argue that these events had a negative impact on the polls. The events include two very unpopular wars. Other writers, combining rally points and force over a broader period, say that they make no difference. Still others, evaluating rallies as one of many influences simultaneously affecting popularity, argue that they do.[13] We suggest that they indeed have a positive impact on the polls, once they are separated from the effects of force, and that force does not have an impact once it is separated from rallies. Since there are far more uses of force than rallies, the point has obvious importance.

This finding needs wider recognition among presidents and those who write about them. If presidents can be lured into using force to help at home, they are lured by a mirage: by the special effects of a very limited number of cases that the presidents themselves help to create. These cases do not require the use of force or even a particular external, independent event.

All of this raises serious questions about the nation's foreign policy, or that portion of policy decided at the White House level. The short-term and personal is potentially at odds with longer-term national issues. Domestic circumstances shape foreign policy acts, although some of these acts reshape the domestic conditions, at least for a time. Moreover, the public is cast against itself, or rather the *name* of the public is taken to justify acts that may not be in the public's interest and strategies that the public would not support. If people were asked what they thought of a president following reactive strategies in foreign policy, based on the domestic conditions, they would probably disapprove strongly.

It is pleasant to think that we do not elect presidents who can be lured into Faustian bargains, but there is nothing in the selection process that suggests this. From the first announcement to the final debate, candidates learn to care about short-term impact and the polls. The candidates who best succeed at this become president. It is not surprising that they and the advisers who helped make the victory possible carry on their skills in the White House. Certainly, they have company and support along the way. If they were to get sidetracked into more altruistic long-term planning, a few media stories on declining popularity would always bring them back. To many people frustrated by the hostage crisis in the Carter years, Grenada gave them a chance to feel patriotic and the Gulf War gave them an even greater chance.

The Carter-Reagan contrast demonstrates the problem in sharpest form. We saw that Reagan emphasized the military-rhetorical pattern whereas Carter did not, engaging in few uses of force or rallies. Although their public support was similar, it was widely perceived at the time that Carter's "weakness" in foreign policy hurt him with the public and threatened his reelection. At this point, early in the 1980 election year, the Russians advanced into Afghanistan.

Carter's response was to denounce the Afghanistan invasion strongly. Although the United States was not involved in the action, he gave a speech to the nation on the subject on January 4. He used the occasion to ask Congress for stronger support for intelligence activities and a renewal of the draft registration, which had been out of existence since 1974. Carter's action and requests stayed in the news for much of January: The event qualified as a rally without the use of force. The polls jumped considerably, bringing Carter back above the 50 percent approval mark, although by April he dropped below again. Afghanistan can even be shown to have had some impact on the election. While voters in post-election surveys criticized Carter for his handling of the hostage crisis, some spoke positively of his stand on Afghanistan.[14] Was Carter exploiting an issue that might otherwise have been treated differently? Or was he, in good democratic fashion, merely doing what he thought a majority of Americans wanted? Probably he was doing both.

The dilemmas of making foreign policy in a public-relations White House preclude any easy solution, and yet some initial steps appear. If people are made more conscious of the intertwining of foreign policy and the polls, they can begin to give more thought to their approval responses, evaluating the kind of behavior they do and do not want. It is unlikely that a majority of the public would approve of the reactivity this chapter reveals. Hence, simply knowing that bad economic news greatly increases the chance of a use of force can set in motion influences that would decrease the linkage between these events. Presidents can choose different kinds of emphases in their foreign policy agendas: There is not only one model to choose. Therefore, both presidents and the public can begin to evaluate these choices more carefully. Finally, the results indicate limits for even the most cynical of White House strategists. The effects are partial and typically short in duration. In short, we can begin to separate the polls from the American public. Their influence on foreign policy, and the views they reflect, are probably not the same.

6

The Presidents in Office

WHITE House staffer Barbara Honegger has observed that remarks about Ronald Reagan's ethical problems often were met by the response, "Compared to whom?"[1] This question not only capsulizes the kind of relativist ethics so popular in the 1980s but also reveals a problem peculiar to the presidency. The reason White House people could use "Compared to whom?" as a kind of unanswerable question is that the president is thought to be incomparable. How can we hold a president to an ethical standard if there is no one else in that unique situation, facing the particular problems and challenges of the time. Even if we tried to do so, we would see that surely another of these unusual beings must have acted in the same way, even if we do not know that for sure. Accordingly, Richard Nixon could point out that, although he was blamed for Watergate, many of his predecessors would be found as guilty for other acts if only the facts were known.

Americans tend to look at their government and its problems one president at a time. This focus is encouraged by news media who focus on the present rather than the past, the individual apart from the pattern. It is embraced by citizens who want a concrete embodiment of democratic government to celebrate and identify with. It is supported by the presidents themselves, who rarely mention their predecessors in public, thus dramatizing their singular status and protecting themselves from invidious or demeaning comparisons.[2] As Johnson reminded people when he was being criticized for the war in Vietnam, he was the only president they had.

This attention distorts the problems we see and blinds us to those that are lost in the hazy background. Trends are missed. New precedents are announced that need not exist. All the variation and pattern are missing. If there is a very uneasy balance at best, as this book argues, between presidential action and democratic support, then we need to be able to answer "Compared to whom?"

This book finds patterns common to all presidents and also individual variation. Presidents make choices within constraints, but they do make choices. Moreover, some presidents have made the same choices. They disregarded public opinion or wooed it steadily. They bombarded Congress with new legislation or treated it gingerly. They cultivated reputations for activity or popularity or tried to devise some balance between the two. The comparison allows us to explore these similarities more fully. Are they built into the office in any way that people should recognize and perhaps compensate for? Or are these merely a coincidence of idiosyncratic factors occurring in what is after all a small number of presidents? If the public wants more input into how its support will be used and solicited by the White House, these questions are important.

In addition, the profiles can provide a new and deeper perspective on the many accounts of individual presidents. Readers can find plenty of biographies, psychobiographies, oral histories, work from presidential libraries, and accounts from reporters and former White House staffers. Presidents are analyzed and psychoanalyzed in rich detail. The research and the insights are impressive; yet the accounts again emphasize presidential uniqueness. We see each individual portrait but none of the larger picture. There also is some danger of intellectual inbreeding since so many of the sources and authors knew and worked with one another. The Carter insiders and the Reagan insiders all want to make the same point. Particular images of presidents and favorite stories about them thus quickly grow into accepted facts. It will be interesting to see when the comparison confirms these impressions or adds new insights.

Political scientist James David Barber has classified individual presidents along broad personality dimensions to predict "performance in the White House." He characterizes them on two dimensions as active or passive and positive or negative, according to their activities; on such dynamics as their love of politics or sense of duty; and on their following of internal versus external cues.[3] The approach and measures of this book are very different, but we also look at performance in the White House and can say how presidents compare with one another in their activity and the taking of internal or external cues. Although we cannot "test" the Barber classifications, we should be able to add a new point of view. Here, then, are the presidential profiles in comparative perspective, with their choices, activity, and public support.

THE PRESIDENTIAL PROFILES

Truman

Truman's profile in this book stresses sharp contrast between his low regard for public opinion and his considerable activity. Truman not only ranks lowest of all our modern presidents in the polls, when we control for the circumstances of his times, but he went out of his way to show his low regard for the polls. He fought with reporters and with Congress, and his low regard seemed a matter of personal style, one that was carefully cultivated. One of his diary entries records the characteristic Truman lines: "Congress meets—too bad too. I'm to address them soon. They won't like the address either."[4] As Truman himself tells the story, he told his World War I command pretty much the same thing, long before he came to the White House: "I didn't come over here to get along with you. You've got to get along with me."[5] It is interesting that even the First Lady carried this style forward. When reporters urged Bess Truman to take more of a public role, she snapped, "I am not the one elected. I have nothing to say to the public." She shocked one columnist, who complained to her that the president had used the phrase "horse manure" in a nonagricultural context, by retorting that she was delighted she had finally gotten him to say "manure."[6]

Against this disregard for public opinion, the activity of the Truman years is impressive. Truman ranks high in military and legislative activity in foreign policy. This ranking for 1949–52 excludes his greatest accomplishments: the ending of World War II and the historic postwar legislation. Although we do not have direct comparisons for the Truman years in overall legislative activity and success, the size of the program is clear. Truman pioneered what would become the modern foreign assistance program, presided over the restructuring of foreign policy making in the National Security Act of 1947, and worked with Congress on an Atomic Energy Act that would determine how the development of atomic and nuclear energy would be governed. At the same time, he continued to push the domestic programs of the New Deal. He was not always successful, as his frequent fights with Congress and record-high number of vetoes show. Indeed, he was the only president to *campaign* for his own election on the platform of how bad Congress was. This was the Republican-dominated 80th Congress, which he admitted much later probably had not been that bad.[7] While we have no clear-cut quantitative measures, it appears that Truman emphasized activity over success.

This contrast is corroborated in several individual accounts. James David Barber, for example, in his study of presidential personalities, characterizes Truman as an active-positive type. According to Barber, Truman showed high self-esteem and a "self-acceptance" of his strengths and limits. The limits were a lack of charisma and ease in dealing with the public, and the strengths involved the capacity to make vigorous decisions.[8] Another writer, Alonzo Hamby, sees the same contrast, but interprets it differently. Truman showed both insecurity and responsibility: a resentment of public criticism along with the attempt to avoid it wherever possible, as well as the determination to do whatever he needed to do to be successful.[9]

Whatever the personality dynamic at work, it is worth emphasizing how much Truman's behavior appears to have been deliberately selected. Truman, we must remember, was a successful politician, a "natural," a member of Missouri's political machine who rose to success in Congress and favor with Democratic party leaders sufficient to be nominated for the vice presidency. He was always the pragmatic politician, as biographer Cabell Phillips asserts.[10] If he campaigned against the 80th Congress, he used the 79th to pass record-breaking legislation and admitted that he would have to work with the 81st, the Democratic Congress that came to power with his election, even though he would have to "kiss and pet too many . . . SOB so-called Democrats" in the process.[11] Although Truman could not control the good and bad luck that occurred during his term, he could affect what he wanted to be known for.

Eisenhower

Eisenhower was sometimes characterized as the political innocent who reigned without ruling, enjoying his popularity and staying above the political fray. His passion for organization and delegation made him appear less active than the other presidents. This joke made the rounds about his busy chief of staff: "What if Adams should die and Eisenhower would become President?"

Eisenhower was certainly no political innocent, as work by Stephen Ambrose and Fred Greenstein makes clear.[12] He had won his way to the top in the harsh school of military politics and demonstrated the same skills in the European Command and in NATO. He had won a presidential election and reelection; maintained one of the highest records of personal popularity; and achieved, for a Republican facing Democratic majorities in Congress for much of his time in office, a very respectable record of legislative success. These are all political triumphs of the highest order. Greenstein also points out how much of Eisenhower's theory and practice of leadership took place behind the scenes, with a "hidden hand" and a skill at organization and working through others.

This does not mean, however, that we should take the revisionism too far. From our comparative perspective, the initial popular impression is correct in one way: Eisenhower seemed to be less active in many areas when compared to the other presidents. He ranked relatively low in legislative activity and low on the various foreign policy dimensions. In foreign policy, he was the least active of all the presidents in his second term. Among the various routine activities associated with the office, he ranked as high as average on only one: the frequency of public speaking. This does not contradict the hidden-hand thesis; in fact, it complements it. Eisenhower was at work behind the scenes.

The Eisenhower profile becomes clearer when we see the relationship between popularity and these visible public acts. Legislative activity hurts popularity, as we saw in Chapter 4, while many of the other activities have no effect. Only speech making, among the acts under a president's control, has a positive effect; in this, Eisenhower engaged at an average level. If Eisenhower was concerned with maintaining public support, then he conducted his activities correctly. Eisenhower also had few of the international rallies of Reagan and Kennedy, two of the other popular presidents. Eisenhower's popularity, therefore, was at least partly a product of his *not* acting in a visible public fashion.

A picture emerges of behind-the-scenes skill used at least partly to maintain popularity. Eisenhower has been characterized as a passive-negative type, following the conventional impression that he did not enjoy political activity and worked primarily from a sense of duty.[13] However, this does not account for his great political skill and the popularity he maintained throughout his career. He was liked in the military, liked when he did army liaison with Congress, and liked in the White House. People liked Ike long before the 1950s, and it can be argued that Ike saw to it that they did. Biographer Stephen Ambrose observes how his "eagerness to be well liked coupled with his desire to keep everyone happy" created difficulties in dealing with Generals Montgomery and Patton in the closing months of World War II: "Thus he appeared to be always shifting according to the views and wishes of the last man with whom he had talked. . . . Everyone who talked to him left the meeting feeling that Eisenhower had agreed with him, only to find out that he had not."[14]

Combining behind-the-scenes activity with skill at being liked, Eisenhower seems much closer to the passive-positive mode. And since politicians are not usually "liked" in American culture, although they can be voted for, Eisenhower's reputation as political innocent may have been his own creation. Military men gain esteem by appearing to stay out of politics, even if they must engage in it continually. Presidents, too, can gain public support, as Eisenhower showed so well, by avoiding the normal public political battles.

Greenstein points out that Eisenhower was "acutely attentive to winning and maintaining public support" and admits that the famous grin might have been consciously applied. During his first campaign, Eisenhower gave advice to the political professionals around him on how body language and an animated impression could instill a happy enthusiasm into audiences.[15] On the other hand, he disliked blatant appeals to popularity, "glory grabbing," and publicity gimmicks. He observed, as early as his wartime command, that modesty and media attention were not necessarily in conflict with each other.[16] Even his striking popularity as president, and the chief feature of his administration, showed something of the hidden-hand leadership style.

Eisenhower and Truman, both skilled politicians, were opposite in many ways. Truman sought conflict, and Eisenhower avoided it. Truman went out of his way to show publicly that he did not care about opinion. Eisenhower worked behind the scenes to maintain that opinion at very high levels of support. Both, it seems clear, made choices about what they would do and be known for.

Kennedy

Although Kennedy is more difficult to profile because of his short time in office, biographers characterize him somewhat easily as an active-positive type. To such writers as Barber and Arthur Schlesinger, Jr., to whom the active-positive mode is the highest presidential form, Kennedy followed in the footsteps of FDR, the original model for the type. Schlesinger and Theodore Sorensen, both Kennedy aides, wrote about the programs he wanted to accomplish and the more modest results.[17] It is possible that he would have accomplished more in his fourth year, but reelections are not normally times for domestic or foreign policy accomplishments. By October of his third year, his approval rating had fallen below 60 percent for the first time. Presumably there would have been a hard run for reelection. It does not seem unfair, then, to compare Kennedy with the other first-term presidents.

According to this comparison, Kennedy did appear active on several dimensions, although not always strongly so. He was higher in legislative activity than might be expected, and he maintained a good success rate, primarily because of his high popularity. In foreign policy he was active rhetorically and average or high militarily, depending on how we treat the various military activities of the time. Contrary to some popular impressions, he was not high in diplomatic activity, speeches to the nation, or foreign trips. The most striking component of Kennedy's administration was his high popularity, buttressed by several international rally points. Even when we control for these events, Kennedy emerges as one of the most popular presidents, tying with Eisenhower in public support. This was his rating at the time and owes nothing to any subsequent idealization because of his assassination.

Activity and popularity do not usually go together. Kennedy combined them through another trait associated with the active-positive mode: flexibility. Active-positive types are supposed to prize flexibility and can adjust to circumstances and learn from them.[18] We see Kennedy's flexibility throughout his administration—in his fluid advisory system and pragmatic and often ad hoc responses to events. The pragmatism was evident in his presidential campaigns beginning as early as 1956. It seems likely that the same pragmatism was at work balancing the activity he needed to maintain popularity. While Kennedy was active, he did not allow activity to go so far as to endanger his public support.

Kennedy could not be like Eisenhower, however, in anything but popularity. As a Democratic president of his era, he had to be an activist, pursuing an ambitious legislative agenda. He also lived with great illness and pain, which required him to spend portions of his working day lying down. Because of this, the impression of vigor and energy in the White House was all the more important. From the first keynotes of the inaugural address, according to this interpretation, vigor and activity were consciously projected by Kennedy and those around him, in the same way that Truman and Eisenhower projected their chosen traits.

Johnson

Johnson's profile in this book accords well with the individual accounts, offering a study in dramatic contrasts. Johnson, like Truman, was low in popularity and high in activity. Of all the presidents, he scored highest in legislative activity, even when we discount for the circumstances of the time. This means that Johnson's legislative record cannot be explained merely by the large number of Democrats in Congress. Even after we discount for the differences among presidents in congressional party support, Johnson remains at the top. He was active in foreign policy as well as domestic legislation. While his success rate suffered with his declining popularity, the accomplishments were still substantial, given the number and scope of the programs he proposed. One writer points out that in 1965 alone, Congress passed eighty of the administration's eighty-three major proposals. These dealt with civil rights; Medicare; elementary, secondary, and higher education; poverty; air pollution; jobs; model cities; Appalachia; Housing and Urban Development; urban mass transit; arts and humanities; among many other subjects.[19]

This activity was not surprising from one who was, by all accounts, a dynamo of energy, driving others and himself. According to Johnson himself, a typical day began at 6:30 A.M. and proceeded, with a brief respite for lunch, a nap, and phone calls, until well past midnight.[20] Johnson's favorite bedtime reading apparently was congressional bills. He drove others at least as hard as himself, earning the name "Caligula's Court" for his White House staff. Aides were expected to keep his schedule, and those who had the misfortune to be away on Sundays or holidays when Johnson might need them were severely upbraided. Even Johnson admitted that his most loyal aides worked "like dogs."[21]

What stands out by its absence in all this activity is Johnson's poor record of speaking to the public. Although he is the highest ranking of all the presidents in some forms of activity, he is the lowest on this. This was not a minor matter of ceremony, since in a time of war, frustration, and dissent, the nation might want to hear from its president. Nixon, for example, gave eleven speeches on Vietnam in his first term, while Johnson gave one. Johnson's refusal to talk about Vietnam persisted in the face of pleas from his advisers to address public confidence and "take command of a contest that is more political in its character than any in our history except the Civil War."[22] But Johnson remained silent. This peculiarity has been briefly touched on by biographers as a "sensitivity to criticism": Since Johnson felt that he performed poorly in front of mass audiences, he consequently performed more poorly—and he soon abandoned the enterprise entirely.[23] His style was personal, a matter of one on one. The famous Johnson treatment could not be felt across the air waves. It did not work for a mass public.

This one instance of inactivity needs closer attention from biographers, as it relates to Johnson's public standing in important ways. Certainly public speaking helps support. Nixon maintained his standing in part because of this activity; Johnson did not. Johnson's decision *not* to speak fits with his other personality traits. Barber calls Johnson the "prime example" of an active-negative type, as shown by his driven workaholic personality, his need for accomplishment, and his rigid holding to inner conviction even when external facts do not support it.[24] It is therefore not surprising that Johnson held to a rigid course in Vietnam, against a shrinking number of advisers, or that he chose not to speak to the public during this time. Johnson had to satisfy only one critic ultimately. He did not have to be liked.

The famous Johnson treatment was not designed to endear him to fellow senators; it established power over them and achieved what Johnson wanted done. His dealings with his staff can be understood in the same way. The man who browbeat his aides and insulted them in public was not trying to be liked, even a little bit. It was only one step from the senators and staff to the public once he reached the White House. According to this interpretation, his high activity, low popularity, and low public speaking fit together in an interesting way.

Johnson could be hurt by negative public reaction, asking wistfully why the American people did not like him after all he had done for them. But he was asking for appreciation more than liking. Like the senators for whom Johnson did favors, the public should have acknowledged how generous, and thus how powerful, he was. Some people might argue that he differentiated the American citizens from those colleagues and subordinates he saw every day. It is more likely, however, that the same dynamic was at work in both instances. Doris Kearns apparently believes the latter interpretation. She remarks carefully that LBJ did not seek power as an end in itself but "to influence and dominate external behavior and conditions." Since "he could no longer find satisfaction in the capacity to manipulate and influence other individuals," she continues, "Johnson became deeply conscious of the effect he might have on the daily lives of ordinary men and women for generations to come."[25] If this interpretation is correct, the importance of "influencing external behavior and conditions" took precedence over Johnson's desire to be liked by the American people.

The contrast between Johnson and the incumbents who cared more about public approval is seen in the proposal put forward by Senator George Aiken of Vermont. "Let's declare that we have achieved our objectives in Vietnam and go home," the senator remarked.[26] Although Johnson did not accept Aiken's proposal, it foreshadows the kind of public-relations approach to national problems that would be seen more frequently later: An international event could be redefined by a White House statement. In one case, a president pursued a course of policy not supported by a majority of Americans. In the other case, he was urged to give a military endeavor a verbal and symbolic solution styled so as to be publicly palatable. Each approach raises its own kind of worries for democratic government.

Nixon

Nixon selected his first-term activities carefully. He ranks high in foreign policy activity and speeches to the nation and foreign travel but low in legislation and domestic trips. The selectivity is seen most clearly in his relations with Congress, where he gained a high success rate for a Republican president by sending over very few bills.

Note that most of these activities happen to be those that help popularity: foreign policy advances rather than domestic policy legislation, major speeches rather than domestic trips. Yet, at the same time Nixon took unpopular actions: announcing inflation controls and continuing the war in Southeast Asia and expanding it to the bombing of Cambodia. Administration spokespersons, including Vice President Spiro Agnew, made speeches against the dissent and protest at home, thereby increasing the dissent. If Nixon took actions to help his public support, he also acted against it, and the negative actions had somewhat more impact. Not surprisingly, his first-term popularity was slightly below average when compared to that of the other presidents. He ranks below Carter and the more popular presidents and above Truman, Johnson, and Ford. Nixon took negative actions in his first term, but compensated for them by positive acts. The three presidents he outranks did not make the same compensations.

If Nixon had served only one term, he would probably be profiled as mixed, or average, on the dimensions of activity and popularity, a president who attempted to balance the various things he wanted to do. Although he won a major reelection victory (positive), he engaged in a series of acts (negative) that engendered the Watergate crisis and ended in his resignation from office. Note that Nixon's activities changed in his second term as the negative reaction grew. As Watergate began to dominate the political agenda in 1973, Nixon did little to compensate for it. This president who had traveled so frequently before cut back his foreign trips: Watergate became the sole subject of the few speeches he gave. At the same time, there were negative activities, including the firing of the Special Prosecutor and the

Attorney General and the various statements about withholding the tapes.

Barber characterizes Nixon as active-negative, emphasizing the unconstitutional acts that brought on the crisis. But, fortunately or unfortunately, we cannot compare unconstitutional actions among the presidents since we do not have the relevant comparative information. Considering the actions that we do have information on, we might best characterize Nixon as negative and mixed in activity compared to the other presidents.

Ford

Ford's circumstances were in many ways the harshest of all. He took office with no electoral mandate and minorities in both houses of Congress, which were soon reduced even further by the "Watergate" election of 1974. However, he left his own mark on his presidency in two decisive ways.

First, he ranks low in public support, even after we control for his circumstances. Ford made hard choices right away—the Nixon pardon and amnesty for draft evaders—that showed he was not in the business of seeking public favor. Even apart from these choices, however, Ford's popularity was lower than would have been expected. In this, as in his fights with the Congress, he resembles Truman. Both rank among the highest veto presidents of the century, although Ford had more of his vetoes overturned. Truman averaged twenty-two vetoes a year, and Ford averaged nineteen. Many presidents had less than five. This combativeness with Congress might have seemed surprising in a former party leader: Ford had been Minority Leader in the House for many years. Yet he had been known as a tough partisan in the House, willing to take on political battles when they arose. He had gained the leadership in the first place in a fight that defeated the sitting minority leader, Charles Halleck. As minority leader, he was described as taking an "activist" role when the Democrats occupied the White House, subsiding to a quieter more supportive role when the Republicans won the White House after 1968.[27] Ford never said that he had to be universally liked.

Second, Ford ranks high in activity, again independent of

circumstances. Simply by counting the number of positions he took on legislation, we see that he was more active than his Republican predecessors, Eisenhower and Nixon. When we control for his circumstances, in particular the Republican weakness in Congress, he ranks as one of the most active presidents, second only to Johnson. Critics might say that Ford had no business being as active as he was. But while Ford was low on congressional success, he managed some substantial accomplishments along the way. He held the threatened reform of the intelligence agencies to a minimum and managed to slow some of the Democratic spending programs. He won a major arms sale bill after a two-year fight. Ford was also active in the more ceremonial activities: He ranks the highest of all the presidents in domestic travel, high in foreign trips, and average in his speeches to the nation.

Note that Ford's activities seemed calculated to keep his public support low. He was high on domestic trips, associated with a decline in support, and average in public speaking, which helps support. He was high on military activity, too, although only one of the several uses of force became a rally event. His very high legislative activity was also inversely related to public support. He had no positive announcements to make about peace or prosperity; on the other hand, he decided to make two very controversial announcements, which reminded the nation of Watergate and Vietnam. Presidents who want to maximize their popularity could take Ford as a kind of negative model and *reverse* everything he did. But for presidents who would like to have an impact in a very short time with few resources on hand, Ford is a positive model.

Like Truman and Johnson, Ford combined activity with a disregard for public opinion. Ford's speech on the Nixon pardon suggested a further similarity among these three presidents. There were only two themes in this very short speech, each supported by the rhetoric and pictures Ford called to mind. One theme stressed the powers of the presidency: the historic office, the constitution, "this desk," Harry Truman's plaque that says "The Buck Stops Here." Ford referred to himself as president eight times. The other theme emphasized Ford's "conscience," and he used the word itself six times, along with several references to God and other religious subjects. Ford argued essentially that he pardoned Nixon not only because he had the power to do so as president, but because he believed it was the right thing to do. Ford knew, of course, that the decision would be unpopular: He had earlier told Congress that the American people would not stand for such a thing. Just as Truman could predict in advance the uproar to come from his MacArthur firing, Ford knew what would follow his action.

Ford therefore appears as an active-negative type, along with Johnson and Truman, following conscience or inner conviction, stressing activity, and disregarding public support. Barber places Ford in the active-positive category. Barber, who admits that there is less biographical data on Ford than on most of the other presidents, is apparently impressed by Ford's love of teamwork and his speeches of conciliation when he first took office. Barber sees conciliation and the spirit of teamwork as active-positive traits.[28] In contrast to Barber, we would say that the combativeness and inner conviction is much clearer than the conciliation when we look at his actual behavior in office. The former minority leader knew the virtues of teamwork, but Ford's game was football, before he turned to politics. And even as he addressed Congress and spoke of conciliation, his first veto was only two months away.

Carter

Of all the modern presidents, Carter is the most difficult to profile, except by such terms as "median" and "mixed." In popularity, Carter was directly at the median, when we take into account the circumstances of his time. His administration ranks lower than those of both Reagan terms, both Eisenhower terms, and Kennedy, and higher than those of both Nixon terms, Ford, Johnson, and Truman. He is close to the midpoint also in legislative activity and success. Although he was active overall in the number of positions he took on legislation, his activity and success were average considering his party majorities in both House and Senate. Carter did about as well as could be expected, in both activity and success, in comparison with the other presidents. He was active in some ceremonial activities and average in others. Like Ford, he was high on the acts that did not help popularity, and less high on public speaking. On the most visible foreign policy, he also showed a mixed record. Many people felt that he failed in dealing with the hostage crisis, succeeded dramatically in the Middle East peace treaty signed at Camp David, and achieved a mixed result in the Panama Canal treaties.

What these rankings say is that Carter was by no means an unpopular president, as some might characterize him. He was certainly no legislative failure either, with his average activity and success ratings. In short, Carter's performance improved dramatically when we compare him with the other modern presidents.

And yet the rankings highlight one problem that Carter faced in his administration, one that probably contributed to his poor reputation. Average in all dimensions, he was distinctive in none: He presented a "blurred" or mixed impression. That impression was heightened by his tendency to change activities from year to year. For example, he was high in legislative position taking in one year and low in others, showing much more variation than the other presidents. Congress could have complained with some justification that Carter switched his signals. The same tendency was criticized in foreign policy, when the Carter administration tried different approaches and gave contradictory statements, often within a short period.[29]

It is probably wrong, however, to attribute this mixing to inability or failure on Carter's part. In the complex setting of American politics, where activity often hurts public support, Carter can be seen as trying to balance both, to maintain enough support to do the things he wanted done. This accords with Erwin Hargrove's interpretation of Carter as a skilled politician who had strong principles and policy goals and believed in the "politics of the public good."[30] Carter may have been in conflict himself in the battle between principles and pragmatism: hence the different signals and the average popularity ranking. Still, this balancing could have been as much intended as Kennedy's style or Truman's very distinctive one. Carter clearly chose neither of these styles. Given the need for balancing, the adjustments also make sense. By his third year, Carter had greatly improved his relations with Congress. This followed a time of very high activity in his first year and very low activity in his second. The correct balance took a while to work out.

Reagan

Before we can profile Reagan, we have to separate his well-known personality from his performance in the White House: what we know about the individual from what we see as the actions he took in office. While it is true that all presidents work with the help of a small group of aides and advisers, the split between the individual and the administration is sharpest in the Reagan case. As an individual, Reagan appears to fit the passive-positive type. Chiefs of staff and secretaries of state alike have spoken of Reagan's lack of interest or inability to focus on substantive problems of the presidency. Aides reported that they had about six or seven minutes to make him concentrate before he was distracted to more pleasant subjects. Apparently foreign leaders experienced the same conversational dynamic when they talked to the U.S. president.[31] Passivity is more than a lack of action; it allows others to take action. If he lived life as a movie, as many writers suggest, then he needed cues and directors to guide him. As two critics wrote:

> There was, of course, a bit more to it than that—lines had to be memorized, proper emotions expressed—yet the actors knew that the director and his cohorts behind the cameras were united in an effort to make them look good when they appeared on the screen. This reliance on the guidance of coworkers, whose job it was to make the stars shine, carried over into Reagan's political career and helps to explain his remarkable passivity and the broad delegation of authority that puzzled so many Washington observers when he became President.[32]

The Californians were not surprised, according to several observers, since he had practiced the same style in the State House.[33] As the star in the presidential drama, Reagan still had directors to tell him what to do.

The so-called passive-positive presidents can be very effective, as we see for both Reagan and Eisenhower, who were two of the most popular. As a political style, passivity has its advantages. The knack of allowing unpleasant subjects to be dealt with by others behind the scenes strengthens the impression that all is well. This, in turn, increases public support. The style can be strategically effective also, shielding presidents from the usual White House conflicts and protecting them from blame. As both Alexander Haig, Jr., and David Stockman point out in their highly critical accounts of their White House years, Reagan advisers brought their complaints to a genial president who appeared to agree with them but did nothing to change things once they left his office.[34]

The criticism is almost identical to that levied against Eisenhower by the European generals. Reagan, too, appeared to shift his views according to the last person with whom he talked. Avoiding such controversies in politically charged circumstances is not necessarily a sign of presidential incompetence. Haig's complaints stemmed from conflicts between the secretary and state and national security adviser over their respective responsibilities in foreign policy. Stockman's arose from controversies over the pace and direction of economic policy. In Reagan's case, this style also shielded him from the worst effects of the Iran-Contra scandal. Both the Tower Commission and the congressional investigating committee compiled a list of illegal and unconstitutional actions that made some people think of impeachment. Yet both the Commission and the committee "excused" the president with the reprimand that he had not been paying enough attention. He was excused like one of the slow students in a class who does not have to do the same work as the others.

Just as other officeholders consciously projected styles they desired to be known for, Reagan made clear that he should be perceived in a particular way. Even superficially unattractive traits can round out the presidential image and serve a useful purpose: Truman admitted that he got into fights, Johnson confessed that he worked his staff too hard, and Reagan sheepishly agreed that he did not always pay attention to the business of government. Not only were people willing to excuse the president for his actions, but Reagan asked to be excused. At the time the news first broke of the mining of Nicaraguan harbors, Reagan gave his annual address to the White House correspondents black-tie dinner. He stated his reaction to the news with characteristic humor: "What's all that talk about a breakdown of White House communications: How come nobody told me? [Laughter]. Well, I know this: I've laid down the law, though, to everyone there from now on about anything that happens, that no matter what time it is, wake me, even if it's in the middle of a Cabinet meeting. [Laughter]."

Each punch line reinforced the comic notion of a president who did not pay attention while deflecting the serious issue that the United States had taken hostile action against another country. People would later discover that Reagan knew of the mining in advance. In January 1986, Reagan signed the secret intelligence finding authorizing the sale of weapons to Iran that became known as the arms-for-hostages deal. When this became public, Reagan used the same defense. In a hastily called press conference, he admitted this: "A few months ago, I told the American people I did not trade arms for hostages. My heart and my best intentions still tell me that's true, but the facts and evidence tell me it is not." Somehow the president did not know what he had done. Congress agreed that Reagan should have been more actively involved in the events occurring around him.

Reagan's *administration* was not passive, however. When we look at his actions, his White House was quite energetic on several dimensions. It was Reagan himself who made the speeches, did the travel, and signed the troop orders and legislation. Reagan was particularly active in what we call the military-rhetorical kind of foreign policy, calling attention to various situations of international hostility around the globe and giving speeches about them. Many of these situations involved a U.S. use of force. In addition, Reagan was the most vigorous president overall in the various forms of ceremonial activity: tying with Nixon in major addresses, second only to Ford in domestic trips, and highest in foreign travel. The oldest president turned out to be one of the most active. Finally, the legislative record of the Reagan years was at least average. Both activity and success in Congress were about what could be expected, given his circumstances. Reagan held very close to the presidential mean in both legislative position taking and success. Budget victories in the early years were followed by budget defeats; yet most people would agree that national policies had changed by the time the Reagan years were over. In qualitative terms, these included a major shift between defense and domestic budget priorities, as well as a shifting of priorities within foreign policy programs from economic to defense spending. Using the same standards for Reagan as for the other presidents, we would place the Reagan White House with the Kennedy White House as an example of the active-positive mode.

Barber agrees that the Reagan case shows the "uncoupling" of the president from White House decision making.[35] It also shows the uncoupling of personality from performance and a new kind of presidential choice. Activity and popularity do not go together. Being liked conflicts with managing the problems of government. Faced with these tradeoffs, Reagan made a choice different from that of his predecessors, splitting the personality who can be liked as president from the administration that must engage in controversy. He was unlike Eisenhower because his choices included a more activist administration. Reagan tried to have it both ways. The particular choice may have been necessary given the personality and priorities of the administration, but it held implications for the office of the future. The same choice, although a somewhat different division of responsibility, will be seen in the Bush administration.

The Real and the Ideal

What about presidential greatness? Where are the presidents like those who founded the nation, held the union together, and led the nation in the time of major wars? Have we missed criteria we ought to consider in the profiles, or are the moderns of lower stature than those of the past?

To answer these questions, we should look more closely at the presidential greatness rankings. Only Truman among the modern presidents places high in the historians' rankings of the greatest presidents. Truman typically makes a near-great rating, below those highest in rank: Washington, Jefferson, Madison, Lincoln, Wilson, FDR. Truman is grouped with such figures as John Adams and Theodore Roosevelt in the second-highest rank. Other modern presidents range from above to below average, with Nixon ranked low. In the widely cited Murray-Blessing ranking, for example, Truman makes the near-great category; Johnson, Eisenhower, and Kennedy are rated above average; Carter and Ford are rated average; and Nixon is ranked in the lowest "failure" category. Nixon is grouped along with Grant and Harding, who also had major scandals in their administrations, and Andrew Johnson, who faced a Senate impeachment trial.[36]

If we look at the very small number of presidents who are rated highly, one thing becomes clear. Each had circumstances that allowed the greatness accolade, either before or during his time in office. The first presidents were revolutionary leaders or writers of the Constitution. Lincoln, Wilson, and Franklin Roosevelt saw the nation through its three most dramatic wars. True, these highest-ranked individuals responded to the circumstance successfully when others might not have done so: their place in history is well deserved. But we cannot avoid the conclusion that without the particular circumstances, the range would be much narrower, and probably comparable to the modern pattern. These circumstances are the good and bad luck we have pointed to throughout this book. According to the ironies of presidential evaluation, the most critical circumstances become the presidents' good luck. For example, one study "predicting presidential greatness" reveals the following likely traits: being in office during a war; being a war hero before assuming the presidency; and being assassinated, thus carrying presidential luck to its logical extreme. Greatness is also helped by being in office a long time and is negatively correlated with having a scandal in office.[37] The patina of crisis becomes the patina of greatness as time goes by.

Truman is elevated above the other modern presidents, not because of his style or his legislative record or his actions in the Korean War. He had the good fortune, we can say, of being in office when the nation ended World War II with victory and faced the first critical peace-time decisions. Other presidents might not have done as well as Truman at this time; but Truman would not be in the same rank if he had been president at many other times. Truman's assessment, by the way, makes another comment on the polls. In the weeks after Germany's defeat in World War II, 87 percent of the American people approved of the way Truman was doing his job. By the end of 1951, 23 percent approved. But the polls, with their 60 percentage point fluctuation, made no difference to the historians' evaluation. Perhaps Truman was right in ignoring the polls as he did.

The evaluations supposedly reflect those who strengthened the presidency and who weakened it in the eyes of historians, so there is an emphasis on scandals and heroic events. Nevertheless, beyond the few exceptional cases a vast range of performance remains largely undifferentiated. It is this normal range within which most presidents work. The modern presidents do well in the overall comparisons. Carter and Ford are the average, while several exceed the average. What remains unclear is what these average expectations are. Of the three ranked above average, two enjoyed high popularity, and one exhibited high activity. These three also were beneficiaries of a much better national economy than were Ford and Carter. Johnson's activity was helped by large partisan majorities in Congress, a boon of fortune not granted to Ford. It is possible that the rankings recognize vigorous activity and strong public support, but they appear most heavily influenced by good and bad fortune.

It is doubtful that the profiles in this chapter have missed criteria—some ineluctable component of greatness. We have focused on activity in a variety of forms and on popularity and the president's relations with the public. Activity includes acts in foreign and domestic policy, as well as the range of ceremonial choices that can so well express a president's style. An administration more vigorous than average should be captured by this dimension. Popularity, including the president's choices and the public's response, can show the range of positive and negative approaches as well as skill and leadership potential. A president with charisma or an unusual ability to inspire the country should be tapped by this dimension. But the two dimensions do not usually go together, and high activity or high popularity is not always a good thing. Each has its dangers and costs. Once we control for circumstances, we find a narrower range for presidential performance than the historians' ratings suggest. It is within this range where the more realistic and useful evaluations must begin.

THE IMPLICATIONS

Comparing the presidents to one another leads us to several new insights. In several cases, the comparison confirms earlier individual accounts but challenges some perspectives, too. It points out that Eisenhower was less active on many dimensions compared to the other presidents. Carter, far from the failure that some popular commentary call him, appears to have been at least average in activity, success in Congress, and public support. He was the median president in many ways. The profile of Ford as active and combative could not have emerged without this kind of comparison. All the presidents gain sharper focus in the process. We see Kennedy's pragmatism and flexibility as he balanced his actions with his popularity. Understanding Johnson's attitude toward public relations is essential to understanding the larger dynamic at work in his presidency. The carrots and sticks that Johnson brought with him to the White House were the tools of a person who wanted to be acknowledged as powerful, not be liked. It is therefore not surprising that the war escalated along with his Great Society programs. Both show this power on the largest scale.

Another insight from these results is the extent to which the presidents themselves chose what they would be known for. Kennedy announced in his first inaugural address that he would be vigorous, and everyone took him at his word. Eisenhower projected his grin and confidence-inspiring manner, and Reagan did the same in his own way. Truman and his First Lady went out of their way to show that they were not slaves to public opinion. Johnson pointed out the energy that went into his own sixteen-hour workdays and those of his staff. Indeed, Carter may have been disliked by political and media professionals because he did not project as clear an image as the other presidents. He did not give them a personality they could relate to. While these are small points in themselves, they accord with a much larger pattern of action that we find among the administrations. The choice is not entirely theirs, but presidents do appear to have this discretionary impact.

The comparison also offers an alternative second opinion to the personality traits that James Barber assigns. The classification scheme and approach are quite different, but we can characterize presidents as more or less active in their White House performance (active-passive in Barber's scheme), as more or less concerned with the public's opinion and being liked, and as more or less likely to follow external as opposed to internal cues (positive-negative for Barber). Our classification focuses on only selected actions, but we have tried to show how they are supported by broader activities and background traits. In addition, the scheme provides observable measures that other researchers could test and discuss. Our active extrovert (Kennedy) could thus be distinguished from the active introverts (Ford, Truman, Johnson) and from the less active extrovert (Eisenhower). These results agree with Barber on seven of the ten dimensions. They agree for Kennedy and Johnson on both dimensions and differ for Truman, Eisenhower, and Ford on one of the two dimensions. Barber calls Eisenhower passive-negative, but we would say passive-positive; Barber calls Ford and Truman active-positive, but we would say active-negative. The difference comes from the assignment of positive and negative. For this, we look at how the presidents regarded their popularity at the polls and in other political settings—when they appeared to choose conflict or to be liked.

This leaves three presidents who fit less easily in the categories. Carter is difficult to classify because he was so balanced between the extremes. Nixon mixed activities also. Reagan was difficult because we must ask what it is we are evaluating—his passive personality or active performance. To these three we assign mixed or combination ratings. A summary of the presidential profiles is given in Table 6.1.

What else do the comparisons tell us? Profiling the presidents as a group gives a broader picture and overview of the modern

Table 6.1

The Modern Presidents Compared

Being Active and Being Liked

Truman	Active/Negative
Eisenhower	Less Active/Positive
Kennedy	Active/Positive
Johnson	Active/Negative
Nixon	Mixed/Negative
Ford	Active/Negative
Carter	Mixed/Mixed
Reagan	Less Active/Positive[a]

[a]This characterization distinguishes the individual president from the active record of the administration.

office, a perspective not afforded by the individual studies. First, we see that there are no clear chronological trends. The relatively inactive presidents were scattered throughout the time period, and so were the extrovert or positive types. The variety suggests that no expectations connected with the office constrained these particular choices—at least so far. Reagan demonstrated that a passive-positive individual could have an active administration, and Bush, as we will see, selected his activities carefully while following a positive style. Each delegated to others certain necessary but unpopular aspects of the presidential job. The Reagan and Bush years together set a powerful precedent. Therefore, it seems worth pointing out to future incumbents that the choices are wider than the most recent presidential history suggests.

The infrequency of the active-positive combination also is of interest. Despite the clear preference for presidents of this style in much of the writing on the presidency, it is not the dominant pattern. People may equate presidential leadership with an active-positive mode, but they do not necessarily elect such presidents. The selection system may have one bias, however. Three of the four presidents who were clearly not positive in their style came to office through succession: Truman, Johnson, and Ford. Although two of these would later win elections, they became president in the first place without passing the electoral hurdles the others faced. Excluding the three accidental presidents, all of the others, except Nixon, can be called positive. Nixon did not rank as far on the negative side as Johnson, Truman, and Ford, when one counts both of his terms. The three accidental presidents not only cluster together at the negative end of the scale but also exhibit other similar traits.

The selection process appears to reward the positive style: those who garner liking and public support, who somehow demonstrate that they can win the biggest of all popularity contests, the presidential election. This holds true for the period when party caucus selection was dominant and for the newer period of primary selection dominance. But why should all the accidental presidents be so clearly less positive in their style and behavior? It is possible that this, too, is a product of a kind of selection. Throughout the period, presidential candidates have had a key influence, if not always a dominant one, on the selection of vice presidential nominees. Vice presidents who are less able or less interested in winning the same kind of liking as the presidential candidates might be the preferred officemates; they are less likely to be used for invidious comparisons. The selection ensures that we have only one president in office at a time.

The effects of political recruitment are seen in other ways. The three accidental presidents also were legislative leaders, offering a visibility and knowledge of Washington politics attractive in vice presidential candidates. Ford and Johnson were elected party leaders, while Truman was a senior influential senator and leader on key committees. As a border-state senator, Truman had played a key role in winning support for New Deal programs. Although such leaders are known for their ability to compromise, they are party leaders first, willing to fight when necessary to hold party lines. It is not surprising that they would follow active-negative styles in the White House, with their party convictions and skill in moving legislation through Congress. Ford was an expert in veto strategy long before he became president.

It is also interesting that those presidents with direct Washington experience of politics appear to have been more active than the outsiders. Of the four presidents characterized as less active or mixed, three (Eisenhower, Carter, and Reagan) were outsiders.

Nixon was the only exception. Profiles of eight presidents do not allow us to make any definitive conclusions, but the patterns do suggest that political background is an indicator of presidential style. The habits of the general, the California governor, and the activist minority leader accorded with behavior seen in the Oval Office and provide a fuller understanding of that behavior. Hence, it might not be necessary to seek examples from childhood, but to look at the more recent political and adult experiences to predict performance in the White House.

This account fits well with the institutional perspective given in the preceding chapters. Just as the common constraints can explain similarities among the presidents, the narrow range of political backgrounds helps to make sense of the variety. The backgrounds provide learning and experience while screening for their own desirable traits. Another kind of learning also occurs. Since a few other individuals have held the unusual job assignment of being a modern president, the new presidents have some models to choose from. Although they would not admit it, perhaps they do make their own informal comparisons.

Each of the various styles raises its own particular kind of worries: that presidents will too easily adopt their acts to follow public opinion, that they will disregard this opinion too much, that they will be so in conflict themselves that one part of the administration works against the other. There is no obvious preferred presidential style, and there is no obvious model among the modern officeholders. Presidents can fail to act or act in the wrong ways. Negative-style presidents can make decisions that American citizens do not approve of. Positive-style individuals can make the same decisions but convince the public that (a) they did not make the decisions, (b) while the facts suggest they made them, they did not mean to make them, or (c) there are more important things everyone should be considering. It is worth stressing the drawbacks of this active-positive style, since it has been so favored by writers in the modern period. A style made famous by Franklin Roosevelt in the crises of depression and war will work very differently in a time of less severe crisis.

Finally, the profiles remind us that the presidency is a very human office. If the problems are clear, the virtues are evident, too. Exceptionally skilled political people work in a complex situation where all good things do not go together. Recognizing the modern range of presidential performance as the typical range—barring the most extreme crises—we need to develop more realistic criteria for judging it. This is the on-the-job description of the president's job. We have no reason to believe any other officeholders could do better.

7

Broccoli and Yellow Ribbons

"I don't live by the polls," George Bush assured reporters in a question-and-answer session in March 1990, a time when his high popularity and choice of particular activities led to worries that he did live by them.[1] In the following months, the questions became more persistent as both the popularity and the pattern of activity continued. Wasn't the president out of Washington quite a lot? Was he planning to make any legislative proposals? Shouldn't he say more about the longer-than-expected recovery period that other people were calling a recession?

As the memory of the Persian Gulf War victory faded, the voices reached a crescendo. A *Newsweek* story spoke of a "dramatic redefinition of the office" and proposed that Bush be brought home to eat his broccoli—that is, to pay attention to domestic problems. Even *USA Today* spoke of a "tide of discontent" and suggested that the president had canceled a foreign trip because of domestic political pressure. As people criticized Bush for jogging around the world and ignoring the economy, Republicans began to worry about the upcoming reelection.[2] By this time, of course, the polls had fallen, too. In March 1991, while waving the Gulf War flags and yellow ribbons, 86 percent of the public told the Gallup pollers that they approved of the way the president was doing his job; by December 1991, with only a few faded ribbons left on the storefronts, Bush's approval had fallen below 50 percent.

One advantage of comparison is that we can place these phenomena in perspective, setting the swiftly changing events of the moment against the clearer patterns of the past. Interpretations have their greatest urgency while presidents are still in office, but it is at this point that they are most subject to error. Hence a profile of Bush, like those of the other presidents, needs a comparative base.

Consequently, we must ask what explains the course of this president's first years in office and how similar or different that course has been from those of the presidents before him. Has Bush jogged around the world more than his predecessors? Has it made any difference? What were the distinctive features of his public-opinion ratings? Is it true that the Bush years have brought a redefinition of the office, and if so, how is it to be defined?

THE ERRATIC REFERENDUM

When we look at Bush's popularity during his first thirty months in office, two things stand out. His polls were strikingly high— higher than those of many of the other presidents in a comparable period, and they were much more erratic, showing greater volatility in support from one month to the next. On the surface, we can see the contrast shown in Figure 7.1, where Bush's polls are compared to the average approval of the other first-term presidents during their first thirty months in office.

Bush averaged 68 percent approval during his first years, second only to Kennedy and tying with Eisenhower in overall support. The next most popular presidents were 10 points or more below Bush. Ronald Reagan was 20 points below him, averaging 48 percent during the same time. Bush *is* comparable to the other modern presidents: He is not setting any new records. Still, he compiled a record of popularity in his early years that had not been seen for a very long time. In addition, the trend of his popularity was different. Most presidents decline in popularity through their first three years, independent of any other circum-

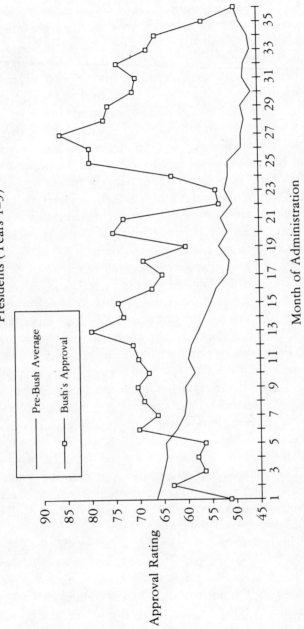

Figure 7.1 Bush's Popularity Compared to That of Other First-Term Presidents (Years 1–3)

stances. Bush's popularity showed no such decay: Indeed, when we control for circumstances, we see a very slight upward trend. Like Bush, Reagan began his term low in public support, with only a 51 percent approval rating. But, although Reagan climbed in the polls in his first year and fell below the 50 percent approval mark in his second and third years, Bush did not fall below the 50 percent level until the end of his third year.

The volatility of his support is equally striking. Eisenhower's polls fluctuated about 5 percentage points around his average, and Kennedy's varied by about 6 points. This means that most of the time the polls would not swing by more than 5 or 6 points from month to month.[3] Bush's polls, by contrast, fluctuated from month to month by about 9 points. Eisenhower and Kennedy maintained their popularity fairly steadily over the period. Bush's popularity swung higher and fell lower.

We can look at this volatility in another way. On only three occasions in the first thirty-month period did Kennedy's polls swing more than 5 percentage points from one month to the next.[4] They swung up with the Bay of Pigs crisis, went down the next month, and climbed again with the Cuban Missile Crisis. Eisenhower's polls remained very stable: On only five occasions did his polls swing more than 5 percentage points, and even then they remained for the most part in the 6–7 point range. By contrast, Bush's polls swung more than 5 percentage points thirteen times in the thirty-month period. For example, they climbed with the Panama invasion, fell the next month, and then fell even further. They climbed again with the Gorbachev summit, but plummeted the following month. They then shot up with the Persian Gulf crisis, plunged because of a congressional budget fight, and skyrocketed upward again because of the Gulf War.

This volatility is not merely a matter of a public opinion more erratic in the present than it was in the Eisenhower and Kennedy years. Ronald Reagan's polls fluctuated by more than 5 percentage points on only two occasions in his early years. The fluctuations appear distinctive to the Bush administration. Why?

EXPLAINING PUBLIC SUPPORT
FOR BUSH

The general model of public support, which we first proposed in Chapter 2, should help to explain these fluctuations. We expect public support to be the result of the decay over time, negative and positive dramatic events, economic conditions, plus the activities that the individual president engages in. We will now apply this model to Bush's first three years in office.

Bush's relatively high ratings, from the summer of his first year on, were exclusively associated with international events. When domestic problems intervened or were forced on the White House, the polls returned close to the presidential average. The same dynamic was seen throughout the three years. To illustrate this briefly, we can see how closely changes in the polls mirrored dramatic events.

In Bush's first year, as change swept through eastern Europe and appeared to herald a new age of democracy, his polls rose, although he had little to do with these events. The U.S. invasion of Panama and the subsequent surrender of Noriega brought the trend higher. The decline in the polls that began early in his second year, with no dramatic international news in the spotlight, was arrested by the Gorbachev summit in early summer. When Bush was forced into a battle with Congress about the budget, his poll ratings fell sharply again, but returned the next month when he sent forces to Saudi Arabia. The budget battle continued, bringing the polls down close to the normal presidential average by the end of his second year.

Bush's third year showed the same fluctuations but in a more extreme form. His poll ratings shot upward from the congressional battles as preparation for the Gulf War began. After the victory in Operation Desert Storm, they began a steady decline from March to the end of 1991 with the return to problems of the economy. While the dramatic coup attempt in the Soviet Union may have slowed the decline, his polls continued to fall. And so with the bad economic news of the fourth quarter of

1991, Bush's polls were once more barely above those of the other presidents.

These dramatic events were both positive and negative in their predicted impact. The historic changes in Europe and the former Soviet Union occurred independently of Bush's actions. These we termed good luck, the positive nondiscretionary events of Chapter 2. Along with Kennedy, Bush had a significantly greater amount of good luck in his first thirty months.[5] Positive discretionary acts also occurred: the invasion of Panama and the separate uses of force over a six-month period in the Gulf. These were highly publicized rally points, made dramatic in part because of the efforts of the administration. All these events help popularity. Yet, in even the best-managed White House, domestic politics can intervene. Bush made two decisions that increased controversy, or negative discretionary events: He sent the nomination of John Tower as Defense Secretary to a Congress already known to have problems with that nomination, and he reversed his campaign pledge not to raise taxes, admitting that a tax increase might be necessary. Finally, he encountered the bad luck that Republican presidents are vulnerable to when they have Democratic congresses when controversy over the budget became a highly visible conflict late in his second year. These negative dramatic events lower popularity.

Drama and the White House

Dramatic events take work on the part of the White House: Bush by no means passively inherited these good effects. For example, Bush gave eleven speeches to the nation in this thirty-month period, excluding the inaugural address and obligatory State of the Union addresses. Seven of these addressed the crisis and then war in the Persian Gulf, one described the invasion of Panama, and one spoke more generally of Central American problems. This left one speech for the budget and one for education policy. The budget speech directly followed two speeches on Iraq in the summer and fall of 1990, and the education speech directly followed four on the war in the Persian Gulf. Bush sent very few foreign policy messages to Congress during this period, but of the six he did send, two concerned Iraq and one concerned Panama. This left three for all other foreign policy legislation.

His informal news conferences, too, were directed toward these international events. Presidents have grown to dislike the formal news conferences of previous years, so they are held with decreasing frequency. Although the White House could control the agenda to some extent, there was always the risk of the surprise question or the unpleasant subject. Bush redesigned the news conference to be much more a presidential instrument, with frequent informal sessions that were limited to specific subjects: a nomination, a meeting with the Egyptian president, a particular issue that the White House chose to address. In this way, reporters were restricted in the kinds of questions they could ask and held closely to the president's agenda.

At the peak of the Panama crisis, Bush held three news conferences in three weeks. In August, during the Iraqi invasion of Kuwait and the beginning of the Persian Gulf crisis, he held ten news conferences. The frequency increased to almost one a day when the Gulf War began. Reporters have been criticized for helping Bush keep his preferred international agenda by not asking hard questions on domestic issues.[6] Yet with the new, narrowly circumscribed news conferences, reporters have not had that much opportunity to do otherwise.

Consider the president's schedule during August 1990, the month in which his polls jumped more than 15 points. The following events occurred in which the president made a public appearance.[7] In addition to the ten news conferences on the Gulf, Bush gave two other news briefings on the same subject, plus a briefing for congressional leaders. He made five speeches, again on that subject. He delivered a major address to the American people, a speech to the Veterans of Foreign Wars, and a speech at the Aspen Institute. Each discussed the crisis. He also addressed the members of Congress and spoke to the U.S. troops in the Persian Gulf over Armed Forces Radio. In the remaining public appearance, Bush conducted a combined news conference on the budget and the Gulf crisis. All these attention-focusing events were scheduled between the announcement about raising taxes and the budget battles with Congress that began in the fall.

It is not only the discretionary international events that have been dramatized by White House activities, the good luck is utilized, too. During the attempted Soviet coup, Bush gave daily informal news conferences from 19 August through 25 August 1991. Two additional meetings with reporters followed in the next week. Certainly Americans wish to hear from their president in a time of international crisis, and Bush was available, to say the least. But, somehow, the end of the coup attempt left the president looking stronger, at least in the American press. "All Americans should agree with the way President Bush handled this matter," a Democrat in Congress was quoted as saying.[8]

White House attention to these dramatic events went beyond speeches and news conferences. In August 1990, when the military operation in the Persian Gulf was still in its early phase, a ten-page memorandum was sent to all relevant military personnel, laying out what would be the operation's public-relations policy. Even though drafts on military public-relations policy had been prepared in the mid-1980s, this draft was devised in the office of Secretary of Defense Dick Cheney. The memo set forth the rules for military censorship of press stories about the war and for an escorted pool system of press coverage. Reporters selected into pools to cover the war had a military escort "at all times," according to the memo, thus restricting their observation and interviews. Within months, television viewers saw news of the war along with the legend, not seen since World War II, "Reports reviewed by military censors." Viewers also saw very few casualties or the damage inflicted on the other side, as Ted Koppel of ABC's "Nightline" pointed out. The escorted pool system was new. World War II reporters did not have the same restrictions.[9]

The White House may have left many of the details to the secretary of defense, but it took a direct hand in much of the policy. Daily polls were made available through the summer and fall to monitor the shifting public opinion on the Gulf. Administration spokespersons could then, if they wished, shift the emphasis of their various announcements to reflect these opinions. They could explore the shifting proportions of the public who came to support negotiation or invasion as well as those who would, in any case, "Support the Troops." The pooling system for journalists, experimented with in the invasion of Panama, was tightened under White House auspices. Presidential advisers also proposed arrangements whereby the small-town press, expected to be more sympathetic to the war, would have free transportation to Saudi Arabia. The president and his aides were said to have watched all the early news briefings to decide who were the best military briefers. After an early performance in which he shone, Lieutenant General Thomas Kelley was promoted and set up for daily rehearsals so that he could perfect his style.[10] Later, it was the White House that decreed there would be no televised ceremonies of the American coffins returning home. White House aides and the secretary of defense said frankly that they had learned from "the lessons of Vietnam."[11] They meant the public-relations lessons.

It is true that Bush's popularity climbed with these events, but it is also true that they represented considerable White House effort and attention.

Other Activity

Presidents make other choices about their activities that can help or hurt them at the polls: give speeches to the nation, take foreign trips, and engage in domestic travel. Bush was high among the presidents in these activities. In domestic travel in his first thirty months he was second only to Ford, and in foreign travel second only to Carter. He also was second in major addresses—after his predecessor, the "Great Communicator"—although his pattern of speaking was distinctive, as we will see. All these second-rank positions add up to considerable ceremonial activity and confirm the impression of many observers that Bush did not like to stay in Washington. Still, it is true that he did not jog around the world as much as Jimmy Carter did in his first thirty months, and he is comparable to the slightly less energetic joggers, Nixon and Ford.

A closer look at the major addresses shows a more distinctive pattern. Throughout his first year, following the inaugural and State of the Union speeches, Bush remained silent until the fall, when he spoke on drugs and the invasion of Panama. It was seven months during which the American people were not addressed by their newly elected president, far under the typical rate for presidential speaking. It is perhaps most comparable to Lyndon Johnson when he hid from the nation for eleven months during the Vietnam War. Bush's second year repeated the pattern. After the constitutionally required State of the Union address, he made no speeches for seven months, until the speeches on the Gulf crisis. All other presidents gave major economic addresses, most at the rate of one a year. Typically these followed shortly after the State of the Union address and marked the occasion for sending economic legislation to Congress.[12] Bush gave no such addresses in his first thirty months in office. His one speech on an economic subject—the budget controversy with Congress—was sandwiched between two speeches on the Gulf crisis.

Without the addresses on Panama and the Gulf, Bush would not even have shown an average level of public speaking. We saw previously that presidents averaged about five major addresses a year during their first terms. Bush averaged two speeches a year, one required by the Constitution.

Presidents do appear to carry out these activities reactively, in ways designed to help them at the polls. Major addresses and foreign travel follow drops in popularity. Major addresses are also more likely to occur following hard choices and positive dramatic events, when presidents apparently try to explain or capitalize on these events. Domestic travel is most clearly associated with poor economic conditions. When the economy is poor, presidents do not speak to the nation or take foreign trips. They do travel domestically, however, perhaps to explain to selected audiences what the economic news means and what should be done. Bush followed the presidential norm to some extent. He was more likely to take domestic trips when the economic picture was worsening and after times of bad luck. He was less likely to travel abroad during poor economic times or when his popularity was falling. And he was much more likely to give a major address following a positive dramatic event. His speaking was not related to risks or falls in popularity. Like the other presidents in many ways, Bush was most distinctive in his concentration of speaking around positive dramatic events.

Not all these activities help a president's popularity. Controlling for the circumstances of the time, speeches to the nation do have a positive impact on public support, foreign travel makes no difference, and domestic travel shows a negative impact. We do not know if the presidents know this or even if they care, since they might need to travel for other reasons. Nevertheless, it will be interesting to see whether Bush's high activity on the three dimensions translates into public support.

An additional measure can be included: foreign policy messages to Congress. These particular messages can help distinguish dramatic events in foreign affairs from more traditional foreign policy activity. Bush ranks low among the presidents in these messages; only Reagan and Ford sent fewer legislative requests in a comparable period. This lower legislative initiative is not merely a Republican response. Eisenhower ranks high in foreign policy messages in his early years, while Nixon sent about as many of these messages as the Democratic presidents. Overall, presidents do not make these requests reactively or strategically, nor do the requests affect their public support. This is understandable since the messages would be shaped in part by the congressional agenda and its process of deliberation each year. We would not expect these messages to affect Bush's public support. We therefore ask how the key influences on the polls, identified for the other modern presidents, help explain Bush's public support in his early years in office.

The Key Influences

Two influences stand out: dramatic events, both good and bad, and Bush's own choice of activities. (See the results shown in Appendix B.) As we might suspect, dramatic international events had a substantial positive impact on Bush's ratings, whether they were discretionary or inherited good luck. With each of these international rally points, Bush gained about 5 points in the polls. Negative events, too, had a substantial effect, driving the polls downward by more than 10 percentage points on the average with each major domestic conflict or frustration encountered along the way. Since the positive events occurred so frequently, keeping Bush's popularity high, the few negative events stand out in their impact. In this way, Bush was being charged for his high popularity much like sports competitors who must play against their own averages. Budget fights with Congress are fairly routine occurrences on the Washington scene. Ronald Reagan had them all the time. But it appears that Bush's skirmish with Congress in his second year, occurring within the context of the Gulf crisis and its attendant support for the president, brought his polls down sharply.

Bush's ceremonial activities also made a difference, but not always in the ways he might have wished. Bush gained an additional 4 points on the average when he spoke to the nation during an international event. Although the events and the speeches tended to go together, the results showed that each had a separate positive impact. Bush's other activities, however, produced negative effects. For each day of his domestic travel, he lost about 1 percentage point, and for each day of foreign travel, he lost more than 1 point. A five-day trip to Europe cost about 6 points in the polls. Bush is like the other presidents in the positive effects of his speeches and the negative effects of domestic travel; he is unlike them in showing a significant negative impact for foreign travel. Even his foreign policy messages to Congress appeared to accompany drops in the polls. According to these results, Bush was correct in cutting short a foreign trip in the fall of 1991 at the time his approval ratings were falling. But he was incorrect in setting out for a trip across the nation, because this activity would likely bring the polls still lower.

Again we see the paradoxical consequences of high popularity. The dilemma of the Bush administration in its early years emerges sharply. Polls that are artificially high, as sustained by a few international events, are unstable. Anything will bring them down. It is not that Bush made any mistakes on his trips, but that they returned attention to all the rest of the nation's agenda—and the artificial support disappeared. It is unlikely that the legislative messages themselves attracted any attention, but occurring as they did in times without dramatic events, they accompanied drops in the polls.

Notice also that it was not foreign policy in itself that was Bush's strong point, as opposed to domestic policy, but only a particular kind of foreign policy activity. When Bush engaged in many foreign policy activities, traveling abroad as head of state and chief diplomat or sending foreign policy messages to Congress, his poll ratings fell. It was only when he was associated with dramatic international events that his polls rose sharply. These dramatic events, accompanied by speeches and other efforts by the administration, accounted for the high popularity. Everything else brought the polls down. The other presidents, too, could not count on foreign affairs generally to help public approval, but only a very narrowly defined foreign policy area. Bush merely showed this distinction in its sharpest form.

Two other key influences on the polls showed little effect in Bush's first thirty months: the economy and the decay over time. Bush's polls did not show the decline over time or the reaction to the economy found for most of the modern presidents. They were very much *event driven*. This phenomenon accounts for the volatility in support that is so striking when compared to that of the other presidents. It also explains why these two common influences did not show more of an impact. It was only by the end of the third year that the economy caught up with the Bush administration. Economic misery began to take its toll, and approval fell steadily past the 50 percent mark and continued to decline. At this time, economic news supplanted the international news as the leading stories. The shift in the news focus and the corresponding shift of the economy on the polls is surely no coincidence. Journalists, turning from the problems in Russia and Kuwait to the problems at home, wrote about the recession— and Bush's falling approval ratings.

How different, then, was the Bush administration from its predecessors? These key influences can still explain the fluctuation in the polls, but they should also be able to identify areas of distinctiveness. We can refine the analysis by focusing on Bush's month-by-month differences in popularity.[13] We ask not whether the chief influences had an impact, but whether they had one in

the Bush years significantly different than what we have seen
before. While there is distinctiveness, it is mainly a matter of
degree. Dramatic events and Bush's own activities made more of
a difference. In other words, they brought his polls up more
sharply and brought them down more sharply. The major addresses continued to show a positive impact, while the other
activities—foreign and domestic travel and congressional messages—were strongly negative. Dramatic events also showed a
substantial influence, especially the negative-predicted events.
This supports the interpretation of Bush's polls as primarily event
driven. Since approval was maintained at an artificial high point
through a series of dramatic positive events, any other events and
presidential activities drove the polls down.

All uses of force do not help presidential popularity, although
the particular cases that become rally points do help. This general
finding holds for the Bush years. Although Bush participated in
dramatic uses of force, he was also high in the overall use of
force. This use of force, however, showed no significant impact
on the polls within the month, in the following month, or by a
variety of measures.[14] Only very specific events shaped the polls
of this president.

In what is the clearest difference from his predecessors, Bush
did not experience the normal decay over his first thirty months
in office; rather, he gained about 1 percentage point each month
when compared to the past administration averages. His popularity did not increase, but neither did it decrease; hence the interesting positive increment against the normal declining trend. Most
presidents come to office along with artificially high public expectations, aroused by the election victory and inauguration. The
inflated support then decays into their third year. Bush, however,
did not have a particularly inspiring election campaign in 1988:
Many people felt that he won through the Democrats' default.
His initial low poll ratings reflect this electoral dissatisfaction—he
began his term with only 51 percent of the public's support.
Bush, therefore, had no artificial support to lose. His decline
came later, much more suddenly, following another kind of inflated expectation. By the end of his third year, his thirty-sixth
month, Bush's polls converged exactly with the average for the

other modern presidents. Fifty percent of the public approved of his performance in office.

These results help us compare Bush to the other occupants of the office. He was subject to the same influences, although in different degrees, revealing a picture of support that was primarily event driven and very vulnerable to other influences. Bush's exaggerated popularity was costly: Sooner or later, inflated expectations collapse. The model does well in identifying the influences at work and also allows some projections for the future. Bush's polls should stabilize at considerably lower levels without so many dramatic international events. Paradoxically, Bush would probably find that his other activities had less negative impact. Even though economic conditions should become more of a factor when they are not overwhelmed by dramatic events, the Bush White House showed itself able to focus attention on international affairs, thus minimizing negative economic effects. There would be enough support, in other words, for Bush to pursue a somewhat wider range of choices than his predecessors.

The following section looks more closely at what these choices were.

BUSH IN COMPARATIVE PERSPECTIVE

In the previous chapter, we profiled the modern presidents on dimensions of activity and public support. Using the same scheme, we can characterize Bush as positive, with the emphasis on pragmatism, being liked, and following external rather than internal cues. This is evident in the pragmatism seen throughout the campaign and years in the White House, the high popularity and attention to public relations, and the apparent hesitancy to take unpopular or controversial positions. The activity is somewhat more difficult to characterize because it was so selective: Bush was very active on some dimensions and inactive in others. Overall, we can call Bush an example of the active-positive style, although we need to look at what the various mixtures are.

Bush's peculiar mixture of foreign policy activity should now be clear. Like Reagan, Bush was active in the use of force and in the foreign policy speeches that talked about this force. He was significantly higher than the other presidents, including Reagan, in the use of force in his first years in office.[15] According to the Congressional Research Service listing, there were four U.S. uses of force in 1989 alone: in Libya, Panama, the Philippines, and the three nations participating in the Andean War on Drugs.[16] He was also the most active president in speaking about foreign policy in his early years, with Nixon ranked second and Reagan third. Bush's speaking almost always accompanied a major use of force. By this account, Bush not only continued the military-rhetorical style of the Reagan years but also carried it further. On the other foreign policy dimensions, Bush was less distinctive. He was high in foreign travel, although not as high as Carter in his first thirty months, and he was low in foreign policy legislative requests.

It is interesting how much of this activity in foreign policy clustered around a few selected events. Without Panama and the Gulf War, Bush would rank low in foreign policy speeches to the nation, since he gave only one. He would rank even lower in legislative messages, since a number of his messages concerned these two subjects. He would also be lower in the use of force. This is not to say that Bush deliberately selected these events in order to appear presidentially active, merely that he did not spend his activity on other events.

The informal news conferences gave a sense of presidential energy while directing attention to specific subjects. The major addresses and the uses of force did the same. Thus, behind the surface activity was a more mixed picture. Perhaps even more clearly than his predecessors, Bush decided what he would be active about.

Bush's legislative record also showed a selectivity that the superficial facts do not capture. On the surface, Bush was high in activity and low in success. He showed above-average activity in his early years, measured by the number of positions he took on legislation, although he was low in more visible presidential initiatives. Early assessments could point to only a few bills in the way of substantive domestic policy initiatives.[17] The large number of positions he took were heavily concentrated in a few bills: More than a dozen occurred on the White House–sponsored Clean Air Bill, for example. At the same time, he was low in legislative success. His success rate in his first year was lower than that for all the presidents except Ford, while his success rate the following year was close to the record low, exceeded only by Reagan in his second-to-last year in office. Reagan won 44 percent of the votes on which he took a position as a lame-duck president ending his time in office. Bush compiled his 47 percent success rate in the second year of his presidency.

"How can members turn the president down when . . . he said give us a chance to be as effective here at home as we have been overseas?" Whip Newt Gingrich pleaded in one key vote on the House floor. Yet Congress had no problem saying no, even though the vote occurred in early March 1991, immediately after the victory in the Gulf War.[18] Overall, a president's popularity does help congressional success, when we correct for other influences. Bush's popularity, however, so closely connected with a few international events, did not translate into success in Congress. Activity, as position taking, also helps success. Nevertheless, Bush was an active and popular president with a very low record of congressional success, even compared to those of the other Republicans. Adjusted for his high popularity at the time and the number of positions he took on congressional roll calls, Bush's success rate would be even lower.

Why should this be so? If Bush was the pragmatic, compromising politician that many saw him to be, why could he not win more bipartisan support in Congress? Why were there not more legislative compromises?[19] The answer becomes clearer when we look at his veto record: Bush apparently chose *not* to make bipartisan legislation, or at least chose not to spend his energy in this way.

The vetoes present another dimension of Bush's relations with Congress. On the surface, they show Bush high in both activity and success. Only Ford vetoed more bills than Bush in the first three years in office. And, unlike Ford, Bush had a perfect record: Ford was overridden twelve times by the necessary two-thirds vote of Congress.[20] This need not mean that the Democratic Congress was intimidated by a popular president. Bush had enough Republicans in Congress to defeat Democratic override attempts; Ford did not. It does show us more, however, of Bush's legislative strategy. While he was not proposing or winning legislation of his own, he was stopping Democratic legislation. For example, he vetoed a civil rights bill, a minimum-wage bill, foreign aid appropriations, and a bill to bar employers from hiring permanent replacements for workers on strike. This was not the kind of strategy designed to win legislative support.

A veto strategy has political costs. As political scientist Barbara Sinclair observes: "The frequency with which Bush found it necessary to threaten vetoes and the number of significant bills he actually did veto [were] indicators of weakness, not strength."[21] Sinclair points out how the failure to compromise legislation led to many confrontations between the Bush administration and Congress, forcing Bush to veto bills, such as the civil rights bill, that would have political costs. The president and the Republicans in Congress could not, or did not, negotiate to get the kind of bills Bush would sign. Despite the costs, Bush seems to have chosen this legislative strategy over others.

Clearly Bush's positive approach to the public, in attempting to win support, was not followed in his approach to Congress, where he was not trying to be liked. Here, Bush pursued a more passive and combative strategy, stopping legislation rather than fighting and compromising for legislation of his own. Yet, the mixture came together and made its own kind of political sense. Placing the burden on Congress to perform the unpleasant tasks of policy making in a time of restricted budgets, Bush minimized his losses. All he had to do was say what Congress was doing wrong. If the president conducted foreign policy well and Congress made domestic policy poorly, the stage was set for the reelection of 1992. It is unclear what other approach Bush could have pursued if public popularity were his main goal.

LOOKING AHEAD

This anatomy of the early Bush years shows the usefulness of comparison. What we have done here could be done for other presidencies in progress, providing a sharper perspective for ongoing events. We can isolate the main influences on Bush's popularity and point out his similarities to and differences from other presidents. While the key influences continue to be important, the results show how much of Bush's popularity was event driven, supported by great White House effort.

The results point to the dilemma of the Bush administration. *Exaggerated popularity is costly.* When events artificially inflate support, any other activities will bring poll ratings down. And when the exaggerated support collapses, as it does inevitably, the fall can be all the more devastating. Bush was not elected by 80 percent to 90 percent of the citizens; no American presidents are. He was elected by 53 percent of the two-party vote in a year when the other major party did not mount that much competition. It was this margin he struggled to maintain at the end of his third year, at a time of economic recession. He was not helped by the memory of how high his polls had been.

Besides placing ongoing events in perspective, the results raise questions for the future. We have come a long way from Harry Truman to George Bush—from the president who fired MacArthur to the one who managed the Gulf War, from the one who scorned the polls to the one who appeared to make major choices in terms of them. However, it would be wrong to conclude that the choices have narrowed in any important ways. No trend was apparent over the years in the profiles traced out in the preceding chapter. Presidents continue to have a range of choices.

What we do have to ask is whether popularity is becoming more consciously manipulated, whether the professionalization of White House decision making renders the polls no longer useful as a means of tapping public opinion. If polls measure the public's reaction to the job the president is doing, they can function as a kind of continuing referendum, whether valuable or not. But if, instead, they merely show public reaction to events that are predicted to have that reaction, they say nothing at all. If political scientists can predict events that will raise or lower a president's public-opinion polls, presidents can do so, too.

We can foresee administrations that would continue to be event driven, powered by positive dramatic events, with negative instances of conflict kept to a minimum. The polls would fluctuate greatly between the peaks and troughs of the dramatic news stories, but no one—in the public or the White House—would ask how the presidents were doing their jobs.

The Reagan and Bush administrations were both highly professional in matters of public relations. Reagan, the professionally skilled performer in communicating to mass audiences, was advised by others with political expertise. Bush, himself a skilled Washington professional, was surrounded by advisers like himself. Both showed a selective and mixed activity that worked well in maintaining public support: Reagan separating the amiable and passive individual from the activity of the administration, and Bush distinguishing areas of high and low activity. In each case, the activities they delegated to others consisted of the controversies and the problem areas of governing. The Reagan administration was said to be a hard act to follow; however, Bush has surpassed Reagan in some ways.

Two administrations do not make a trend, but they do set a powerful precedent. We need to think of the consequences of the increased professionalism of maintaining public support: what it means for the conduct of government and what changes it might bring in the role of the public in a democracy. Two episodes in modern American history, Watergate and Vietnam, cast grave doubts on decision making in the White House. Somehow, the most recent administrations have changed the perspective on these events. They have been redefined from problems of decision making to problems of public support. The Iran-Contra affair suggested that there need be no more Watergates. Illegal and unconstitutional acts might continue, but they would not result in impeachment or resignation, given proper management at the White House. The Gulf War suggested that there would be no more Vietnams. The nation would continue to go to war, but the wars would not be unpopular, nor would they show the casualties and civilian damage that might make them so. Each in its own way was a public-relations victory. However, these might not be the lessons the public wants their presidents to learn.

8

A Guide to Presidents
and the Polls

THERE is a new voice of the people in American politics. It sings a continuous and beguiling tune with great range and variety. We hear it clearly but do not know what it says or what it means. Although the polls have not supplanted elections as the democratic base for a president's actions in office, at times they can supersede them. They withdraw support from winners of landslide elections, discourage some presidents from running for reelection and encourage others, and affect White House actions and the legislative agenda. Given their importance, it is surprising how cavalierly we treat them and how little we ask about what they actually mean.

Since the time of the Truman administration, a nationwide sample of Americans have been asked on a regular basis if they approve or disapprove of the job President _____ is doing. This question is used in the various network polls and forms the basis for most of the news stories about a president's public support. Many people do not evaluate the president's job performance, however. They respond to the president as a person or, linking two patriotic symbols, say how the *nation* is doing. Merely dividing events into those that dramatize either the nation's conflict and problems or its unity in the face of external threats allows us to explain a great deal of the fluctuations in the president's approval ratings. This leads to some ironic consequences. The Bay of Pigs invasion was planned by the U.S. government and failed because of many mistakes; yet Kennedy's polls rose at this occurrence. Eisenhower's did the same when a U.S. spy plane was downed after flying illegally over Communist territory. The spy plane incident led to the Soviet cancellation of an important summit meeting. Presidents do not need to be blamed to have their polls rise after international incidents—they can also do little or nothing. Bush's polls rose after a slow beginning in his first year as revolution swept previously Communist eastern Europe. Although he had not contributed to these historic trends, a significantly higher percentage of Americans approved of the way he was doing his job.

What this means is that we often evaluate presidents based on their good and bad luck in office. As we saw previously, Kennedy and Bush had significantly more good luck than the other presidents; Eisenhower had significantly less bad luck. It is not surprising that these presidents had higher poll ratings overall than most of their contemporaries.[1] Economic circumstances, too, can be powerful conditioning factors. While presidents can make marginal adjustments, they cannot overcome endemic problems or worldwide economic trends. For all their efforts, some presidents face better economic conditions than others. Hence, the ratings that form the basis of news stories—and set their own additional effects in motion—are an amalgam of influences only some of which reflect the president's job performance or are even under the president's control.

Further, there is a growing disparity between what the professionals—presidents and political experts—know and what the public knows about these phenomena. The public rallies around the president in times of national drama, while the professionals predict when the drama will occur as well as how long it will last and what kind of impact it will have. When the public guides presidents, by offering evaluations of the job they are doing, the polls might have value; but when things are turned around so that the presidents guide the polls, they become much more questionable. Journalists have an impact, too, with the same magnifier effect seen in presidential nominations. Changing the major stories—from international to economic news, for example—changes the view of a president's performance. Soon the trends accumulate. Attention focused on low approval ratings makes them fall further. Suddenly a president is in trouble, although nothing else has happened to make a difference in the world or in the White House. The international events continue; the economic trends developed from the past. Since popularity makes a difference, the reporting has changed the conditions within which a president governs. All this suggests that much of the tune we listen to so attentively is not the voice of the people at all.

This book has sought to make the polls and presidential performance more accessible to the public. It places the presidents in comparative perspective, identifying the chief patterns among administrations as well as individual differences. At this point, it is worth summarizing the most important findings to capsulize what the politically literate citizen needs to know. We can then raise a few far-reaching questions about the polls and the presidency in the future.

THE CHIEF INFLUENCES

Say that a president comes to office with 65 percent of the public approving of the way he is doing his job on inauguration day. By the end of the year, his support is slightly below 50 percent, and it falls further in his second year. Although he recoups somewhat in his third year, an average of 55 percent approve of his job performance. Imagine the news stories that would be written and the advice given. What happened? What went wrong? And what did he begin to do right in his third year that he had not done before?

Readers of this book will recognize this hypothetical president. He has the *average* support at the beginning and the *normal* decay over time. Nothing happened. This is the decay curve we expect, independent of other influences, for all the modern presidents. The polls begin to decline almost immediately and continue to fall into the third year, turning upward again as the next election approaches. They fall even more quickly and decrease more sharply in a president's second term. This ebb and flow of polls with the electoral cycle suggest that the support is inflated to start with: Election and inauguration festivities continually renew expectations that cannot be fulfilled. It also suggests that the initial honeymoon is costly in setting a standard that presidents cannot continue to meet.

Of course, if our hypothetical president encounters economic difficulties during his term, his polls will decline further in line with these economic events. Dramatic events that reflect the state of the nation also affect the polls, whether or not the president is involved in the event or has any control over it. We therefore can see why presidents are tempted to address foreign policy, and foreign policy of a particular kind, rather than domestic issues. Dramatic international events involving hostility are strongly positive in their impact, whether or not the United States engages in force. Reagan denounced the Soviet downing of a Korean airliner, without taking any other action, and gained support in the polls. On the other hand, dramatic peace-making events show little effect on popularity, while domestic controversies lower support. This does not necessarily mean that war is more popular than peace. Uses of force by the United States, without the accompanying drama and visibility, have little effect on the polls, at most a slightly negative effect. This holds independently of the more strongly negative effects on popularity produced by the Vietnam and Korean wars.

One kind of event stands out for its large positive impact: a highly publicized international incident, of brief duration, involving the use of force by the United States. If presidents speak to the nation at the same time, the effect is doubled. For each dual event—the force and the speech—presidents gain about 8 percentage points in the polls. Thus, a use of force one month, with a speech, followed by a victory in the next month, also with a speech, makes a spectacular impact. A president could gain 20 points on the average by the second month of the event.

It becomes clear that much of the surface fluctuation we see is only the polls returning to normal from changes in the economy and the impact of these events. So Bush's polls appeared to fluctuate wildly in his first years in office, from the high 80s in percent approval down to the high 40s in one year alone. Dramatic international events brought the ratings up, and then other activity (or no activity) brought them down. While Bush was distinctive in the volatility of his support, he showed the same kinds of influences at work as the other presidents.

Individual choices also make a difference. Presidents can select and time some of the dramatic events and help to focus attention on them. They can pursue a legislative agenda and take positions on votes in Congress. They can engage in many support-gathering activities as well, giving speeches to the nation and taking foreign and domestic trips. Although these actions can fulfill a number of objectives simultaneously, we see that they are taken reactively, with an eye toward public support, by their timing. Presidents hide, making no speeches to the nation, during times of bad luck or worsening economic conditions. They do speak to explain difficult choices they have had to make and to dramatize the international events predicted to help them. Some of these choices have major import. For example, the presidents are also more likely to engage in force of any kind as well as dramatic uses of force during bad economic times. The sharper the deterioration of economic conditions is, the much more likely will be the use of force. This curious and disturbing relationship is far stronger than could be expected by chance.

It is at this point that the differences between presidents come into sharper focus. We see their performances apart from circumstances and the common institutional constraints. Both Johnson and Nixon, for example, spent their first term fighting the war in Vietnam, but they handled their public relations far differently. Nixon spoke to the nation frequently, while Johnson remained silent. Nixon's strategy appeared more successful overall than Johnson's. Both presidents were high in negative dramatic events, and Nixon's economic conditions were worse than Johnson's. Nevertheless, along with the speaking and other choices, Nixon maintained higher levels of public support through a time of protest and demonstration. Ford and Reagan pose an even sharper contrast. Reagan was relatively high in choices that helped at the polls, while Ford was highest in activities that hurt or made little difference. Both presidents were active in the use of force by the United States. Whereas Reagan's military action was almost always accompanied by the speaking and drama that give polls a substantial lift, Ford's almost never was. On the one time Ford spoke to the nation during a military action— the recapture of the crew of the *Mayaguez*—his polls did rise substantially.

By the choice and timing of activity, presidents can affect their poll ratings. Some do so more consistently and effectively than others, as we can see in the following popularity rankings. The left column ranks the presidents by their raw public-approval standing over the years of their first elected term.[2] This is the popularity the presidents are known for. The right column ranks them by their popularity, after adjusting for economic conditions and the dramatic events of the time. Only some of these events, remember, are under presidential control.

Kennedy ⎫ tie		Reagan
Eisenhower ⎭		Eisenhower ⎫ tie
Nixon		Kennedy ⎭
Johnson		Carter
Reagan		Nixon
Ford		Ford
Carter		Johnson
Truman		Truman

Kennedy and Eisenhower, who experienced similar economic conditions and good circumstances, tie in the rankings. Truman, significantly lower in the polls than the other presidents, remains lowest in rank. The sharpest changes occur with Carter and Reagan. Carter faced some of the worst economic conditions of the period and a mixture of negative and positive events. Once we correct for these effects, he appears above average in public support. Carter illustrates what happens when we evaluate presidents for bad luck. Reagan's shift is even more striking: from a below-average position in the standings to the highest in rank. Reagan's economic conditions were far worse than Kennedy's or Eisenhower's, but no worse than Carter's. He spoke to the nation more, however, than the other high-ranked presidents, and he timed activities in ways that helped his support. Then, too, the economic circumstances we adjust for are the objective, "real" circumstances. Reagan apparently convinced people they were better off financially than they had been before he came to office, even if this were not objectively true. His polls were shaped by the perceived conditions; the ranking adjusts for the objective conditions. To some extent, Reagan made his own good fortune.

The presidents do group together in ways that tell more about their styles and choices. The top-ranked presidents—Reagan, Eisenhower, and Kennedy—showed a positive style, with its emphasis on being liked and following external rather than internal cues. Bush also fits this pattern. The lowest-ranked presidents—Johnson, Ford, and Truman—showed a more negative style, with its emphasis on conviction and internal cues. Each demonstrated in his own way that being liked was not the most important thing. The median presidents, Carter and Nixon, showed mixed styles that fit with other contrasts seen within their administrations. We begin to see more of the range and variety of the modern presidency. The presidents faced the same influences, but they responded to them in different ways.

EVALUATING THE
EVALUATIONS

The People versus the Polls

Seeing the polls more clearly helps us uncover the problems, too. It is hard to avoid the impression that something is wrong. The largest number of citizens approve of the president's job before he has any chance to do it. His support declines, and so does his capacity to win in Congress, as his experience in office grows. Presidential acts are taken reactively, in ways that help the polls. Foreign policy and presidential popularity appear intertwined. Use of U.S. force and other dramatic international events follow negative domestic occurrences much more frequently than could be expected by chance. Presidential speeches on foreign policy also follow negative events, although initiatives in diplomacy and foreign policy legislation do not. Some foreign policy acts do affect the polls, but this impact has little to do with the substance of policy and much more to do with how events are presented and perceived.

Yet, all this happens in the name of the public and with the legitimacy of public support. In one way, it is hard to quarrel with either the presidents' or the reporters' attention to public opinion in a democracy. Few people want presidents to go far in *disregarding* strongly felt opinion, or at least not too often or to any critical degree. They would probably feel uncomfortable with Truman's assertion that neither Jesus nor Moses needed polls to guide him; they would not understand why the American president found the comparison relevant. It is interesting that the three presidents we identified as least public regarding—Truman, Johnson, and Ford—all came to office accidentally, through vice presidential succession. Quite possibly, a person willing to make frequent unpopular decisions in the White House would be screened out by the presidential selection process.

The problem is not that presidents are overly public regarding, too willing to sway with the winds of popular passion. Almost all of the modern presidents made at least one hard choice in office, a dramatic discretionary act predicted to lower their support. Kennedy is the only exception. Eisenhower invoked the controversial Taft-Hartley Act, showing that a domestic problem could not be solved in any other way. Although Reagan made no hard choices in his first four years, he decided on a second-term Cabinet shakeup that dramatized problems within his administration. He also persisted in the planned trip to the Bitburg cemetery in Germany against strong sentiment from Congress and the public. As early as his second year, Bush announced it would be necessary to raise taxes. Most of these events did incur the predicted drop in support.

The problem is not that presidents are concerned with public approval but that they will manipulate events to appear so, to appear in line with public opinion when they are not. Their decisions would still be unpopular, but they would be made to seem more palatable or the public's attention would be directed to other things. Bad economic conditions are unpopular; they can be faced and addressed or disguised in various ways. Negotiating with terrorists is unpopular, as is the idea of begging nations for cash. Public-regarding presidents can therefore decide not to take these unpopular actions, or they can try to hide them and divert attention when they come to light. Wars are unpopular if the resulting damage and death far outrun the cause. So presidents who care for public opinion would weigh these risks carefully or they would take actions to keep the damage and death from public view. The examples from recent administrations are not meant to single out particular presidents for criticism; they point to a general problem that has become more visible in the last several years.

Less extreme cases reveal the same confusion of public opinion with what the public might want. People do not like the idea that any actions in foreign policy are taken to win their approval or that any hard choices are suppressed. They want to hear from presidents in domestic hard times and wish they would travel the country more to find out what opinion really is. Since someone must address the problems of government, they might like the presidents, whom they have elected to office, to try. If these things are true, the polls are not expressing what the public wants.

We might like to think that a president could resist the many temptations and keep national priorities straight. Nevertheless, from the first days of the campaign to the final presidential debate, candidates learn to look to short-run objectives and watch the polls. Those who succeed at it best become president. It is not surprising that they and their advisers continue to exercise their skills in the White House; they are caught in a phenomenon not of their own making.

Journalists assume that poll ratings and the public's opinion are the same thing. They reward presidents with favorable stories when the polls are high and punish them when the polls fall. It is not the decline in the polls the White House must fear as much as all the press stories that will come in its wake, stories that, in time, make the polls fall further. Because of their own continuing attention to the polls, the media fix the presidents' attention on them. In all these ways they "teach," or condition, presidents to watch the reports of public opinion every step of the way. Journalists often think of themselves as guardians and interpreters of public opinion. But just as a large number of Americans may not like what presidents are doing in their name, they may also dislike how their name is used in news stories. If they do not like to think of themselves as manipulated by public-relations experts in the White House, they are equally unwilling to be "interpreted" to themselves by professionals in the media. Either role inverts the democratic basis of the government that made the polls important in the first place.

The problem extends beyond presidents and journalists. Presidents also are caught by false expectations of the office that continue to work throughout American culture, expectations that are reflected in citizens' opinions and in popular and academic writing. The presidency is an institution shaped by expectations—from the public; from officials, including past presidents; and from the basic constitutional design. These expectations continue over time, forming the constraints and choices that individual presidents face. They also form the basis for citizen evaluations, people rating the individual occupants of the White House against the job presidents in general are expected to do. These expectations can be realistic, inappropriate, or highly idealized; in any case, they affect the office and the individuals in very profound ways.

We began this book by identifying a set of widely held expectations about the office. We then used these expectations—and nothing else—to predict the chief influences on presidential evaluations. These expectations led to the positive and negative prediction of events that dramatized the state of the nation, whether or not the president took any action in the event. They led to the surmise that presidents would be held accountable for things over which they had no control and for their good and bad luck. The resulting analysis showed that these influences could explain much of the similarity and differences among presidents. They could be applied to the presidents as a group and to administrations in progress. Therefore, if we do not like the poll results—for what they say about the American public or for the ways they constrain presidents—we should reexamine these basic expectations.

Toward More Realistic Appraisals

Presidents should be active, popular, and successful, according to some idealistic accounts of the office. They should exercise "leadership" and rally the country around their objectives and goals. Failure to do so, for whatever reason, is often counted as an individual failure. Somehow it is the president's fault when the early promise fades or the country drifts into conflict and disarray. Yet, as we have seen, such expectations are unrealistic, building in disappointment and decline across time. Presidents cannot stop this decay in popularity or manage the economy in more than marginal ways. On average, they control less than half of the positive and negative events in their administrations. Of the various ceremonial acts at their disposal, only major addresses are likely to produce a positive impact, if they are timed carefully and well. Without some good luck in the international arena, the only other way for a president to bolster sagging approval runs the risk of war. Even the uses of force, however, will not contribute to a president's popularity without considerable effort on the part of the White House.

Further, activity often works against popular support. In idealized portraits, presidents use their popular mandate in vigorous support of programs, winning Congress and the public to their point of view. In reality, the choices are more complex and limited. In the first place, the size and success of the legislative agenda are heavily shaped by factors presidents cannot control. And, when presidents do try to rally the nation for legislative objectives, they risk a drop in the polls and a corresponding loss of success for their programs in Congress. Active position taking on votes in Congress and domestic travel (rallying the congressional members' own constituencies) hurt public support.

Tradeoffs are necessary. When presidents take positions, helping their success in Congress, they lower their public approval. But approval helps congressional success. Every 10 percentage point gain in public approval yields a 7 percentage point gain in congressional success. Presidents thus face a delicate situation: in order to increase congressional success—by bolstering approval—they must decrease the number of positions they take. As their positions decrease, their congressional success rate falls. Popular presidents thus find built-in limits, while their less popular peers confront the dilemma in which efforts to make headway in Congress set them further behind in the polls. The dilemma has no obvious solution, as presidents facing serious economic conditions know. With their polls at a low ebb, they can least afford bold new proposals; they can then be criticized as ineffectual and even less able to do their job. Since the polls fall with worsening economic conditions and rise with dramatic international events, presidents are most able to provide legislative leadership when the country needs it least and are least able to supply that leadership when domestic conditions demand it.

Presidents appear to recognize these tradeoffs and balance their activity and success. Although some presidents are more activity-oriented or success-oriented than others, the differences are not extreme. Carter and Reagan were the most evenly balanced: as if the most recent occupants of the White House were learning lessons from the past about the fine line they had to tread. Carter was very high in activity his first year and low in his second. By his third year, he had it right.

If they cannot rally the nation around a legislative agenda, what can presidents do? The one kind of rallying we find is very specific: highly visible international events, typically short in duration, with publicity supplied by the White House. These narrowly circumscribed events, often called rally points, do have a substantial poll impact that lasts from one to four months. But surely this is not the rallying that the presidential idealists have in mind. Moreover, these rally points have their own built-in limitations. Their impact is brief, they require White House effort and management, and they risk unintended international consequences. Reagan's speech about the Korean airliner was an international as well as a domestic political event; it was not risk-free. Finally, after all the drama was over, the problems at home remained.

The real leadership, American style, is probably more a matter of juggling: Juggling the checks with the balances, the hard choices with positive acts, and the hopes for the legislative agenda with the appraisals about congressional success. It is carried out, moreover, on narrow margins of support, the kind to be expected in a plural society, with two major political parties competing for power and diverse opinion and claims on government. Presidents are elected typically with less than 60 percent of the popular vote. Why should we expect their polls to be higher? If we ask that presidents be merely symbolic figures—strongly supported by all Americans—then we constrain them to only those activities that can bring near-unanimous support. We discourage them from pursuing the activities we elected them for. People made jokes that George Bush had finally come out against drugs, crime, and dirty air. He had also fought a war against a villainous international figure. He then took steps to show his distance from the Congress, an institution becoming increasingly unpopular because of its own scandals and disarray. We can expect more of those positions in the future if we demand artificially high levels of support.

The range of realistic performance becomes clearer from the various profiles in Chapter 6. The modern presidents have made different choices about their activity and popularity. Citizens who are serious about the task of evaluating presidents have to decide which particular balance they find best. Perhaps future presidents can do better, but it is the real, rather than an idealized, standard they should try to exceed.

One of the easiest ways to a new realism is to revise what we expect by popular support. Presidents typically win elections by little more than 50 percent of the popular vote, even when they hold these narrow margins in most of the states. If we merely ask that they govern in a plural society by the same kind of margin that elected them, most of the problems of a public-relations presidency would disappear. There would be far fewer poll stories and less attempts on the part of the White House to make all the minor manipulations. More could be risked, since most of the presidents most of the time can hold their electoral constituency: They can hold to a level of majority support. It is when we ask them to do more than they were elected to do that the problems begin.

It is important to point out that this does not mean to *lower* standards but to begin to develop them. The great presidents of American history typically faced circumstances of an unusually critical kind: They helped found the nation, preserve the union, and lead the country in two of its major wars. These are what we have called presidential good luck. It is true they responded to circumstances successfully when others might not have done so, but we are trying to evaluate performance apart from the good and bad luck in office. If the modern range is the typical range, as we argued in Chapter 6, then we need to develop standards for evaluating it.

The past presidents had another advantage over the moderns: They did not have public-opinion polls. Lincoln, for example, was criticized in his first term as being unpopular and unsuccessful. A leading article of the day was entitled "The Unpopular Mr. Lincoln." According to one historian, "Friendly critics viewed him as honest, well intentioned, but rather lacking in force; hostile ones, as weak, vacillating, and opportunistic."[3] He was criticized for his inability to organize his administration, for allowing corruption in the appointment of generals, and for having no policy in the crisis. His talents as a public speaker helped little, since he never addressed Congress in person and had no means to address the citizens at large. It was not clear if he could win reelection, and many Republicans urged him not to try. To paraphrase Truman's famous question, "I wonder how far Lincoln would have gone if he had taken a poll?" it is likely that the polls would have been even more discouraging than the advice he received at the time. Without support from key factions in the North and with his own administration in disarray, we can imagine the poll stories at the time. It is doubtful that he would have won the chance for a second term, victory in the war, and the beginning of his legendary place in history.

"Who, then, can measure the strength that is given to the President because he holds Lincoln's office, lives in Lincoln's house, and walks in Lincoln's way?"[4] Clinton Rossiter argues that great myths and idealized expectations are important parts of a president's support. According to this argument, a new realism might undercut support, making a president's problems even more difficult by removing some of the mythic splendor. We have to ask, however, if the hypothetical loss would outweigh some very real gains. Without unrealistic expectations to start with, presidents would no longer need to face the inevitable decay of support. They would not be held accountable for unsolvable problems or be asked to maintain support beyond their initial electoral referendum. They could govern proudly as representatives of a pluralistic society with between 50 and 60 percent of the public approving of their job. Wouldn't they be less pressed to maintain public relations, less timid about tackling hard problems, and less tempted to choose and time their actions for an impact on the polls? Would they lose support in Congress? Their support now is contingent on many externalities and is vulnerable to falling approval levels. Might not the public respect them more?

Expectations are difficult, perhaps impossible, to change. However, the implications for democracy—for what the voice of the people is supposed to mean—are serious enough for us to think further about these questions.

Self-correcting Effects

Additional reform might come more easily with increased consciousness on the part of the presidents, the news media, and the public. Presidents seem to react more to the polls than the public does to the presidents. Actions that appear timed to help presidential popularity do not necessarily help. All of the ceremonial acts are reactive in various ways, and yet they do not all have the desirable impact. While the use of force is oddly timed to coincide with bad economic times, force is not a popular strategy overall. Only particular international events ever made a difference in the polls. In short, much of the effort expended on maintaining public approval does not seem worth the results.

The White House appears to learn its public-relations lessons quickly, supported by a skilled and attentive professional staff. It is unlikely that the reactivity would continue if it were found to have little impact. The early years of the Bush administration taught an additional lesson. What goes up artificially comes down swiftly. Bush differed from the other presidents in that almost all his activities outside of dramatic international events had negative impacts. Even his foreign travel lowered his poll ratings. Such knowledge could change the strategies of future incumbents of the office. Presidents face costs for a few months of spectacular popularity that might be counterproductive in the long run. Perhaps, too, opinions are less responsive and subject to manipulation than the experts believe. Rule by resonator and the daily tracking polls will take presidents only so far.

The same kind of awareness could improve news coverage. As news representatives begin to understand the dynamics at work, it will become responsible journalism to point out as a matter of course the expected decline over a term or the artificial inflation of approval ratings following dramatic international events. Reporting a president's popularity at the end of a war would be not only distasteful but also unnecessary—it would not be news. Going somewhat further, patterns common to all administrations do not make newsworthy stories. It would be news, and worth a speculative essay, only if a case did not follow these accustomed lines.

Of course, journalists as well as presidents are subject to temptations. A story on a sudden high in presidential popularity can be followed by another story when the popularity declines to its normal level. That makes two news items instead of none. It is also easy to write this kind of horse-race story, found so frequently in election campaigns, with its suspense and drama of an individual's contest against political odds. The games of politics, including a president's manipulation of the polls, are easier to cover than the complex issues of government. Finally, journalists, like presidents, are in the business of communicating with the public. Fascination with the skill exhibited by fellow professionals leads to coverage that not only condones the more extreme White House public-relations efforts but also encourages them. Journalists encourage them when they report a president's "game plan" for reviving failing poll ratings or when they imply that such are the primary, if not exclusive, subjects of White House decision making.

George Bush could have accused reporters that *they* lived by the polls. Stories featured his high popularity in the early months of his administration, when he experienced near-record approval ratings. As his third year in office drew to a close, stories tracked his falling polls to below the 50 percent mark. While the administration appeared to be reacting to the falling polls, the press followed the administration's reaction. As noted in *Newsweek,* "The President first sensed trouble around Labor Day, when he read a 'misery index' in the *Wall Street Journal.* "[5] In the weeks that followed, there were numerous news reports that the economy showed signs of worsening. The search for an economic policy began. In Congress, Bush dropped his threat to veto civil rights legislation, despite his earlier denunciations of it as a quota bill. Later, he ordered his top aides to negotiate a compromise on extending unemployment benefits, even though he had vetoed similar measures twice before. He cut back foreign travel, and in early December his abrasive chief of staff, John Sununu, finally resigned. Covering these events, the press commented not only on the substance of these actions but also in terms of Bush's "game plan" for the 1992 election. Questions of presidential strategy seemed to attract at least as much attention as questions of national leadership. As the economy worsened and a host of domestic issues arose, the press cared less about in what direction Bush was (or was not) leading the nation and wondered if he could "pull it out" in the closing innings of his first term. From the Gulf War to the administration's plight at the end of 1991, the national news had told a story of the polls.

Many journalists are worried about the impact on the news of the people who write about it. They know that horse-race stories do not substitute for coverage of issues, and they recognize that news creates its own self-fulfilling prophecies. These worries, expressed most frequently about presidential campaigns, have led to some internal reforms. The media used to announce the "winners" of presidential debates, for example, before the viewers could form their own impressions. These announcements were felt to have an impact on the campaign, as in the 1980 Carter-Reagan debates. The networks discontinued the practice because it was both silly and unfair and now let citizens make up their own minds without interpreting the event for them. Poll coverage should be watched as closely as election coverage for the way it inhibits presidents, creates its own momentum, and seeks to interpret public opinion. As the new referendum, polls not only influence who wins a subsequent election but also affect the course of an ongoing government and the choices made in the White House.

"Voters are not fools," political scientist V. O. Key wrote in the last book of his distinguished career.[6] Key went on to say that voters could distinguish policies and positions of candidates on issues important to them. Far from being puppets manipulated by the candidates and parties, they could make keen and influential evaluations. American citizens are not fools either, whether or not they vote or are asked to take part in the new referendum. It seems clear that the traditional approval question is not tapping an adequate depth of opinion. Surface questions lead to superficial answers and a superficial view of public relations. Americans are thus made to seem more foolish and gullible than they are. Few people would want to change a question that has been asked since the 1940s, but it could easily be followed by one or two more probing questions. It would be interesting to find out what people approved and disapproved of and how they separated their feelings about the president from their job evaluation. These specific questions are asked only from time to time. Somehow the traditional question does not allow enough of the citizens' evaluations to come through.

Americans agree with Key. We think ourselves capable of evaluating our presidents and feel that we should do so. But this evaluation requires a standard of comparison. We therefore need better information than we have had to date about what are the typical patterns. Evaluation also requires that we separate individual responsibility from what is predetermined or chance. We need to see individual presidents apart from their luck and institutional constraints. It does not take any special statistical skill to compare individuals against an average or to follow the commonsense logic of adjusting for good and bad fortune. Armed with this information, citizens can become better critics of both the presidents and the journalists who report the polls. Citizens also need information about their own opinions that is as accurate as what presidents and political scientists possess. This knowledge provides its own corrective influence. Simply knowing that bad economic times greatly increase the probability of a president using force can help to decrease the linkage between these events. Understanding the chief influences on the polls makes people more self-conscious when responding to these influences. Knowing that a more alert public is watching them might hold presidents to higher standards of performance. Most critically, as Americans begin to realize it is their name that is taken so often in vain, they will wish to make clearer what they do definitely disapprove of.

As the first practical democratic experiment of modern times was getting underway, Thomas Jefferson observed that an informed citizenry would be essential. This was not a casual comment or one that should be too quickly taken for granted. For watchers of American presidential politics, the observation has a particular relevance today.

Appendix A

I. EVENTS CLASSIFICATION AND CODING RULES

Events are included if they appeared in two of the following three annual summaries: *The World Almanac and Book of Facts* (New York: World Almanac, various issues); Arthur M. Schlesinger, Jr., ed., *The Almanac of American History* (New York: Putnam, 1983); and Gorton Carruth, ed., *The Encyclopedia of American Facts and Dates,* 8th ed. (New York: Harper & Row, 1988). It should be noted that most chronologies include similar lists of events. Indeed, our events were found to be very similar to those examined by Ostrom and Simon (1985) and MacKuen (1986) in their studies of years within this period. Following accepted conventions, all events were coded as occurring in the month they were first announced and were treated as discrete (see Ragsdale [1984], Ostrom and Simon [1985], and MacKuen [1986]). In only two instances did more than one event occur in a single polling period. In one (04/1952, see the list of events below) a positive and negative event canceled each other out, and in the other (06/1970) two negative events were coded as one.

Events are coded as in the categories listed below, following the literature on general support. The following decision rules were applied:

A. Nationally Unifying Events: Positive-predicted

1. The first major engagement of American military units abroad or units under American auspices; the first major engagement of Communist military units abroad; other aggression perceived as a threat to U.S. interests or the security of its citizens.
2. Actual threats to the health of the president, or sudden dramatic threats to others representing the nation. (Incidents within an ongoing war are not included.)
3. Successful accomplishments carried out by the president or others representing the nation. Announcements of an end to divisive events. Routine diplomatic trips abroad are not included.

B. Nationally Divisive Events: Negative-predicted

1. All protests, demonstrations, or serious occasions of domestic conflict, whether or not the president was involved.
2. Scandals and new events within a scandal that question the president's judgment.
3. Acts announcing a controversial decision or extending or increasing an already controversial situation; events dramatizing difficulties with the economy.

Events were also coded as discretionary and nondiscretionary—that is, whether the surface impression suggested some control by the president over the timing or occurrence of the event. Hence, responses to international events occurring independently are coded as nondiscretionary, whether or not any covert activity might be thought to have occurred. Clearly, this is a necessary simplifying assumption since actual knowledge of covert activity would be incomplete at best. Overall, these decision rules allow straightforward assignment of events in the categories and 100 percent intercoder reliability was obtained.

II. EVENTS

Following the classification scheme outlined above, events were coded as follows: P = Positive-predicted; D = Discretionary; N = Negative-predicted; and ND = Nondiscretionary.

Poll Date	Event	Coding
03/1949	Coal strike	N-ND
10/1949	Steel strike	N-ND
07/1950	North Korea attacks South Korea	P-ND
09/1950	Wage-price controls	N-D
05/1951	Truman fires MacArthur	N-D
04/1952	Japanese Peace Treaty announced	P-D
04/1952	Truman nationalizes steel industry	N-D
06/1952	Court rules against Truman on steel case	N-ND
03/1953	Soviets fire on U.S. bomber	P-ND
08/1953	Korean armistice announced	P-D
10/1953	Eisenhower invokes Taft-Hartley	N-D
07/1955	Soviets shoot down U.S. spy plane	P-ND
10/1955	Eisenhower has heart attack	P-ND
06/1956	Eisenhower has major surgery	P-ND
10/1957	Eisenhower orders army to Little Rock	N-D
10/1957	Sputnik launched	N-ND
06/1958	Sherman Adams scandal breaks	N-ND
07/1958	Eisenhower sends Marines to Lebanon	P-D
07/1959	Steel strike	N-ND
11/1959	Eisenhower invokes Taft-Hartley	N-D
05/1960	U-2 incident	P-ND
05/1961	Bay of Pigs invasion	P-D
08/1961	Berlin Wall crisis	P-ND
11/1961	Second Berlin Wall crisis	P-ND

Poll Date	Event	Coding
03/1962	First American orbits Earth	P-D
05/1962	Steel crisis	N-ND
10/1962	Integration crisis in Mississippi	N-ND
11/1962	Cuban Missile Crisis	P-ND
05/1963	Integration crisis in Alabama	N-ND
05/1965	Dominican Republic crisis	P-ND
08/1965	Vietnam draft doubled	N-D
04/1966	Vietnam protests	N-ND
08/1966	Race riots in Chicago	N-ND
09/1966	Race violence in Atlanta	N-ND
08/1967	Race riots	N-ND
11/1967	Vietnam protest	N-ND
02/1968	Tet offensive	N-ND
04/1968	Johnson announces end to bombing	P-D
05/1968	Campus protests	N-ND
09/1968	Soviets move into Czechoslovakia	P-ND
11/1968	Johnson halts bombing in Vietnam	P-D
12/1968	Lowest unemployment in fifteen years	P-ND
04/1969	Campus protests about Vietnam	N-ND
08/1969	Successful moon launch	P-D
12/1969	Huge antiwar rally	N-ND
06/1970	Cambodia invasion	N-D
06/1970	Protest and killings at Kent State	N-ND
02/1971	Laos invasion	N-D
04/1971	Antiwar demonstrations	N-ND
09/1971	Nixon imposes wage-price controls	N-D
02/1972	Vietnam peace proposal announced	P-D
04/1972	Increase in war and bombing	N-D
01/1973	Vietnam peace accord	P-D
02/1973	Watergate burglars convicted	N-ND
03/1973	McCord letter to Sirica	N-ND
05/1973	Ervin Committee begins	N-ND
06/1973	Price freeze announced	N-D
07/1973	Dean testifies	N-ND
08/1973	Agnew investigation revealed	N-ND
09/1973	Ehrlichman, Liddy, and others indicted	N-ND
10/1973	Saturday night massacre	N-D
11/1973	Gap in tape revealed	N-ND

Poll

Date	Event	Coding
11/1973	Six Watergate figures sentenced	N-ND
04/1974	House judiciary hearings begin	N-ND
04/1974	Nixon ordered to pay back taxes	N-ND
05/1974	Judiciary hearings continue	N-ND
08/1974	*U.S. v. Nixon* announced (8/30)	N-ND
08/1974	Articles of Impeachment voted	N-ND
08/1974	Tapes incriminate Nixon	N-ND
10/1974	Ford pardons Nixon	N-D
05/1975	Cambodia falls	N-ND
06/1975	*Mayaguez* incident	P-ND
09/1978	Camp David Accords signed	P-D
12/1979	Hostages first seized in Iran	P-ND
01/1980	Soviets invade Afghanistan	P-ND
02/1980	Inflation sets new record high	N-ND
04/1980	Helicopter rescue plan fails	N-D
05/1980	Race rioting	N-ND
03/1981	Assassination attempt on Reagan	P-ND
08/1983	Soviets attack Korean airliner	P-ND
10/1983	Grenada invasion	P-D
03/1984	Record deficit balance of payments	N-ND
04/1984	Bombing of Nicaraguan harbors divulged	N-ND
01/1985	Cabinet shakeup	N-D
04/1985	Bitburg controversy	N-D
07/1985	Hostage incident (06/14–06/30)	P-ND
08/1985	Reagan surgery (07/13)	P-ND
01/1986	Space shuttle explodes	P-ND
04/1986	Libyan hostilities	P-ND
05/1986	Air strike on Libya	P-D
11/1986	First Iran-Contra revelation	N-ND
12/1986	Reagan claims Iran-Contra ignorance	N-ND
03/1987	Tower Committee report	N-ND
03/1987	Donald Regan resigns	N-ND
05/1987	Iran-Contra hearings	N-ND
05/1987	Persian Gulf attack on U.S.	P-ND
06/1987	Iran-Contra hearings continue	N-ND
06/1987	U.S. escorts Kuwaiti tankers	P-D
07/1987	Iran-Contra hearings continue	N-ND
10/1987	Stock market plunges	N-ND

Poll Date	Event	Coding
11/1987	Iran-Contra report by Congress	N-ND
12/1987	U.S.-U.S.S.R. treaty signed	P-D
01/1988	Meese investigation	N-ND
04/1988	Justice Department investigated	N-ND
04/1988	Marines enter Panama	P-D
05/1988	Senate ratifies INF treaty	P-D

III. POOLED ANALYSIS OF PRESIDENTIAL APPROVAL

Studies of presidential approval have either modeled approval ratings for each administration (for example, Kernell 1978; Ostrom and Simon 1985), or have analyzed pooled approval ratings for numerous administrations (for example, Mueller 1970; Ragsdale 1984). Since our goal is to present a general model of approval within and across presidencies, we analyze pooled approval ratings.[1] By pooling monthly presidential support ratings for eight administrations, presidential approval may be partitioned into three distinct and exhaustive components. The first component consists of interadministration differences in approval. These differences are captured by the inclusion of indicator variables that distinguish between administrations. The second component, overlooked in the literature to date, consists of variations in approval over the course of the presidential term common to all administrations. The final component consists of distinct variables reflecting the performance of the economy and the occurrence of good and bad events within administrations. Pooled analysis is thus particularly useful for disentangling these multiple components. The approach allows us to isolate statistically the variation unique to individual administrations, identify temporal patterns common to all administrations and, with those general influences controlled, evaluate the specific effects of the economy and good and bad events.

These components may be expressed more formally as:

$$Approval_{it} = \mu_t + \gamma_i$$

$$+ \ \beta_2 Misery_{it}$$

$$+ \ \beta_3 Positive\ Events_{it}$$

$$+ \ \beta_4 Negative\ Events_{it}$$

$$+ \ e_{it}$$

$i = 1, 2, \ldots, N$ (total number of administrations)
$t = 1, 2, \ldots, T$ (total number of months)

where:

γ_i is the intercept change attributable to president i.

μ_t is the intercept change attributable to month t.

$Economy_{it}$ is the effect of the economy ($MISERY$ or $INFLA$-$TION$) for president i in month t.

$Positive\ Events_{it}$ is the occurrence of a positive-predicted event for president i in month t.

$Negative Events_{it}$ is the occurrence of a negative-predicted event for president i in month t.

e_{it} is the error term.

IV. POISSON REGRESSION ANALYSIS

The presidential activities analyzed in Chapter 3 and the foreign affairs matters examined in Chapter 5 take on only nonnegative integer values, the typical definition of events. For events, Ordinary Least Squares Regression, suitable for variables measured at the interval/ratio level, is inappropriate. In addition, techniques such as Probit or Logit that are designed for dichotomous dependent variables also are not appropriate for events. Instead, Exponential Poisson Regression (EPR) analysis was employed. This technique is ideally suited to events count data. For an excellent discussion of this methodology, see Gary King, "Statistical Models for Political Science Events Counts: Bias in Conventional Procedures and Evidence for the Exponential Poisson Regression Model," *American Journal of Political Science* 32 (3 [August 1988]): 837–63; and King, *Unifying Political Methodology* (New York: Cambridge University Press, 1989). For a complete discussion of the modeling employed in this analysis, including issues of simultaneity, see Paul Brace and Barbara Hinckley, "Presidential Activities from Truman Through Reagan: What Difference Did They Make?" paper presented at the annual meeting of the Southern Political Science Association, Tampa, Florida, October 1991.

V. POOLED ANALYSIS OF PRESIDENTIAL-CONGRESSIONAL RELATIONS

Our analysis of presidential-congressional relations parallels and extends the analysis of presidential influence in Congress presented by Douglas Rivers and Nancy Rose.[2] They found that presidential success was tied to their public approval when the number of the presidential submissions were incorporated in the analysis.

Our analysis consists of three endogenous variables—approval, activity, and success—and conditioning or exogenous variables to be discussed below. From the reasoning presented in Chapter 4, we expect approval, activity, and success to be reciprocally related. Approval is expected to affect a president's congressional success but their success, in turn, could be expected to increase their approval ratings. In a similar manner, we could expect activity to increase success and heightened success to increase activity. Our central interest is in the nature of the reciprocating relationships between approval, activity, and success. These nonrecursive relationships require the application of special estimation procedures.

First, we apply pooled cross-sectional time series analysis, wherein we pool seven units (presidencies) by four time points (years).[3] Second, the nonrecursive relationships are modeled as a system of three endogenous variables and ten exogenous variables, as follows:[4]

[1] $Approval_{ti} = a + b_{11} Success_{ti} + b_{12} Activity_{ti} + Z_{11} Economy_{ti} + Z_{12} Positive Events_{ti} + Z_{13} Negative Events_{ti} + Z_{14} YR1_t + Z_{15} YR2_t + Z_{16} YR3_t + Z_{17} YR4_t + e_{ti}$

[2] $Activity_{ti} = a + b_{21} Success_{ti} + b_{22} Approval_{ti} + Z_{21} Split Cong. Control_{ti} + Z_{22} Opposing Cong. Control_{ti} + Z_{23} Pres. Party + Z_{24} YR1_t + Z_{25} YR2_t + Z_{26} YR3_t + Z_{27} YR4_t + e_{ti}$

[3] $Success_{ti} = a + b_{31} Approval_{ti} + b_{32} Activity_{ti} + Z_{31} Split Cong. Control_{ti} + Z_{32} Opposing Cong. Control_{ti} + Z_{33} YR1_t + Z_{34} YR2_t + Z_{35} YR3_t + Z_{36} YR4_t + e_{ti}$

$t = 1, \ldots, 4$

$i = $ Eisenhower, $\ldots$, Reagan

In this analysis, cycles in approval, activity, and success are explicitly incorporated by use of the time-point dummy variables that capture temporal fluctuations over the course of presidential administrations. The best way to demonstrate the usefulness of this approach is to consider the results of the analysis with and without the inclusion of these time-point variables. Comparing the following estimates with those presented in Appendix B, we can see that some very notable differences emerge.

The different results underscore the importance of controlling for the temporal cycles that influence these important relationships. First, the relationship between activity and approval emerges as plausible and statistically significant with the inclusion of the time-point variables. Second, the relationship between approval and success rate also emerges as plausible and significant when these time-point indicators are included. The inclusion of the time-point indicators has virtually no effect on the estimated effects of success on presidential activity. These variables do have the effect of reducing the magnitude of the influence of approval on activity, and rendering this relationship statistically insignificant. With this single exception, the time-point controls in these pooled models produce strong, plausible, and statistically significant relationships. In either case, the substantive conclusion about the effects of approval on activity remains the same.

Without Time Points Included as Instruments

	Approval		Activity		Success Rate	
Intercept	−43.30	−.69	245.09	.96	−.55	−.01
Approval	—	—	−9.63	−2.41*	.87	1.39
Activity	−.14	−1.09	—	—	.15	4.25**
Success	−1.66	2.51**	6.49	4.25**	—	—
Adjusted R^2	.19		.59		.39	

*Significant at $\alpha = .05$.
**Significant at $\alpha = .01$.

Appendix B

RESULTS OF ANALYSIS FOR CHAPTER 2

Analysis of Presidential Approval[a]

Variable	First Term				Second Term[c]			
	Using MISERY		Using INFLATION		Using MISERY		Using INFLATION	
	b	t	b	t		b	t	b	t
Misery/Inflation	-.98	-2.65***	-.16	-3.38***		-1.37	-1.43*	-.51	-4.14***
Positive Events	4.24	2.91***	4.28	2.96***		6.79	1.93**	4.76	1.49*
Negative Events	-1.80	-1.31*	-1.48	-1.08		-1.64	-.61	-2.69	-1.11
Truman	54.51	16.91***	62.34	13.84***	Eisenhower II	84.62	11.77***	114.79	11.37***
Eisenhower I	86.97	26.99***	95.80	19.81***	Nixon II	59.28	7.65***	118.99	6.98***
Kennedy	88.03	24.70***	95.77	19.81***	Reagan II	81.11	9.42***	236.30	5.88***
Johnson	67.02	21.24***	77.01	15.65***					
Nixon I	74.61	22.03***	86.37	15.21***					
Ford	64.66	15.55***	81.56	10.36***					
Carter	66.57	16.30***	90.20	9.31***					
Reagan I	71.74	16.07***	106.37	8.02***					

Analysis of Presidential Approval[a] (continued)

| | First Term | | | | Second Term[c] | | | |
| | Using MISERY | | Using INFLATION | | Using MISERY | | Using INFLATION | |
Variable	b	t	b	t	b	t	b	t
Month 1 →								
Month 48[b]								
N =	342				116			
Adjusted R^2 =	.75		.77		.56		.63	

Note: b refers to parameter estimate; t refers to T-statistic.

*Significant at α = .10 (one-tailed test).

**Significant at α = .05 (one-tailed test).

***Significant at α = .01 (one-tailed test)

[a]For a discussion of the pooled technique employed in this analysis, see Appendix A.

[b]The time-point indicators are illustrated in Chapter 2. All time-point coefficients beyond the sixth month are significant at or below the .05 level.

[c]A model excluding Nixon and one combining first and second terms show no difference in results.

Chapter Note:

The explanatory usefulness of each category (Events, Economy, and Time) of variables was also evaluated. To test these categories, models were run given categories excluded and the others remaining, providing estimates of the restricted sum of squared error. Computing the F-statistic for each category with appropriate degrees of freedom indicated that each category was statistically significant at the .01 level. In addition, interrelationships between categories of independent variables were estimated and in no instance did multicollinearity emerge as a problem. The overall explanatory power of the first-term model (with an R^2 of roughly .75) is similar to past studies that have analyzed fewer administrations. See, for example, Kernell (1978) and Charles Ostrom and Dennis Simon, "Promise and Performance: A Dynamic Model of Presidential Popularity," *American Political Science Review* (June 1985): 541–66. Models were also run using GLS to correct for autocorrelation. Those results were not appreciably different from those presented above.

RESULTS OF ANALYSIS FOR CHAPTER 3

Analysis of Influences on Presidential Activity[a]

I. The First Term

Independent Variables	Major Addresses		Foreign Trips		Domestic Trips	
	MLE	t	MLE	t	MLE	t
Approval $_{t-1}$	-.02	-1.66**	-.03	-2.97***	-.004	-.98
Inflation	-.03	-2.41***	-.03	-3.88***	.02	4.20***
Good Luck	.49	1.52*	-1.11	-2.45***	-.24	-1.45*
Bad Luck	.13	0.35	-.46	-1.52*	-.01	-.03
Hard Choice	1.03	2.52***	-.29	-.64	.17	.82
Congressional Election	.04	0.17	.11	.76	.30	3.59***
Presidential Election	.35	1.29*	.65	3.01***	.30	2.61***
Eisenhower	1.11	1.86**	11.34	.20	-.11	-.46
Kennedy	1.17	1.89**	12.85	.22	.56	2.28**
Johnson	.60	1.29*	12.39	.22	.03	.19
Nixon	1.68	2.63***	13.71	.24	-.30	-1.22
Ford	2.53	2.31**	14.74	.26	-.33	-.83
Carter	3.78	2.47***	16.05	.28	-1.85	-3.08***
Reagan	6.47	2.57***	18.39	.32	-3.00	-3.29***
Intercept	1.91	1.45*	-8.45	-0.15	-1.01	-2.15**

N = 342

Analysis of Influences on Presidential Activity[a] *(continued)*

II. The Second Term

Independent Variables	Major Addresses		Foreign Trips		Domestic Trips	
	MLE	t	MLE	t	MLE	t
Approval $_{t-1}$	.006	.33	-.01	-.89	.04	3.45***
Inflation	-.05	-1.47*	-.05	-3.05***	.03	1.76**
Good Luck	-.23	-.31	-.03	-.06	-1.43	-1.97**
Bad Luck	.42	1.10	-1.53	-4.42***	-0.20	-.91
Hard Choice	-.18	-.24	-9.86	-.20	-1.63	-1.62*
Congressional Election	-.25	-.62	-.74	-2.56***	-0.71	-2.59***
Presidential Election	.003	.007	1.36	5.67***	-1.69	-1.69**
Nixon	2.71	1.67**	3.64	4.26***	.68	.68
Reagan	11.66	1.49*	11.97	3.01***	-1.44	-1.44*
Intercept	2.83	.81	5.09	2.72***	-4.48	-2.71***

N = 113

Note: MLE refers to Maximum Likelihood Estimate; *t* refers to T-statistic.

*Significant at α = .10 (one-tailed test).

**Significant at α = .05 (one-tailed test).

***Significant at α = .01 (one-tailed test).

[a]Poisson regression was employed in the analysis of these events. For a discussion of this technique, see Appendix A.

RESULTS OF ANALYSIS FOR CHAPTER 4

Presidential Success and Activity in Congress

Average Annual *Success Rates*		*Average Number of* *Positions Taken (Activity)*	
Kennedy	84.5	Johnson	265.2
Johnson	81.5	Carter	217.2
Eisenhower	79.2	Reagan	189.2
Carter	76.4	Kennedy	186.7
Nixon	73.0	Ford	136.0
Reagan	71.9	Nixon	124.5
Ford	57.6	Eisenhower	91.7
Average	75.2	Average	177.1

Analysis of the Predeterminants of President-Congressional Relations[a]

	Position Taking			Presidential Success			Presidential Approval		
Variable	b	t	Variable	b	t	Variable	b	t
Split Congress	153.24	5.28***	Split Congress	-8.80	-2.16**	Economy	-.09	-3.42***
Oppositional Congress	91.37	3.78***	Oppositional Congress	-12.89	-4.13***	Positive Events	.56	.31
Democratic President	192.23	8.15***				Negative Events	-3.52	-1.66*
Year 1	44.21	1.60*	Year 1	83.94	28.51***	Year 1	77.85	12.35***
Year 2	29.10	1.23	Year 2	81.50	27.68***	Year 2	73.36	10.39***
Year 3	14.10	.59	Year 3	80.18	25.58***	Year 3	66.24	10.50***
Year 4	56.58	2.20**	Year 4	77.30	21.47***	Year 4	75.25	8.21***
Adjusted R^2	.56			.42			.36	

Note: b refers to parameter estimate; t refers to T-statistic.

*Significant at α = .10 (one-tailed test).

**Significant at α = .05 (one-tailed test).

***Significant at α = .01 (one-tailed test).

[a]For a discussion of the methodology involved in this analysis, see Appendix A.

RESULTS OF ANALYSIS FOR CHAPTER 4 (CONTINUED)

Analysis of Presidential-Congressional Relations[a]

Independent Variable	Dependent Variable					
	Presidential Approval		Congressional Success		Presidential Position Taking	
	b	t	b	t	b	t
Presidential Approval	—	—	.75	2.75*	-5.86	-3.44*
Congressional Success	1.29	3.33*	—	—	5.85	3.97*
Presidential Position Taking	-.20	-2.64*	.15	4.44*	—	—
Intercept	-9.41		6.06		-21.30	
Adjusted R^2	.40		.43		.45	

Note: b refers to parameter estimate; t refers to T-statistic.
*Significant at $\alpha = .01$ (one-tailed test).

[a] Two Stage Least Squares regression was used in this analysis. For a discussion of this technique, see Appendix A.

Figure B.1 Mapping the Tradeoffs: A Path Diagram of
Presidential-Congressional Relations

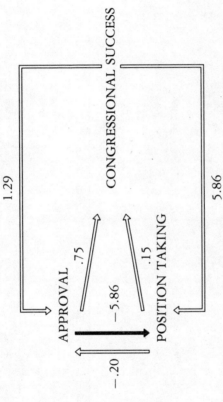

Unstandardized Relationships (All Significant at p = .01)

RESULTS OF ANALYSIS FOR CHAPTER 5

Analysis of First-Term Foreign Policy Events[a]

Independent Variable	Force°		Rally#		Foreign Policy Address		Major Diplomacy%		Congressional Message&		Treaty	
	MLE	t	MLE	t	MLE	t	MLE	t	MLE	t	MLE	t
Approval $_{t-1}$	-.01	-.72	-.004	-.32	.002	.16	-.002	-.10	.005	.66	-.04	-1.29*
Hard Choice	-6.9	-.14	-.74	-.17	1.23	2.03**	1.33	1.25	.65	1.27	-8.91	-.04
Bad Luck	1.32	2.61***	.71	1.47*	.98	2.33**	-8.36	-.12	.11	.31	-8.98	-.07
Misery	.23	2.62***	.15	2.23**	.08	1.12	-.14	-.96	-.07	-1.54*	-.12	-.67
Intercept	-3.67	-2.37***	-2.98	-2.59***	-2.92	-2.71***	-2.84	-1.59*	-1.24	-1.86**	-1.25	-.56
Year 2	.30	.57	-.11	-.25	.21	.49	-.68	-.55	.13	.44	-.31	-.21
Year 3	-.22	-.33	-.26	-.26	.36	.81	-1.19	1.38*	.27	1.19	-9.28	-.12
Year 4	-.23	-.33	.11	.24	-.20	-.40	.06	.05	.13	.39	.90	.71

N = 349

Note: MLE refers to Maximum Likelihood Estimate; *t* refers to T-statistic.

*Significant at α = .10 (one-tailed test).

**Significant at α = .05 (one-tailed test).

***Significant at α = .01 (one-tailed test).

[a]Poisson regression was employed in this analysis. For a discussion of this technique, see Appendix A.

°Hard choice (α = .05) and inflation (α = .01) are significant in a model with all independent variables lagged one month.

#Inflation (α = .05) is significant when substituted for Misery in a model with all independent variables lagged one month.

%Hard choice (α = .01) is significant in a model with all independent variables lagged one month.

&Misery is significant in a model with all independent variables lagged one month.

Analysis of Second-Term Foreign Policy Events

Independent Variable	Force		Rally		Foreign Policy Address		Major Diplomacy		Congressional Message		Treaty	
	MLE	t	MLE	t	MLE	t	MLE	t	MLE	t	MLE	t
$Approval_{t-1}$	−.006	−.21	−.01	−.41	.01	.31	−.03	−1.13	−.02	−.88	−.64	−1.47
Hard Choice	−7.19	−.10	−7.17	−.14	−7.31	−.16	.88	.74	.25	.22	1.95	−.006
Bad Luck	−.69	−.62	−.38	−.47	−.25	−.31	−.89	−.89	.28	.44	−10.91	−.09
Misery	.17	.54	.14	.59	−.41	−1.40	−.36	−1.03	−.31	−1.18	−1.86	−1.50
Intercept	−3.96	−1.28	−2.87	−1.12	−.41	−.15	.99	.34	.93	.42	22.29	.29
Year 2	1.11	.97	.40	.45	.74	.83	.79	.71	.04	.06	−3.26	−.03
Year 3	1.26	1.08	1.07	1.27	.98	1.29	1.09	1.08	.31	.43	19.80	.27
Year 4	.11	.08	.54	.59	−.12	−.13	.63	.57	−.38	−.48	20.21	.27

$N = 113$

Note: None of the above relationships is significant at or below $\alpha = .05$. No significant patterns were found substituting inflation or the "High Misery" variable discussed above for the Misery variable. Alternative lags also revealed no significant relationships. *MLE* refers to Maximum Likelihood Estimate; *t* refers to T-statistic.

RESULTS OF ANALYSIS FOR CHAPTER 5 (CONTINUED)

Analysis of Rally and Nonrally Uses of Force[a]

Independent Variable	First Term Nonrally		First Term Rally		Second Term Nonrally		Second Term Rally	
	MLE	t	MLE	t	MLE	t	MLE	t
Approval $_{t-1}$	−.01	−.52	−.03	−.91	−.04	−1.05	.02	.27
Hard Choice	−6.62	−.14	−7.55	−.06	−7.09	−.06	−8.58	−.04
Bad Luck	1.69	3.15*	−8.02	−.10	−.45	−.39	−8.21	−.07
Misery	.30	2.99*	−.09	−.46	−.07	−.16	.66	.91
Intercept	−5.02	−2.63	−.45	−.15	8.58	−.15	−9.39	−1.27
Year 2	.69	.99	−.83	−.83	8.32	.14	−.09	−.07
Year 3	.23	.29	−1.77	−1.27	9.37	.16	−8.98	−.07
Year 4	.37	.46	−9.31	−.19	8.27	.14	9.11	−.07
	N = 342				N = 113			

Note: MLE refers to Maximum Likelihood Estimate; t refers to T-statistic.
*Significant at α = .01.

[a]Poisson regression was used in this analysis. For a discussion of this technique, see Appendix A.

International Events and Presidential Approval (First and Second Terms Combined)

	Dependent Variable = Presidential Approval									
	Lag of Independent Variable									
	t		t − 1		t − 2		t − 3		t − 4	
Independent Variable	b	t	b	t	b	t	b	t	b	t
Treaty Announcement	-1.92	-.78	-1.77	-.72	-1.72	-.68	-2.96	-1.19	-2.05	-.82
Rally: No Force	3.30	1.61*	4.51	2.18**	2.40	1.21	2.12	1.08	2.71	1.39*
Rally: Force	6.37	2.84***	5.80	2.59***	5.63	2.61***	5.01	2.35***	2.99	1.42*
Force: No Rally	-1.11	-.79	-1.04	-.73	-.23	-.16	-.61	-.44	.86	.62
Non—Foreign Policy Rally	4.43	2.42***	.46	.50	.39	.44	.49	.55	.69	.78
Foreign Policy Speech	-.71	-.76	.90	1.56*	1.09	1.91**	.81	1.42*	-.82	-.14
Message to Congress	-.13	-.22	-.58	-.38	-.97	-.64	.58	.38	-1.97	-1.30*
Major Diplomacy	2.12	1.41*	5.05	2.76***	1.89	1.00	3.04	1.62*	3.14	1.56*
Negative Events	-.96	-.93	-1.16	-1.16	-.93	-.95	-1.59	-1.61*	-1.50	-1.54*
Misery	-.89	-2.79***	-.91	-2.84***	-.91	-2.87***	-.91	-2.86***	-.97	-3.03***
Intercept[a]	54.39	24.35***	54.01	24.29***	50.23	24.12***	49.80	22.38***	49.44	19.10***
Adjusted R^2	.76		.76		.78		.79		.79	
N = 455										

Note: b refers to parameter estimate; t refers to T-statistic.
*Significant at α = .10 (one-tailed test).
**Significant at α = .05 (one-tailed test).
***Significant at α = .01 (one-tailed test).

[a]Quarterly and administration dummy variables were used in this analysis but are not displayed for presentational simplicity. Because of the structure of these data, pooled Durbin Watson d could not be computed. As a regression with dummy variables, this analysis is equivalent to an analysis of variance. The parameter estimates for foreign policy events are the averages for those months in which the events occurred, or the months following the events in the case of the lagged models.

RESULTS OF ANALYSIS FOR CHAPTER 7

Explaining Bush's Popularity[a]: The First Thirty Months

Variable	Dependent Variable			
	Approval		Deviation from Predecessors (Truman to Reagan)	
	b	t	b	t
Positive Events	4.45	2.22*	3.76	1.84*
Negative Events	-14.16	-5.35**	-13.99	-5.04**
Major Addresses	3.86	2.69**	3.40	2.21*
Domestic Travel	-.86	-2.71**	-.81	-2.40**
Foreign Travel	-1.23	-4.30**[b]	-1.29	-4.19**[b]
Congressional Messages	-8.04	-2.83**	-7.26	-2.34*
Economy (Misery)	2.03	1.92*[b]	1.70	1.54
Time into Term	.13	1.31	.84	7.02**
Intercept	56.67	7.95**	-7.46	-.98
Adjusted R^2	.78		.88	
$N = 29$				

Note: b refers to parameter estimate; t refers to T-statistic.

*Significant at $\alpha \leq .05$ (one-tailed test).

**Significant at $\alpha \leq .01$ (one-tailed test).

[a]Generalized Least Squares was used in this analysis.

[b]Two-tailed test.

Notes

Chapter 1: Being Liked and Being President

1. See Jane Mayer and Doyle McManus, *Landslide: The Unmaking of the President 1984–1988* (Boston: Houghton Mifflin, 1988), pp. 43, 44.
2. Ibid., pp. 203–5, 279.
3. Woodrow Wilson, *Constitutional Government* (1908, reprint, New York: Columbia University Press, 1961); Richard Neustadt, *Presidential Power* (New York: Wiley, 1980).
4. Clinton Rossiter, *The American Presidency*, rev. ed. (New York: Mentor, 1960), pp. 28–36.
5. Thomas Cronin, *The State of the Presidency*, 2nd ed. (Boston: Little, Brown, 1980), chap. 3.
6. Ibid., pp. 76–90. See also Harold Barger, "Suspending Disbelief: The President in Pre-College Textbooks," *Presidential Studies Quarterly* (Winter 1990): 55–70.
7. James David Barber, *The Presidential Character: Predicting Performance in the White House*, 3rd ed. (Englewood Cliffs, N.J.: Prentice-Hall, 1985).

Chapter 2: The New Referendum

1. Robert H. Ferrell, ed., *Off the Record: The Private Papers of Harry S. Truman* (New York: Harper & Row, 1980), p. 310.
2. *New York Times*, 9 October 1990, p. A-21.
3. Data for the following sections are taken from the Gallup series found in George Gallup, *The Gallup Poll*, Vols. 2 and 3 (New York: Random

House, 1972); and *The Gallup Poll,* Vols. 1 and 2 (Wilmington: Scholarly Resources, 1978); and later issues of the *Gallup Monthly Report.* The percent approving of the president is recorded monthly, with the small number of missing months included in the series through interpolation. When more than one poll is reported in a month, the result closest to mid-month is taken.

4. First terms thus include Truman (1949–52), Eisenhower (1953–56), Kennedy (1961–November 1963), Johnson (1965–68), Nixon (1969–72), Ford (August 1974–76), Carter (1977–80), and Reagan (1981–84). While Ford's succession to the office was historically unique and his administration short, the significant dimensions of his presidency were found to be remarkably similar to those of the other administrations.

5. Fred Greenstein, "What the President Means to Americans," in *Choosing the President,* ed. James David Barber (New York: American Assembly, 1974), pp. 130–31.

6. For this material, see Barbara Hinckley, *The Symbolic Presidency: How Presidents Present Themselves* (New York: Routledge, 1990), pp. 9–13.

7. Ibid. See especially chap. 6.

8. For the Johnson quote, see Doris Kearns, *Lyndon Johnson and the American Dream* (New York: Harper & Row, 1976), p. 226. For his discussion and the Mondale quote, see Paul Light, *The President's Agenda* (Baltimore: Johns Hopkins University Press, 1982), p. 13.

9. Others have also made this argument. See Thomas Cronin, *The State of the Presidency,* 2nd ed. (Boston: Little, Brown, 1980), p. 115; and Hugh Heclo and Lester Salamon, eds., *The Illusion of Presidential Government* (Boulder: Westview, 1981), p. 292.

10. Henry Chappell, Jr., "Economic Performance, Voting, and Political Support: A Unified Approach," *Review of Economics and Statistics,* LXXII (May 1990): 313–20; Samuel Kernell, "Explaining Presidential Popularity," *American Political Science Review* (June 1978): 506–22; Donald Kinder, "Presidents, Prosperity, and Public Opinion," *Public Opinion Quarterly* 45 (Spring 1981): 1–21; Helmut Norpoth, "Economics, Politics and the Cycle of Presidential Popularity," *Political Behavior* 6, no. 3 (1984): 253–71; Charles Ostrom and Renee Smith, "Presidential Popularity and the Economy." Paper presented at the annual meeting of the Midwest Political Science Association, Chicago, Illinois, April 1990.

11. See Chappell.

12. See Kinder.

13. The Casey and Eisenhower quotes are found in Douglas Hibbs, Jr., *The American Political Economy: Macroeconomics and Electoral Politics* (Cambridge: Harvard University Press, 1987), pp. 142, 185.

14. See Stephen Haynes and Joe Stone, "An Integrated Test for Electoral Cycles in the U.S. Economy," *Review of Economics and Statistics,* LXXI (August 1989): 426–34. See also Hibbs, chap. 8.

15. See Mark Hertsgaard, *On Bended Knee: The Press and the Reagan Presidency* (New York: Farrar Straus Giroux, 1988), p. 116.

16. See, for example, the discussion and quotations in Mark Rozell, *The Press and the Carter Presidency* (Boulder: Westview, 1989).

17. Stephen Ambrose, *Eisenhower: The President* (New York: Simon & Schuster, 1984), p. 344.

18. Fred Greenstein, *The Hidden-Hand Presidency: Eisenhower as Leader* (New York: Basic Books, 1982), pp. 98–99.

19. Letter from Eisenhower to Emmet Hughes, 10 December 1953, quoted in Greenstein, p. 99.

20. Ferrell, p. 211.

21. Speech to the nation, 8 September 1974.

22. Quoted in Larry Berman, "Paths Chosen and Opportunities Lost," in *Leadership in the Modern Presidency,* ed. Fred Greenstein (Cambridge: Harvard University Press, 1988), p. 163.

23. Doris Kearns, *Lyndon Johnson and the American Dream* (New York: Harper & Row, 1976), pp. 214, 215.

24. Ibid., p. 257.

25. Ibid., p. 315.

26. John P. Burke and Fred I. Greenstein, *How Presidents Test Reality: Decisions on Vietnam, 1954 and 1965* (New York: Russell Sage Foundation, 1989), p. 13.

27. Erwin Hargrove, *Jimmy Carter and the Politics of the Public Good* (Baton Rouge: Louisiana State University Press, 1988).

28. James David Barber, *Presidential Character: Predicting Performance in the White House,* 3rd ed. (Englewood Cliffs, N.J.: Prentice-Hall, 1985).

29. Peter Lyon, *Eisenhower: Portrait of the Hero* (Boston: Little, Brown, 1974), p. 778. See also Stephen Ambrose, *Eisenhower: The President* (New York: Simon & Schuster, 1984), pp. 480, 481.

30. See Lowi.

31. Mark Rozell, "The Press Strategies of Presidents Ford, Carter and Reagan: Is It True that 'No White House Can Do Much About a President's Image'?" Paper delivered at the Western Political Science Association, Seattle, Washington, 22 March 1991.

32. See the percentage of the vote for the two major-party candidates, as reported in *America Votes,* vol. 18 (Washington, D.C.: CQ Press, 1988), p. 5. In all cases, the percentage of the two-party vote was higher than that of the total vote, which included votes for third-party candidates.

1948	Truman	52.4
1952	Eisenhower	55.4
1960	Kennedy	50.1
1964	Johnson	61.3
1968	Nixon	50.4
1976	Carter	51.1
1980	Reagan	55.3
1988	Bush	53.9

Chapter 3: Actions and Reactions

1. Samuel Kernell, *Going Public: New Strategies of Presidential Leadership* (Washington, D.C.: CQ Press, 1986).
2. Ibid., pp. 137, 138.
3. See Barbara Hinckley, *The Symbolic Presidency: How Presidents Present Themselves* (New York: Routledge, 1990), chap. 4.
4. The activities are taken from *The Public Papers* (Washington, D.C.: Government Printing Office, 1949–90), various volumes.
5. Quoted in Hinckley, p. 16. For the similarity among the presidents, see chaps. 1 and 2.
6. Presidential election years are positively but not significantly related to domestic travel when Truman and Eisenhower are excluded.
7. See, for example, Lyn Ragsdale, "The Politics of Public Speechmaking," *American Political Science Review* (December 1984): 971–84.
8. Minor remarks were analyzed with the other activities. Because minor remarks and domestic trips typically occur together, results from minor remarks were nearly identical to those for domestic travel.
9. Kernell, p. 96.
10. Kernell, p. 87, as cited in Douglass Cater, "How a President Helps Form Public Opinion," *New York Times Magazine,* 26 February 1961, p. 12.
11. Ibid., p. 87.
12. See Michael Gross and Martha Kumar, *Portraying the President* (Baltimore: Johns Hopkins University Press, 1981), chap. 10.
13. These results hold whether or not the second Nixon administration is included.
14. Cited in Bob Schieffer and Gary Paul Gates, *The Acting President* (New York: Dutton, 1989), p. 308.
15. Mark Hertsgaard, *On Bended Knee: The Press and the Reagan Presidency* (New York: Farrar Straus Giroux, 1988).
16. For the same results from a different analysis, see Dennis Simon and Charles Ostrom, Jr., "The Impact of Televised Speeches and Foreign

Travel on Presidential Approval," *Public Opinion Quarterly* 53 (1989): 58–82.

17. As shown on Cable Network News, 8 January 1992.

Chapter 4: Activity, Popularity, and Success in Congress

1. Richard Neustadt, *Presidential Power: The Politics of Leadership from FDR to Carter* (New York: Wiley, 1980).

2. George Edwards III, *At the Margins: Presidential Leadership in Congress* (New Haven: Yale University Press, 1989); Jon Bond and Richard Fleisher, *The President in the Legislative Arena* (Chicago: University of Chicago Press, 1990).

3. See Douglas Rivers and Nancy Rose, "Passing the President's Program: Public Opinion and Presidential Influence in Congress," *American Journal of Political Science* 29 (May 1985): 183–96; and Richard Brody, *Assessing the President: The Media, Elite Opinion, and Public Support* (Stanford: Stanford University Press, 1991), p. 21. Rivers and Rose look at presidential success from 1954 through 1974. As Appendix A shows, the difference between these results and our own, on the one hand, and those by Edwards and Bond and Fleisher, on the other, is the addition of these other influences into the analysis. In particular, once we control for the effects of time, popularity has a strong effect on presidential success.

4. Paul Light, *The President's Agenda: Domestic Policy Choice from Kennedy to Carter* (Baltimore: Johns Hopkins University Press, 1982); Theodore Lowi, *The Personal President* (Ithaca, N.Y.: Cornell University Press, 1985).

5. For the way this measure of activity was derived, see Gary King and Lyn Ragsdale, *The Elusive Executive* (Washington, D.C.: CQ Press, 1988), p. 42. The total number of bills, rather than the percentage of those bills, was found to be the best comparison among presidents. Due to the increasing congressional work load, the number of non-presidential bills has increased greatly. If a percentage was used, this would give the misleading impression that presidential activity has declined. On the increasing congressional work load, see Norman Ornstein et al., *Vital Statistics on Congress, 1987–88* (Washington, D.C.: American Enterprise Institute, 1987), p. 159.

6. Roll calls have their limits, of course, in measuring activity and success, as earlier authors who have used them have pointed out. Roll calls can exaggerate success—by including noncontroversial votes where success is assured and by excluding all bills stopped in committee and thus not subject to roll-call vote. Also, roll calls do not measure the actual

priorities of presidents, treating all legislation equally and including far more than the three or four proposals the administration may be actively working for. Nevertheless, scores based on this roll-call measure correlate highly with several alternative measures. And since these overall activity and success rates are widely reported and discussed, the measure has the advantage of tapping the most obvious and visible effects that people would like to have explained.

7. The annual figure is taken to accord with the annual measures for legislative activity and success. Note that the timing of roll calls over the months of a year is a congressional decision, independent of the White House, largely determined by the actions of committees and the leadership. Therefore, monthly measures of activity or success or cumulative measures within a year say nothing about presidential politics. Since most legislation either occurs annually or is scheduled to be decided within one yearly congressional session, annual measures seem the most appropriate and so require comparable annual approval ratings. Since these annual measures reflect general tendencies only, we weigh the results against the proposition that public approval affects legislative success. We thus ask whether popular presidents do indeed win more votes on Capitol Hill and how important this popularity is in the context of other influences.

8. Aage Clausen, *How Congressmen Decide: A Policy Focus* (New York: St. Martin's, 1973); Clausen and Carl Van Horn, "The Congressional Response to a Decade of Change, *Journal of Politics* 39 (August 1977): 624–66; John Kingdon, *Congressmen's Voting Decisions*, 2nd ed. (New York: Harper & Row, 1981).

9. See Light.

10. The effects of administrative life cycles on presidential-congressional relations can be seen by examining the bivariate correlations between presidential approval and success rate in Congress for each year of the presidential administrations:

Presidential Approval	Success Rate
Year 1	.728
Year 2	.721
Year 3	.325
Year 4	− .603

Given the striking variation in these results over the course of a term, it is clear that the effect of presidential life cycles must be included in the analysis.

11. Readers should understand why presidents facing split-party congresses appear to take the most positions. Since these concern only Republican presidents, they point out that the Republicans facing split-control took more positions than those facing opposing-party congresses.

12. We rank the presidents based on the differences between their administrations (the residuals) from the analyses of success and activity shown in Appendix B. For example, the residuals from the analysis of activity represent the level of activity above (or below) that accounted for by party, cycles, or success rate. Positive residuals indicate a level of activity above what the model would predict, given the objective circumstances controlled for by the model. Conversely, negative residuals indicate that an administration was on average less active than the model would predict. The same procedure was applied to the residuals from the analysis of success.

13. Kearns, p. 227.

14. Lawrence O'Brien, *No Final Victories: A Life in Politics from John F. Kennedy to Watergate* (New York: Ballantine, 1974).

15. Mark Peterson, *Legislating Together: The White House and Capitol Hill from Eisenhower to Reagan* (Cambridge: Harvard University Press, 1990), p. 243.

16. Ibid., p. 233.

17. Rowland Evans, Jr., and Robert Novak, *Nixon in the White House: The Frustration of Power* (New York: Vintage, 1972), p. 11.

18. See Peterson, p. 251.

19. Erwin Hargrove, *Jimmy Carter: The Politics of the Public Good* (Baton Rouge: Louisiana State University Press, 1988).

20. Ibid., p. 67.

21. Ibid., p. 192.

22. Charles O. Jones, *The Trusteeship Presidency: Jimmy Carter and the United States Congress* (Baton Rouge: Louisiana State University Press, 1988), p. 201.

23. Paul Peterson and Mark Rom, "Lower Taxes, More Spending, and Budget Deficits," in *The Reagan Legacy,* ed. Charles Jones (Chatham, N.J.: Chatham House, 1988), p. 214.

24. James MacGregor Burns, *Leadership* (New York: Harper & Row, 1978), pp. 388, 389.

Chapter 5: Long Views and Short Goals

1. Bob Woodward, *Veil: The Secret Wars of the CIA: 1981–1987* (New York: Simon & Schuster, 1987), pp. 323, 336; Theodore Draper, *A*

Very Thin Line: The Iran-Contra Affairs (New York: Hill and Wang, 1991), p. 84.

2. Draper, pp. 81–84.

3. Barbara Hinckley, *Less Than Meets the Eye: President, Congress, and Foreign Policy* (New York: Twentieth Century Fund, forthcoming), chap. 5.

4. John Mueller, "Presidential Popularity from Truman to Johnson," *American Political Science Review,* March 1970, pp. 18–24; George Edwards III, *The Public Presidency* (New York: St. Martin's, 1983); Charles Ostrom and Dennis Simon, "Promise and Performance: A Dynamic Model of Presidential Popularity," *American Political Science Review,* June 1985, pp. 1096–1119.

5. For the most recent list, see Ellen Collier, ed., *Instances of the Use of United States Armed Forces Abroad, 1798–1989* (Washington, D.C.: Congressional Research Service, The Library of Congress, 1989). Another list available is limited to nuclear-capable force from 1953 to 1976. See Barry Blechman and Stephen Kaplan, *Force Without War* (Washington, D.C.: Brookings Institution, 1978), and its use in the Ostrom and Job study, cited below.

6. Charles Ostrom and Brian Job, "The President and the Political Use of Force," *American Political Science Review,* June 1986, pp. 541–66. A change in one standard deviation of an economic misery index increased the probability of the use of force by 20 percent. See also Patrick James and John Oneal, "Influences on the President's Use of Force," *Journal of Conflict Resolution* (June 1991): 307–32.

7. A "high misery" variable was created that equaled one when misery was equal to or greater than its mean plus one standard deviation (and zero otherwise). This variable was significantly related to uses of non-rally force ($\alpha = .01$). It was not significantly related to force occurring during international rally events.

8. See, for example, Stanley Kutler, *The Wars of Watergate* (New York: Knopf, 1990), pp. 546–47.

9.   Ranking Presidents on Foreign Affairs Activities Per Month

Rank	Use of Force	Foreign Policy Speech	Major Diplomacy	Message to Congress
1	Reagan I	Nixon I	Nixon II	Truman
2	Reagan II	Kennedy	Johnson/ Reagan II	Nixon I
3	Ford	Nixon II	Eisenhower II	Eisenhower
4	Johnson	Reagan I	Kennedy	Kennedy

5	Kennedy	Reagan II	Carter	Carter
6	Nixon II	Carter	Nixon I	Johnson
7	Carter	Truman/ Eisenhower II	Eisenhower II	Nixon II
8	Truman/ Eisenhower I	Ford	Ford	Reagan I/II
9	Eisenhower II/ Nixon I	Johnson	Truman/ Reagan I	Eisenhower II/ Ford

10. See Hinckley, chap. 5.
11. See John Mueller, *Wars, Presidents and Public Opinion* (New York: Wiley, 1973), chaps. 2 and 3; Michael Sullivan, *The Vietnam War* (Lexington: University of Kentucky Press, 1985), chap. 4.
12. Michael MacKuen, "Political Drama, Economic Conditions, and the Dynamics of Presidential Popularity," *American Journal of Political Science* (May 1983): 165–92.
13. The studies by Mueller, Edwards, and Ostrom and Simon, respectively, were cited in note 4.
14. Miroslav Nincic and Barbara Hinckley, "Foreign Policy and the Evaluation of Presidential Candidates," *Journal of Conflict Resolution* (June 1991): 333–55.

Chapter 6: The Presidents in Office

1. Barbara Honegger, *October Surprise* (New York: Tudor, 1989), p. 3.
2. See Barbara Hinckley, *The Symbolic Presidency: How Presidents Present Themselves* (New York: Routledge, 1990), pp. 60–64.
3. James David Barber, *The Presidential Character: Predicting Performance in the White House,* 3rd ed. (Englewood Cliffs, N.J.: Prentice-Hall, 1985).
4. Robert Ferrell, ed. *Off the Record: The Private Papers of Harry S. Truman* (New York: Harper & Row, 1980), p. 122, entry for 6 January 1948.
5. Cabell Phillips, *The Truman Presidency* (New York: Macmillan, 1966), p. 13.
6. Carl Anthony, *First Ladies* (New York: Morrow, 1990), p. 530.
7. See Phillips, p. 161.
8. See especially Barber, pp. 237, 252.
9. Alonzo Hamby, "Harry S. Truman: Insecurity and Responsibility," in *Leadership in the Modern Presidency,* ed. Fred Greenstein (Cambridge: Harvard University Press, 1988), pp. 41–75.
10. See Phillips, esp. pp. 13–47.

11. Ferrell, p. 168, entry for 1 November 1949.

12. Stephen Ambrose, *Eisenhower: The President* (New York: Simon & Schuster, 1984); Fred Greenstein, *The Hidden-Hand Presidency: Eisenhower as Leader* (New York: Basic Books, 1982).

13. See Barber, p. 134, although Barber admits that Eisenhower's case is difficult.

14. Ambrose, p. 344.

15. Greenstein, "Leadership Theorist in the White House," in *Leadership in the Modern Presidency,* p. 105.

16. Ibid., p. 104.

17. Arthur M. Schlesinger, Jr., *A Thousand Days* (Boston: Houghton Mifflin, 1965); Theodore Sorensen, *Kennedy* (New York: Harper & Row, 1965).

18. Barber, p. 287.

19. Larry Berman, "Paths Chosen and Opportunities Lost," in *Leadership in the Modern Presidency,* p. 135.

20. Ibid., p. 140.

21. Ibid., p. 143.

22. McGeorge Bundy memo, cited in Berman, p. 162.

23. See Kearns, p. 303; Berman, pp. 137, 138; and Kenneth Johnson, ed., *The Johnson Presidency* (Lanham, Md.: University Press of America, 1987), p. 32.

24. Barber, pp. 79–83.

25. Kearns, pp. 214, 215.

26. Berman, p. 163.

27. Robert Peabody, *Leadership in Congress* (Boston: Little, Brown, 1976), p. 142.

28. Barber, p. 391.

29. See, for example, Donald Spencer, *The Carter Implosion: Jimmy Carter and the Amateur Style of Diplomacy* (New York: Praeger, 1988).

30. Erwin Hargrove, *Jimmy Carter and the Politics of the Public Good* (Baton Rouge: Louisiana State University Press, 1988).

31. Alexander Haig, Jr., *Caveat: Realism, Reagan and Foreign Policy* (New York: Macmillan, 1984); Donald Regan, *For the Record* (New York: Harcourt, 1988); Bob Schieffer and Gary Paul Gates, *The Acting President* (New York: Dutton, 1989); Laurence Leamer, *Make-Believe: The Story of Nancy and Ronald Reagan* (New York: Harper & Row, 1983).

32. Schieffer and Gates, p. 168. See also Lerner and Michael Rogin, *Ronald Reagan, The Movie and Other Episodes in Political Demonology* (Berkeley: University of California Press, 1987).

33. Schieffer and Gates, pp. 180, 304.

34. See Haig; David Stockman, *The Triumph of Politics: The Inside Story of the Reagan Revolution* (New York: Harper & Row, 1986).
35. Barber, p. 495.
36. The polls were taken too early for Reagan to be included. For a comparison of the rankings, see Robert Murray and Tim Blessing, *Greatness in the White House: Rating the Presidents, Washington through Carter* (University Park: Pennsylvania State University Press, 1988), pp. 16, 17. See also Dean Keith Simonton, *Why Presidents Succeed* (New Haven: Yale University Press, 1987).
37. Dean Keith Simonton, "Predicting Presidential Greatness: An Alternative to the Kennedy and Rice Contextual Index," *Presidential Studies Quarterly* (Spring 1991): 301–7. Other studies cited in the article had similar results.

Chapter 7: Broccoli and Yellow Ribbons

1. See the informal news conference of 13 March 1990, as reported in *The Public Papers of the Presidents* (Washington, D.C.: U.S. Government Printing Office, 1990).
2. Jonathan Alter, "Dragging Bush Home for Broccoli," *Newsweek,* 11 November 1991, p. 29; Adam Nagourney, "White House Senses 'Tide of Discontent,' " *USA Today,* 7 November 1991, p. 1; Robin Toner, "Dark Skies for Bush," *New York Times,* 18 November 1991, p. A-6.
3. Eisenhower's mean popularity in his first thirty months was 68.3 percent approval, with a standard deviation of 4.8. Kennedy's was 72.8, with a standard deviation of 5.7.
4. These effects are shown in the Gallup Poll data we are using throughout this volume, taking one poll per month, as close to the middle of the month as possible. Some of the "fluctuation" people notice may be the result of looking at different polls.
5. Bush's occurrence of good luck compared to the other presidents is significant at the .05 level.
6. See Alter.
7. Data supplied by Public Affairs Video Archives, Purdue University. We are indebted to Robert Browning, director of the Archives, who made the data available.
8. Some commentators saw the event as helping Bush because it allowed him to play the role of spokesperson on international affairs during the highly visible Soviet crisis. See, for example, *Congressional Quarterly Weekly Report,* 24 August 1991, p. 2323.
9. Jason DeParle, "Long Series of Military Decisions Led to Gulf War News Censorship," *New York Times,* 5 May 1991, pp. 1, 20.

10. See DeParle.
11. Ibid.
12. See Barbara Hinckley, *The Symbolic Presidency: How Presidents Present Themselves* (New York: Routledge, 1990), chap. 2.
13. Specifically, we analyze the net difference in Bush's popularity in a given month from the average in that same month of all other first-term presidents from Truman through Reagan.
14. A model of Bush's approval and its differences from his predecessors' approval, including force, was estimated. This variable fell short of statistical significance in each instance.
15. Frequency of Foreign Policy Activities per Month (Months 1–30)

Foreign Trips (Days)	Force	Foreign Policy Speech	Major Diplomacy	Message to Congress
Carter, 1.58	Bush, .27	Bush, .33	Johnson, .01	Eisenhower, .43
Bush, 1.46	Reagan, .17	Nixon, .27	Kennedy, .0034	Johnson, .37 ⎤ tie
Nixon, 1.03	Ford, .14	Reagan, .17	Ford, .0034 ⎤ tie	Nixon, .37 ⎦
Ford, 1.0	Johnson, .01	Kennedy, .14	Carter, .0034 ⎦	Kennedy, .34
Johnson, .83	Kennedy, .007	Truman, .13	Nixon, .0033	Truman, .33
Reagan, .80	Truman, .006	Carter, .10	Truman, 0	Carter, .24
Kennedy, .69	Nixon, .003	Eisenhower, .07	Eisenhower, 0	Bush, .16
Eisenhower, .20	Carter, .003	Ford, .007	Reagan, 0	Ford, .14
Truman, 0	Eisenhower, 0	Johnson, .003	Bush, 0	Reagan, .01

16. See Ellen Collier, ed., *Instances of the Use of United States Armed Forces Abroad, 1798–1989* (Washington, D.C.: Congressional Research Service, The Library of Congress, 1989).
17. Paul Quirk, "Domestic Policy: Divided Government and Cooperative Presidential Leadership," in *The Bush Presidency: First Appraisals,* ed. Colin Campbell, S. J. and Bert Rockman (Chatham, N.J.: Chatham House), 69–91.
18. Janet Hook, "Hill's Acclaim for Bush in War Won't Bring Peace at Home," *Congressional Quarterly Weekly Report,* 9 March 1991, p. 581.

19. Also see Quirk and Sinclair.
20. See *Congressional Quarterly Weekly Report,* 27 July 1991, p. 2041.
21. Barbara Sinclair, "Governing Unheroically (and Sometimes Unappetizingly): Bush and the 101st Congress," in *The Bush Presidency,* p. 171.

Chapter 8: A Guide to Presidents and the Polls

1. Following what we did in Chapter 7, Bush's polls are based on his first thirty months in office.
2. Truman's average is based on the years 1949–52 and Johnson's on 1965–68. Ford is ranked for his two and a half years in office.
3. See, for example, David Donald, *Lincoln Reconsidered,* 2nd ed. (New York: Vintage, 1989), esp. pp. 59, 129.
4. Clinton Rossiter, *The American Presidency* (New York: Mentor, 1960), pp. 102, 103.
5. *Newsweek,* 11 November 1991, p. 27.
6. V. O. Key, *The Responsible Electorate* (Cambridge: Harvard University Press, 1966).

Appendix A

1. The specific approach employed is least squares with dummy variables (or LSDV). In this case, forty-eight monthly observations (t) (with the exception of Kennedy and Ford) were pooled across administrations (i). Stimson (1985) and Judge et al. (1985) provide extensive explanations and documentation concerning this technique.
2. H. Douglas Rivers and Nancy L. Rose, "Passing the President's Program: Public Opinion and Presidential Influence in Congress," *American Journal of Political Science* 29 (1985): 183–96.
3. For an excellent discussion of this methodology, see James Stimson, "Regression in Time and Space: A Statistical Essay," *American Journal of Political Science* (November 1985): 914–47.
4. For the approach, see G. S. Maddala, *Econometrics* (New York: McGraw-Hill, 1977), p. 332.

References

ALTER, JONATHAN. "Dragging Bush Home for Broccoli." *Newsweek* (11 November 1991): 29.

ALTSCHULER, BRUCE E. *LBJ and the Polls.* Gainesville: University of Florida Press, 1990.

AMBROSE, STEPHEN. *Eisenhower,* vols. I and II. New York: Simon & Schuster, 1984.

ANTHONY, CARL. *First Ladies.* New York: Morrow, 1990.

BARBER, JAMES DAVID. *The Presidential Character: Predicting Performance in the White House,* 3rd ed. Englewood Cliffs, N.J.: Prentice-Hall, 1985.

BARGER, HAROLD. "Suspending Disbelief: The President in Pre-College Textbooks." *Presidential Studies Quarterly* (Winter 1990): 55–70.

BERMAN, LARRY. "Paths Chosen and Opportunities Lost." In *Leadership in the Modern Presidency,* edited by Fred Greenstein. Cambridge: Harvard University Press, 1988.

BLECHMAN, BARRY, and STEPHEN KAPLAN. *Force Without War.* Washington, D.C.: Brookings Institute, 1978.

BOND, JON R., and RICHARD FLEISHER. "The Limits of Presidential Popularity as a Source of Influence in the U.S. House." *Legislative Studies Quarterly* 5 (February 1980): 69–78.

BOND, JON R., and RICHARD FLEISHER. "Presidential Popularity and Congressional Voting: A Reexamination of Public Opinion as a Source of Influence in Congress." *Western Political Quarterly* 37 (June 1984): 291–306.

BOND, JON R., and RICHARD FLEISHER. *Presidential Success in the Legislative Arena.* Chicago: University of Chicago Press, 1990.

BRACE, PAUL. "Cubic Splines in Political Science Research." Unpublished manuscript, 1985.

BRACE, PAUL, CHRISTINE B. HARRINGTON, and GARY KING, eds. *The Presidency in American Politics.* New York: New York University Press, 1989.

BRACE, PAUL, and BARBARA HINCKLEY. "Presidential Activities from Truman through Reagan: What Difference Did They Make?" Paper presented at the annual meeting of the Southern Political Science Association, Tampa, Fla., October 1991.

BRACE, PAUL, and BARBARA HINCKLEY. "The Structure of Approval: Constraints Within and Across Presidencies." *Journal of Politics* 53, no. 4 (November 1991): 993–1017.

BRODY, RICHARD. *Assessing the President: The Media, Elite Opinion, and Public Support.* Stanford: Stanford University Press, 1991.

BURKE, JOHN P., and FRED I. GREENSTEIN. *How Presidents Test Reality: Decisions on Vietnam, 1954 and 1965.* New York: Russell Sage Foundation, 1989.

BURNS, JAMES MACGREGOR. *Leadership.* New York: Harper & Row, 1978.

CARRUTH, GORTON, ed. *The Encyclopedia of American Facts and Dates,* 8th ed. New York: Harper & Row, 1988.

CHAPPELL, HENRY, JR. "Economic Performance, Voting, and Political Support: A Unified Approach." *Review of Economics and Statistics* LXXII (May 1990): 313–20.

CLAUSEN, AAGE. *How Congressmen Decide: A Policy Focus.* New York: St. Martin's, 1973.

CLAUSEN, AAGE, and CARL VAN HORN. "The Congressional Response to a Decade of Change." *Journal of Politics* 39 (August 1977): 624–66.

COLLIER, ELLEN, ed. *Instances of the Use of United States Armed Forces Abroad, 1789–1989.* Washington, D.C.: Congressional Research Service, 1989.

CRONIN, THOMAS. *The State of the Presidency,* 2nd ed. Boston: Little, Brown, 1980.

DEPARLE, JASON. "Long Series of Military Decisions Led to Gulf War News Censorship." *New York Times* (5 May 1991): 1, 20.

DONALD, DAVID. *Lincoln Reconsidered,* 2nd ed. New York: Vintage, 1989.

DRAPER, THEODORE. *A Very Thin Line: The Iran-Contra Affairs.* New York: Hill and Wang, 1991.

EDWARDS, GEORGE, III. *At the Margins: Presidential Leadership in Congress.* New Haven: Yale University Press, 1989.

EDWARDS, GEORGE, III. *The Public Presidency.* New York: St. Martin's, 1983.

EVANS, ROWLAND, JR., and ROBERT NOVAK. *Nixon in the White House: The Frustration of Power.* New York: Vintage Books, 1972.

FERRELL, ROBERT H., ed. *Off the Record: The Private Papers of Harry S. Truman.* New York: Harper & Row, 1980.

GALLUP, GEORGE. *The Gallup Poll,* vols. 1 and 2. New York: Random House, 1949–1971.

GALLUP, GEORGE. *The Gallup Poll,* vols. 2 and 3. Wilmington: Scholarly Resources, 1972–1977.

GREENSTEIN, FRED. *The Hidden-Hand Presidency: Eisenhower as Leader.* New York: Basic Books, 1982.

GREENSTEIN, FRED. *What the President Means to Americans, in Choosing the President,* edited by James David Barber. New York: American Assembly, 1974.

GROSS, MICHAEL, and MARTHA KUMAR. *Portraying the President.* Baltimore: Johns Hopkins University Press, 1981.

HAIG, ALEXANDER, JR. *Caveat: Realism, Reagan and Foreign Policy.* New York: Macmillan, 1984.

HAMBY, ALONZO. "Harry S. Truman: Insecurity and Responsibility." In *Leadership in the Modern Presidency,* edited by Fred Greenstein. Cambridge: Harvard University Press, 1988.

HARGROVE, ERWIN. *Jimmy Carter and the Politics of the Public Good.* Baton Rouge: Louisiana State University, 1988.

HAYNES, STEPHEN, and JOE STONE. "An Integrated Test for Electoral Cycles in the U.S. Economy." *Review of Economics and Statistics* LXXI (August 1989): 426–34.

HECLO, HUGH, and LESTER SALAMON, eds. *The Illusion of Presidential Government.* Boulder: Westview, 1981.

HERTSGAARD, MARK. *On Bended Knee: The Press and the Reagan Presidency.* New York: Farrar Straus Giroux, 1988.

HIBBS, DOUGLAS A., JR. *The American Political Economy: Macroeconomics and Electoral Politics.* Cambridge: Harvard University Press, 1987.

HINCKLEY, BARBARA. *Less Than Meets the Eye: President, Congress and Foreign Policy.* New York: Twentieth Century Fund, forthcoming.

HINCKLEY, BARBARA. *The Symbolic Presidency: How Presidents Present Themselves.* New York: Routledge, 1990.

HODGSON, GODFREY. *All Things to All Men.* New York: Simon & Schuster, 1980.

HONEGGER, BARBARA. *October Surprise.* New York: Tudor, 1989.

HOOK, JANET. "Hill's Acclaim for Bush Won't Bring Peace at Home." *Congressional Quarterly Weekly Report* (9 March 1991): 581.

HURWITZ, JON, and MARK PEFFLEY. "The Means and Ends of Foreign

Policy as Determinants of Presidential Support." *American Journal of Political Science* (May 1987): 236–58.

JAMES, PATRICK, and JOHN ONEAL. "Influences on the President's Use of Force." *Journal of Conflict Resolution* (June 1991): 307–32.

JOHNSON, KENNETH, ed. *The Johnson Presidency.* Lanham, Md.: University Press of America, 1987.

JONES, CHARLES O., ed. *The Reagan Legacy.* Chatham, N.J.: Chatham House, 1988.

JONES, CHARLES O. *The Trusteeship Presidency: Jimmy Carter and the United States Congress.* Baton Rouge: Louisiana State University Press, 1988.

JUDGE, GEORGE G., W. E. GRIFFITHS, R. CARTER HILL, HELMUT LUT-KEPOHL, and TSOUNG-CHAO LEE. *The Theory and Practice of Econometrics,* 2nd ed. New York: Wiley, 1985.

KEARNS, DORIS. *Lyndon Johnson and the American Dream.* New York: Harper & Row, 1976.

KERNELL, SAMUEL. "Explaining Presidential Popularity." *American Political Science Review* (June 1978): 506–22.

KERNELL, SAMUEL. *Going Public: New Strategies of Presidential Leadership.* Washington, D.C.: CQ Press, 1986.

KESSEL, JOHN. *Presidential Parties.* Homewood, Ill.: Dorsey Press, 1984.

KEY, V. O. *The Responsible Electorate.* Cambridge: Harvard University Press, 1966.

KINDER, DONALD. "Presidents, Prosperity and Public Opinion." *Public Opinion Quarterly* 5 (1981): 1–21.

KING, GARY. "Statistical Models for Political Science Events Counts: Bias in Conventional Procedures and Evidence for the Exponential Poisson Regression Model." *American Journal of Political Science* 32, no. 3 (August 1988): 838–63.

KING, GARY. *Unifying Political Methodology.* New York: Cambridge University Press, 1989.

KING, GARY, and LYN RAGSDALE. *The Elusive Executive.* Washington, D.C.: CQ Press, 1988.

KINGDON, JOHN. *Congressmen's Voting Decisions,* 2nd ed. New York: Harper & Row, 1981.

KUTLER, STANLEY. *The Wars of Watergate.* New York: Knopf, 1990.

LAMMERS, WILLIAM. "Presidential Attention-Focusing Activities." In *The President and the Public,* edited by D. Graber. Philadelphia: Institute for the Study of Human Issues, 1982.

LEAMER, LAURENCE. *Make-Believe: The Story of Nancy and Ronald Reagan.* New York: Harper & Row, 1983.

LIGHT, PAUL. *The President's Agenda: Domestic Policy Choice from Kennedy to Carter.* Baltimore: Johns Hopkins University Press, 1982.

LOWI, THEODORE. *The Personal President.* Ithaca, N.Y.: Cornell University Press, 1985.

LYON, PETER. *Eisenhower: Portrait of the Hero.* Boston: Little, Brown, 1974.

MACKUEN, MICHAEL. "Political Drama, Economic Conditions, and the Dynamic of Public Popularity." *American Journal of Political Science* (May 1983): 165–92.

MADDALA, G. S. *Econometrics.* New York: McGraw-Hill, 1970.

MAYER, JANE, and DOYLE MCMANUS. *Landslide: The Unmaking of the President 1984–1988.* Boston: Houghton Mifflin, 1988.

MUELLER, JOHN. "Presidential Popularity from Truman to Johnson." *American Political Science Review* (March 1970): 18–24.

MUELLER, JOHN. *Wars, Presidents and Public Opinion.* New York: Wiley, 1973.

MURRAY, ROBERT, and TIM BLESSING. *Greatness in the White House: Rating the Presidents, Washington through Carter.* University Park: Pennsylvania State University Press, 1988.

NAGOURNEY, ADAM. "White House Senses 'Tide of Discontent.'" *USA Today* (7 November 1991): 1.

NEUSTADT, RICHARD. *Presidential Power: The Politics of Leadership from FDR to Carter.* New York: Wiley, 1980.

NINCIC, MIROSLAV, and BARBARA HINCKLEY. "Foreign Policy and the Evaluation of Presidential Candidates." *Journal of Conflict Resolution* (June 1991): 333–55.

NORPOTH, HELMUT. "Economics, Politics, and the Cycle of Presidential Popularity." *Political Behavior* 6, no. 3 (1984): 253–71.

NORPOTH, HELMUT, and THOM YANTEK. "Macroeconomic Conditions and Fluctuations of Presidential Popularity: The Question of Lagged Effects." *American Journal of Political Science* 27, no. 4 (1983): 785–807.

O'BRIEN, LAWRENCE. *No Final Victories: A Life in Politics from John F. Kennedy to Watergate.* New York: Ballantine, 1974.

ORNSTEIN, NORMAN J., THOMAS E. MANN, and MICHAEL MALBIN. *Vital Statistics on Congress: 1987–1988.* Washington, D.C.: CQ Press, 1987.

OSTROM, CHARLES, and BRIAN JOB. "The President and the Political Use of Force." *American Political Science Review* (June 1986): 541–66.

OSTROM, CHARLES, and DENNIS SIMON. "Promise and Performance: A Dynamic Model of Presidential Popularity." *American Political Science Review* (June 1985): 334–58.

OSTROM, CHARLES, and DENNIS SIMON. "The President's Public." *American Journal of Political Science* (November 1988): 1096–1119.

OSTROM, CHARLES, and RENEE SMITH. "Presidential Popularity and the Economy: Contrasting VAR and SEQ Approaches." Paper presented at the annual meeting of the Midwest Political Science Association, Chicago, April 1990.

PEABODY, ROBERT. *Leadership in Congress.* Boston: Little, Brown, 1976.

PETERSON, MARK. *Legislating Together: The White House and Capitol Hill from Eisenhower to Reagan.* Cambridge: Harvard University Press, 1990.

PHILLIPS, CABELL. *The Truman Presidency.* New York: Macmillan, 1966.

The Public Papers of the Presidents. Washington, D.C.: Government Printing Office, various years.

QUIRK, PAUL. "Domestic Policy: Divided Government and Cooperative Presidential Leadership." *The Bush Presidency: First Appraisals,* edited by Colin Campbell and S. J. and Bert Rockman. Chatham, N.J.: Chatham House, 1991.

RAGSDALE, LYN. "The Politics of Presidential Speechmaking, 1949–1980." *American Political Science Review* (December 1984): 971–84.

RAGSDALE, LYN. "Presidential Speechmaking and the Public Audience: Individual Presidents and Group Attitudes." *Journal of Politics* 49 (August 1987): 704–27.

REGAN, DONALD. *For the Record: From Wall Street to Washington.* New York: Harcourt Brace Jovanovich, 1988.

RIVERS, DOUGLAS, and NANCY ROSE. "Passing the President's Program: Public Opinion and Presidential Influence in Congress." *American Journal of Political Science* 29 (May 1985): 183–96.

ROGIN, MICHAEL. *Ronald Reagan, The Movie and Other Episodes in Political Demonology.* Berkeley: University of California Press, 1987.

ROSSITER, CLINTON. *The American Presidency.* rev. ed. New York: Mentor, 1960.

ROZELL, MARK. *The Press and the Carter Presidency.* Boulder: Westview, 1989.

ROZELL, MARK. "The Press Strategies of Presidents Ford, Carter and Reagan: Is It True the 'No White House Can Do Much About a President's Image?' " Paper delivered at the Western Political Science Association, Seattle, Washington, March 1991.

SCHIEFFER, BOB, and GARY PAUL GATES. *The Acting President.* New York: Dutton, 1989.

SCHLESINGER, ARTHUR M., JR. *A Thousand Days.* Boston: Houghton Mifflin, 1965.

SCHLESINGER, ARTHUR M., JR., ed. *The Almanac of American History.* New York: Putnam, 1983.

SIMON, DENNIS, and CHARLES OSTROM, JR. "The Impact of Televised

Speeches and Foreign Travel on Presidential Approval." *Public Opinion Quarterly* 53 (1990): 58–82.

SIMONTON, DEAN KEITH. *Why Presidents Succeed.* New Haven: Yale University Press, 1987.

SIMONTON, DEAN KEITH. "Predicting Presidential Greatness: An Alternative to the Kenny and Rice Contextual Index." *Presidential Studies Quarterly* (Spring 1991): 301–7.

SINCLAIR, BARBARA. "Governing Unheroically and Sometimes Unappetizingly: Bush and the 101st Congress." In *The Bush Presidency: First Appraisals,* edited by Colin Campbell and S. J. and Bert Rockman. Chatham, N.J.: Chatham House, 1991.

SORENSEN, THEODORE. *Kennedy.* New York: Harper & Row, 1965.

SPENCER, DONALD. *The Carter Implosion: Jimmy Carter and the Amateur Style of Diplomacy.* New York: Praeger, 1988.

STIMSON, JAMES A. "Public Support for American Presidents." *Public Opinion Quarterly* 40 (1976): 1–21.

STIMSON, JAMES A. "Regression in Time and Space: A Statistical Essay." *American Journal of Political Science* (November 1985): 914–47.

STOCKMAN, DAVID. *The Triumph of Politics: The Inside Story of the Reagan Revolution.* New York: Harper & Row, 1986.

SULLIVAN, MICHAEL. *The Vietnam War.* Lexington: University of Kentucky Press, 1985.

TONER, ROBIN. "Dark Skies for Bush." *New York Times* (18 November 1991): A-6.

TUFTE, EDWARD. *Political Control of the Economy.* Princeton: Princeton University Press, 1978.

WILSON, WOODROW. *Constitutional Government.* New York: Columbia University Press, 1908.

WOODWARD, BOB. *Veil: The Secret Wars of the CIA: 1981–1987.* New York: Simon & Schuster, 1987.

The World Almanac and Book of Facts. New York: World Almanac, various years.

Index